T0156123

Communications
in Computer and Information Science 1717

Rationale

The CCIS series is devoted to the publication of proceedings of computer science conferences. Its aim is to efficiently disseminate original research results in informatics in printed and electronic form. While the focus is on publication of peer-reviewed full papers presenting mature work, inclusion of reviewed short papers reporting on work in progress is welcome, too. Besides globally relevant meetings with internationally representative program committees guaranteeing a strict peer-reviewing and paper selection process, conferences run by societies or of high regional or national relevance are also considered for publication.

Topics

The topical scope of CCIS spans the entire spectrum of informatics ranging from foundational topics in the theory of computing to information and communications science and technology and a broad variety of interdisciplinary application fields.

Information for Volume Editors and Authors

Publication in CCIS is free of charge. No royalties are paid, however, we offer registered conference participants temporary free access to the online version of the conference proceedings on SpringerLink (http://link.springer.com) by means of an http referrer from the conference website and/or a number of complimentary printed copies, as specified in the official acceptance email of the event.

CCIS proceedings can be published in time for distribution at conferences or as post-proceedings, and delivered in the form of printed books and/or electronically as USBs and/or e-content licenses for accessing proceedings at SpringerLink. Furthermore, CCIS proceedings are included in the CCIS electronic book series hosted in the SpringerLink digital library at http://link.springer.com/bookseries/7899. Conferences publishing in CCIS are allowed to use Online Conference Service (OCS) for managing the whole proceedings lifecycle (from submission and reviewing to preparing for publication) free of charge.

Publication process

The language of publication is exclusively English. Authors publishing in CCIS have to sign the Springer CCIS copyright transfer form, however, they are free to use their material published in CCIS for substantially changed, more elaborate subsequent publications elsewhere. For the preparation of the camera-ready papers/files, authors have to strictly adhere to the Springer CCIS Authors' Instructions and are strongly encouraged to use the CCIS LaTeX style files or templates.

Abstracting/Indexing

CCIS is abstracted/indexed in DBLP, Google Scholar, EI-Compendex, Mathematical Reviews, SCImago, Scopus. CCIS volumes are also submitted for the inclusion in ISI Proceedings.

How to start

To start the evaluation of your proposal for inclusion in the CCIS series, please send an e-mail to ccis@springer.com.

Nitin Agarwal · George B. Kleiner ·
Leonidas Sakalauskas

Editors

Modeling and Simulation of Social-Behavioral Phenomena in Creative Societies

Second International Conference, MSBC 2022
Vilnius, Lithuania, September 21–23, 2022
Proceedings

 Springer

Editors
Nitin Agarwal
University of Arkansas at Little Rock
Little Rock, AR, USA

George B. Kleiner
Central Economic Mathematical Institute
of RAS
Moscow, Russia

Leonidas Sakalauskas
Vilnius Gediminas Technical University
Vilnius, Lithuania

ISSN 1865-0929   ISSN 1865-0937 (electronic)
Communications in Computer and Information Science
ISBN 978-3-031-33727-7   ISBN 978-3-031-33728-4 (eBook)
https://doi.org/10.1007/978-3-031-33728-4

This Springer imprint is published by the registered company Springer Nature Switzerland AG
The registered company address is: Gewerbestrasse 11, 6330 Cham, Switzerland

Editorial

The growing challenges of societal sustainability, social complexity, behavioural operations research, and cohesion are becoming increasingly acknowledged worldwide. However, there is a conceptual and analytical gap in understanding the driving forces behind them. Thorough multidisciplinary research efforts are in demand for making valuable contributions, starting from concepts and models, and ending with recommendation and decision support systems capable of contributing to the effective global and Europe-wide cultural and social policy formation agendas.

The application of computational intelligence to study issues in the social sciences has been undergoing rapid development during the last decades. The conference MSBC-2022 aimed to create an open panel for an effective dialogue among researchers and practitioners interested in the integration between computer science and social science to strengthen the visibility, recognition, and understanding of the problems of simulation and modelling in the social sciences and provide developmental opportunities for young European scientists and students as well.

The conference MSBC-2022 revealed how the operationalisation of social-behavioural phenomena leads to the development of a paradigm of rational choice for the efficient understanding of their nature and relevant decision-making, thus enabling us to seek social consensus in society. The creation of such a paradigm on the basis of the theory of structural equation modelling, multi-agent modelling, and game theory, together with data science and mathematical sociology methods, allows the development of data-driven operationalisation for evidence-based solutions.

The papers in the Proceedings cover the main topics and streams of the conference, such as computational intelligence applications in social sciences; modelling of complex societal problems; experimental and behavioural economies in creative societies; multiagent systems and agent societies; metrics of social cohesion and sustainability; big data and optimisation in social networks; OR and Ethics understanding of the dynamics of social processes; social policy modelling and evidence-based decisions; web content and behaviour.

This volume contains selected papers of the *2nd International Conference MODELLING AND SIMULATION OF SOCIAL-BEHAVIOURAL PHENOMENA IN CREATIVE SOCIETIES (MSBC-2022)*, held in Vilnius, Lithuania, September 21–23, 2022. The Programme Committee selected the best papers submitted, and an international board of reviewers reviewed all of them. MSBC 2022 received 35 submissions from countries all over the world. The Program Committee selected 14 regular papers and 1 short paper for presentation. All papers have been double-blind peer-reviewed through at least a two-round process.

We cordially thank all the contributors for the success of this conference.

Nitin Agarwal
George B. Kleiner
Leonidas Sakalauskas

Organization

Organised by

EURO Working Group on Ethics and OR
EURO Working Group on Operations Research for Development
Vilnius Gediminas Technical University (VilniusTech)
Hamburg University of Applied Sciences
Lithuanian Operational Research Society (LitORS)

In Cooperation with

Harbin Engineering University, China
Klaipeda University, Lithuania
Ghent University, Belgium
System Economics Association, Russia
National Technical University of Ukraine "Igor Sikorsky Kyiv Polytechnic Institute"
Russian Operational Research Society, Russia

Chairman of the Programme Committee

Nitin Agarwal   University of Arkansas at Little Rock, USA

Chairman of the Organising Committee

Leonidas Sakalauskas   Vilnius Gediminas Technical University,
                                         Lithuania

International Scientific Programme Committee

Nitin Agarwal   University of Arkansas at Little Rock, USA
Fuad Aleskerov   Higher School of Economics, Russia
Elena Andreeva   Hanover Medical School, Germany

International Board of Reviewers

Vladimir Bocharnikov	Pacific Institute of Geography, RAS, Russia
Daiva Bubeliene	Kaunas University of Applied Sciences, Lithuania
Cathal MacSwiney Brugha	University College Dublin, Ireland
Nicolae Bulz	Romanian Academy, Romania
Gordon Dash	University of Rhode Island, USA
Artem Denisov	Kostroma State University, Russia
Vitalijus Denisovas	Klaipeda University, Lithuania
Dorien DeTombe	EWG on Ethics and OR, The Netherlands
Vladimir Gisin	Financial University, Russia
Olga Gorbaneva	Southern Federal University, Russia
Salvatore Greco	ETH Zürich, Switzerland
Ivan Izonin	Lviv Polytechnic National University, Ukraine
Yan Jun	China University of Petroleum (Beijing), China
Nina Kajiji	University of Rhode Island, USA
George Kleiner	Central Economics and Mathematics Institute of the RAS, Russia
Aleksandr Kobylko	Central Economics and Mathematics Institute of the RAS, Russia
Surya Kumacheva	St. Petersburg State University, Russia
Lyudmila Kuzmina	Kazan Aviation Institute, Russia
Nelson Maculan	Federal University of Rio de Janeiro, Brazil
Oleksandr Makarenko	Kyiv Technical University, Ukraine
Vladimir Mazalov	Petrozavodsk University, Russia
Gedimimas Merkys	Kaunas University of Technology, Lithuania
Maria Milkova	National Research University Higher School of Economics, Russia
Antoinette J. Muntjewerff	University of Amsterdam, The Netherlands
Igor Nedelkovski	University "St. Kliment Ohridski", Macedonia
Guennady Ougolnitsky	Southern Federal University, Russia
Maxim Rybachuk	Financial University, Russia
Leonidas Sakalauskas	Vilnius Gediminas Technical University, Lithuania
Yaroslav Sergeyev	University of Calabria, Italy
Nataliya Shakhovska	Lviv Polytechnic National University, Ukraine
Olga Sviridova	Financial University, Russia
Alexis Tsoukiàs	Université Paris Dauphine, France
Svetlana Shchepetova	Financial University, Russia
Alina Steblyanskaja	Harbin Engineering University, China
Steve Taylor	University of British Columbia, Canada
Vladislav Taynitskiy	Saint Peterburg state University, Russia
Sigitas Vaitkevicius	MB Veldra/SP Veldra, Lithuania
Gerhard Wilhelm (Willi) Weber	Poznan University of Technology, Poland

Adilson Elias Xavier	Federal University of Rio de Janeiro, Brazil
Zhinan Wang	Harbin Engineering University, China
Lidiya Zhukovskaya	Central Economics and Mathematics Institute of the RAS, Russia

VILNIAUS GEDIMINO
TECHNIKOS UNIVERSITETAS

ORD
OPERATIONS RESEARCH
FOR DEVELOPMENT

HAW
HAMBURG

KLAIPĖDA
UNIVERSITY

Litors

Lithuanian OR Society

ETHICS
AND OR

GHENT
UNIVERSITY

RuORS

RUSSIAN OPERATIONAL
RESEARCH SOCIETY

Contents

Simulation of Behavioral Processes

Studying Simulated Mobs Using Monte Carlo Method and the Theory
of Collective Action 3
    Samer Al-khateeb and Nitin Agarwal

Dynamic Approach to Modeling Hierarchical Conflict Situations in Small
Groups 14
    Ludmila Borisova and Mira Fridman

A Cognitive Simulation Model of a Regional Higher Education System 27
    Olga Gorbaneva, Anton Murzin, Guennady Ougolnitsky,
    and Stanislav Mikhalkovich

Behavioral Model of Interaction Between Economic Agents
and the Institutional Environment 48
    George Kleiner, Maxim Rybachuk, and Dmitry Ushakov

Attitudes to Vaccination: How the Opinion Dynamics Affects the Influenza
Epidemic Process 63
    Suriya Kumacheva, Ekaterina Zhitkova, and Galina Tomilina

Free-Rider Problem: Simulating of System Convergence to Stable
Equilibrium State by Means of Finite Markov Chain Models 78
    Olga Pyrkina and Andrey Yudanov

Modeling of Sustainability

Econometric Modeling of Adaptation of the Russian Economy to Western
Countries' Sanctions 97
    Viktor Byvshev

Improved Free Disposal Hull Methodology for China Provinces Effective
Social-Economic Development Modeling 115
    Artem Denisov, Wang Qian, and Elizaveta Steblianskaia

Dynamics of the Long-Term Orientation in Russian Society Over the Past
100 years: Results of the Analysis of the Russian Subcorpus of Google
Books Ngram 126
    Timofei Nestik, Vladimir Bochkarev, and Vera Levina

Sustainable Development Issues of the Belt and Road Initiative
in Educational Modeling Cases 137
 Alina Steblyanskaya and Zhinan Wang

Carbon Dioxide Emissions Modelling Along the Route Using Various
Transportation Modes 148
 Maksim Vasiev, Olga Efimova, Evgeniy Baboshin, Irina Matveeva,
 and Olga Malysheva

Data Science and Modeling

Research on the Prediction of Highly Cited Papers Based on PCA-BPNN 161
 Tian Yu and Changxu Duan

Logical Dimension in Modeling 179
 Gisin Vladimir

Quantification of Textual Responses To Open-Ended Questions In Big Data 191
 Gediminas Merkys and Daiva Bubeliene

Optimization of Works Management of the Investment Project 201
 Alexandr Mishchenko, Oleg Kosorukov, and Olga Sviridova

Author Index 219

Simulation of Behavioral Processes

Studying Simulated Mobs Using Monte Carlo Method and the Theory of Collective Action

Samer Al-khateeb[1]([✉]) and Nitin Agarwal[2]

[1] Creighton University, Omaha, NE 68178, USA
sameral-khateeb1@creighton.edu
[2] COSMOS Research Center, UA-Little Rock, Little Rock, AR 72204, USA
nxagarwal@ualr.edu

Abstract. A *mob* is an event that is organized via social media, email, SMS, or other forms of digital communication technologies in which a group of people (who might have an agenda) get together online or offline to collectively conduct an act and then disperse (quickly or over a long period). These events are increasingly happening around the world in recent years due to the anonymity of the internet, affordability of social media, boredom, etc. Studying such a phenomenon is not an easy task due to a lack of data, theoretical underpinning, and resources. In this research, we use Monte Carlo Experiments and our previous research on Deviant Cyber Flash Mobs that leveraged the theory of Collective Action to implement a model that can simulate a mob, estimate its success rate, and the needed powerful actors (e.g., mob organizers) to succeed. This research is one step toward fully understanding mob formation and the motivations of its participants and organizers.

Keywords: Collective Action · Mob · Cyber Mob · Flash Mob · Monte Carlo Method · Randomness · Simulation · Pearson Correlation Coefficient

1 Introduction

A "mob" is an event that is organized via social media, email, SMS, or other forms of digital communication technologies in which a group of people (who might have an agenda) get together online or offline to collectively conduct an act and then disperse (quickly or over a long period) [1, 2]. To an outsider, such an event may seem arbitrary. However, a sophisticated amount of coordination is involved. In recent years, mobs *"have taken a darker twist as criminals exploit the anonymity of crowds, using social networking to coordinate everything from robberies to fights to general chaos"* [3, 4]. More recently, the term *"mob"* has been increasingly used to remark an electronically orchestrated violence such as the January 6, 2021 attack on the State Capital in Washington DC that lead to property damages, government disruption, and injuries or death for some of the protesters [5, 6]. In the same month and year, an army of small investors from all over the world used Reddit to coordinate *"flashmob investing"* [7] to create a stock market frenzy causing GameStop's stock value to rise from \$20 to \$483 in less than a month [8].

© The Author(s), under exclusive license to Springer Nature Switzerland AG 2023
N. Agarwal et al. (Eds.): MSBC 2022, CCIS 1717, pp. 3–13, 2023.
https://doi.org/10.1007/978-3-031-33728-4_1

These events show that our systems (security, financial, etc.) are not equipped to handle such highly coordinated and sometimes flash actions, underscoring the importance of systematically studying such behaviors.

One way to study mobs is to collect data on various mobs and document various mobbers' behaviors, shared orientations, etc. Then run some machine learning algorithms to try to predict the outcome of the mob or the occurrence of the mob. As straightforward as this task might seem, however, it is not. Being able to identify a mob and collect data about it is not an easy task due to the possibility of mobs being coordinated on various platforms, data collection restrictions, lack of critical data, privacy issues, etc.

Another way to study mobs that is more efficient, cost-effective, and still requires theoretical underpinnings, is to use computer simulation. Simulation is used to solve many real-world problems by modeling real-world processes to provide otherwise unobtainable information. Computer simulation has been used to *"predict the weather, design aircraft, create special effects for movies"* [9] among others. Many simulations require events to occur with a certain likelihood. These sorts of simulations are called Monte Carlo simulations because the results depend on *"chance"* probabilities. The Monte Carlo method (or simulation) is named after the Monaco resort town known for its gambling and casinos. It was invented by Stanislaw Ulam, a Polish-American scientist, in the late 1940s when he was working on the Manhattan Project [10]. The Monte Carlo method has myriad applications in various fields such as business and finance, supply chain, oil and gas, science, insurance, and engineering [11]. This method is usually used to estimate the likelihood of a certain outcome or predict the future value of a variable, risk analysis, etc.

In this research, we use the Monte Carlo method guided by constructs extracted from the theory of collective action to implement a model previously published in [12–15] and analyze its performance to have a better understanding of the mob phenomenon defined above. More specifically, this research tries to answer the following research questions:

RQ1: Given the following parameters (Number of Invited People, Threshold Value of the Mob Success, the Number of Simulations (Mobs), the Number of Powerful Actors), what is the chance a mob will succeed?

RQ2: Given the following parameters (Number of Invited People, Threshold Value of Mob Success, and the Number of Simulations (Mobs)), how many powerful actors are needed to have a successful mob?

Next, we provide a brief literature review of the topics related to this paper. Then we discuss the methodology we followed to implement our model and explain our analysis and results. Finally, we conclude with possible future research directions.

2   Literature Review

The mob phenomenon has been studied in various disciplines such as communication studies [16], marketing [17], cultural studies [18], and other disciplines [19]. However, there is a lack of a systematic and computational model of its formation and prediction of its occurrence or its success and failure. This research is one step in this direction.

The Monte Carlo method/simulation *"is a computerized mathematical technique"* [11] used in decision-making, testing statistical procedure robustness [20], and quantitative analysis [11, 12]. It is used to simulate all possible outcomes of a decision to make a better decision (e.g., the one that involves the least risk) [11]. Since its inception during World War II, it has been used in a variety of fields such as project management, research and development, manufacturing, engineering, and transportation [10, 11]. Monte Carlo method use probability distributions (e.g., normal, lognormal, uniform, triangular, pert, or discrete) as input sample. Then it outputs all possible outcomes with the likelihood of their happening [11]. It works by assigning multiple values to uncertain variable, then the average of the multiple results is used as an estimate of the final outcome [10]. It is an example of stochastic modeling [10] which is much better and more realistic than the deterministic modeling because it allows an analyst to see what input(s) has more impact on a specific outcome [11].

A study close to this study was conducted by Sung-Ha Hwang [21]. He used the Lanchester's equations[1], the Monte Carlo method, and adopted the collective punishment hypothesis to develop a model of public good with punishment (cost of acting). The goal of his research was to study the group-size effects on collective action. In his research, the actor can be either a punisher (act), defector (act against), or cooperator (do not act). He found that *"an increase in group size always favors punishers and cooperators"* [21]. This means that the bigger the group size (mob size) with a higher number of punishers and cooperators (act and do not act) the higher the chance of achieving collective action (a higher chance of mob success).

3 Methodology

In this section, we explain the logical framework we previously constructed based on the sociological theory of collective action [12–15], then explain the various scenarios a mobber can face when it comes to his/her decision to act/participate in a mob (or not). Finally, we explain how the model was implemented using Python programming language.

3.1 The Theoretical Model

To model a mob, we examined the sociological theory of collective action and extracted the factors that lead to the formation of a mob and its success (or failure) in cyberspace, physical space, or both, i.e., the cybernetic space.

Collective action can be defined as all activity of common or shared interest among two or more individuals [23]. From the logic of collective action by Mancur Olson [23], we found that one factor that encourages mobbers to participate in a mob is the amount of utility (benefits) they will gain by participating. This is supported by Coleman's argument in his book *"there is a single action principle which governs the actions of the actors in the system: Each actor chooses those actions which maximize his utility given environmental context created by the events..."* [24]. Also, the *utility difference* which is defined as the amount of utility (benefit) gained by an actor (a mobber) from the pair of possible outcomes (success or failure) of the same event (e.g., the mob) will

---

[1] These are differential equations that are used to calculate the strength of the military and were invented during WWII by Frederick W. Lanchester, an English engineer [22].

determine his/her *interest* in participating in that mob. As the amount of *gained utility* increases the *interest* in participating in the mob also increases and vice versa. Another factor that Olson mentioned in his book that can affect mobbers' decision to participate is *control*, i.e., to what extent an individual could affect the outcome of the event [23]. If the mobber has an *interest* in participating in a mob and has *control* over the outcome of the mob, the mobber is considered powerful (e.g., a mob organizer). By summing the power of all mobbers, we can determine the *importance* of a mob. If the importance of a mob exceeds a certain (predetermined) *threshold* value, then we can hypothesize the mob will more likely succeed. Otherwise, the mob is more likely to fail. Here, we named the sum of the power of all mobbers as the *participation rate*. The threshold value can be estimated using various methods, e.g., based on empirical observations of known mobs or shared knowledge from law enforcement agencies, etc.

3.2 Scenarios a Mobber Could Face

Based on the factors mentioned above (i.e., interest, control, and power) a mobber could face four possible scenarios when it comes to deciding what to do when s(he) sees a mob in physical or cyberspace (or gets invited to participate in a mob). These scenarios will determine the decision of the mobber when it comes to acting in a mob or not. The assumption here is their decision will be based only on the aforementioned factors (i.e., interest, control, and power) and a mob will succeed when the mob *participation rate* exceeds a *threshold* value. The four scenarios are:

1. If an individual **has interest** and **control** then the likelihood of the individual participation is the highest, i.e., the individual will **act**.
2. If an individual **has interest** but **does not have control** then the individual **may act** (i.e., has a 50/50 chance of acting **or withdrawing**). So, the likelihood of individual participation is relatively lower than in the previous case.
3. If an individual **does not have interest** but **has control** then the individual has two choices – either will **withdraw**, i.e., will not act, or execute **power exchange** (i.e., relinquish power to possibly gain control over other events (mobs) or to simply gain social capital[2]). These individuals can perfectly exchange power with mobbers of the second scenario above.
4. If an individual has **no interest** and **no control,** then the individual will have two choices – either will **withdraw** or **act against** the group.

We assume powerful actors (e.g., mob organizers) will always have *interest* and *control*, so they will always **act** in the mob.

These scenarios have been coded using Python programming language and the details of the scripts are explained in the next subsection. These scripts are used to answer the research questions mentioned in the introduction section.

---

[2] Social capital, as stated by Pierre Bourdieu, is "*the value that one gain from personal connections such as membership in a family, an ethnic association, elite clubs, or other solidarity groups*" [25].

3.3 Model Implementation

We used Python programming language to create two scripts (available at: https://github. com/SamerAl-khateeb/MobsSimulator-Python), one is used to answer the first research question and the other is used to answer the second research question. We used the `randrange()` method from the `random` library to implement the four scenarios mentioned above. The `randrange()` method was used to give each mobber a random *interest* and *control*; then a 50/50 chance of either *acting* or *withdrawing* (as in the second scenario); to *withdraw* or *power exchange* (as in the third scenario); and to *withdraw* or *act against* (as in the fourth scenario).

Using the first script, i.e., `Mob_Simulator-Q1.py` the user will be asked to enter *the total number of invited people*, the *threshold value of the mob success*, the *number of simulations (mobs)*, and *the number of powerful actors* then the code will report the result of each mob simulated (success or fail), number mobbers who: acted (partici- pated), withdraw, did power exchange, acted against the mob, and the participation rate. We calculate the *participation rate* using two formulas shown in Eqs. 1 and 2 below. Equation 1 takes into consideration the effect of people who *act against* the mob, while Eq. 2 does not take into consideration the effect of people who act against the mob.

$$Participation\ Rate = \frac{(Act\ Counter + Num\ Powerful\ Actors - Act\ Against\ Counter)}{Mob\ Practitioners}$$

$$(1)$$

$$Participation\ Rate = \frac{(Act\ Counter + Num\ Powerful\ Actors)}{Mob\ Practitioners} \qquad (2)$$

The reason we used these two equations is to study the effect of the people who oppose the mob goal (and act against it) on the mob outcome. In the second equation, we ignore the effect of those people. So, the first case is analogous to viewing what happens during a mob as two competing events where some people act while others act against them. However, in Eq. 2, the mob can be viewed as one event represented by only those who act. In both cases, the number of acts against individuals will be there however, in Eq. 1 we count for it, while in Eq. 2, we do not count for it. Also, in both cases, the *participation rate* will be used to determine if the mob succeeded or not, i.e., if the *participation rate* exceeds the provided threshold value that means the event was important enough to attract enough people to participate, so it will be marked as a successful mob, otherwise, it will be marked as an unsuccessful (fail) mob. The script also reports aggregate results, i.e., the overall success and failure rate (out of the simulated mobs how many succeeded? and how many failed?). Finally, the script reports *the average participation rate of all the simulated mobs*.

Running the second script file, i.e., `Mob_Simulator-Q2.py` will prompt the user to enter *the total number of invited people*, the *threshold value of the mob success*, and the *number of simulations (mobs)*. The script will report the result of each mob simulated (success or failure), how many powerful mobbers were needed to make the failed mob a successful one, the number of mobbers who: acted (participated), withdraw, did power exchange, acted against the mob, and the participation rate. For the *participation rate*, we also used Eq. 1 and Eq. 2 as shown above for the same reasons mentioned. However, we do not count for the number of powerful actors as in the case in Mob_Simulator-Q1.py because we are trying to calculate how many powerful actors are needed when the mob fails in both cases, i.e., in competing events and as one event. To do this, we used Eqs. 3 and 4, shown below, to calculate those needed powerful actors.

$$NPA = \left(\frac{STho * MP}{100}\right) - AC + AAC \tag{3}$$

$$NPA = \left(\frac{STho * MP}{100}\right) - AC \tag{4}$$

where *NPA* is the number of needed powerful actors (e.g., mob organizers), *STho* is the success threshold value, *MP* is the number of invited individuals, *AAC* is the number of individuals who act against the mob, and *AC* is the number of individuals who act/participate in the mob. This script will also report aggregate results, i.e., the overall success and failure rate (out of the simulated mobs how many succeeded? and how many failed?). It also reports on average *how many powerful actors are needed to make most of the failed mobs succeed.*

4   Results and Analysis

In this section, we focus on answering the research questions listed in the introduction section using the scripts described in Sect. 3. We used Mob_Simulator-Q1.py to answer the first research question *RQ1: Given the following parameters (Number of Invited People, Threshold Value of the Mob Success, the Number of Simulations (Mobs), the Number of Powerful Actors), what is the chance a mob will succeed?* We set the *number of invited people* to 100 in all the experiments we conducted. We also set the *number of powerful actors* to 0 to simulate the case when we do not know the number of powerful actors. Finally, we set the *number of simulations* for each case to 10,000 simulations (mobs). The *goal* here is to estimate the *average participation rate* that can be resulted from running the model without knowing the number of powerful actors. Knowing this rate will help in estimating the threshold value that we can use to determine the success or failure of a mob.

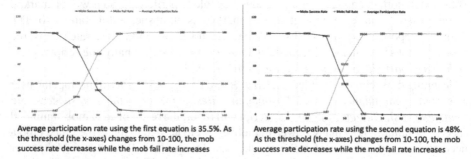

Average participation rate using the first equation is 35.5%. As the threshold (the x-axes) changes from 10-100, the mob success rate decreases while the mob fail rate increases | Average participation rate using the second equation is 48%. As the threshold (the x-axes) changes from 10-100, the mob success rate decreases while the mob fail rate increases

Fig. 1. Change in average participation rate, mob success rate, and mob fail rate as the threshold change from 10–100 (the x-axis).

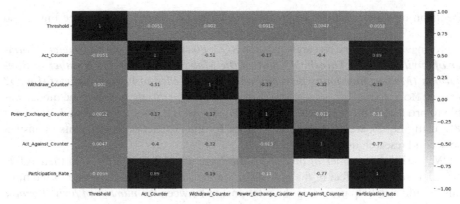

Fig. 2. Correlation between the various mobber types when we used Eq. 1 to calculate the participation rate.

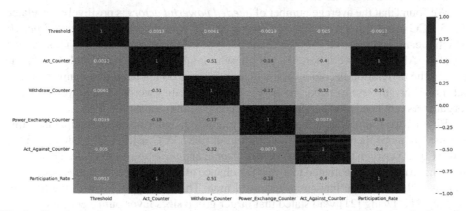

Fig. 3. Correlation between the various mobber types when we used Eq. 2 to calculate the participation rate.

We found that the *mob success rate* depends inversely on the *threshold* provided (i.e., if the *threshold* increases the success rate decrease) with *Pearson Correlation Coefficient* (PCC) of -0.86 when we used Eq. 1 to calculate the participation rate and -0.90 when we used Eq. 2 to calculate the *participation rate*.

We also found that the *average participation rate* regardless of the provided threshold is around 35.5% when we used Eq. 1 to calculate the participation rate and 48% when we used Eq. 2. This means that under the current model, if a mob has less than 35.5% (or 48%) threshold it will most likely succeed, however, if the threshold value is more than 35.5% (or 48%) the mob will most likely fail (see Fig. 1).

Finally, we found a positive correlation between the *participation rate* and the number of mobbers who *act* (0.89 PCC using Eq. 1 OR 1.0 PCC using Eq. 2). Also, we found a negative correlation between the *participation rate* and the number of mobbers who: *act against* (-0.77 OR -0.4); *withdraw* (-0.19 OR -0.51); and *power exchange* (-0.11 OR -0.18). Overall, the mobbers who are against the mob seem to have more negative effects on mob success than people who withdraw or power exchange (see Fig. 2 and Fig. 3).

To answer the second research question *RQ2: given the following parameters (Number of Invited People, Threshold Value of the Mob Success, and the Number of Simulations (Mobs)), how many powerful actors are needed to have a successful mob?* we used Mob_Simulator-Q2.py. Since the average *threshold* value, the model was able to produce without knowing the *number of powerful actors*, was around 35.5% (or 48% using Eq. 2), we used these two values for the next set of experiments to answer the second research question.

We varied the *number of invited people* from 10–100 then 100–1000 then 1000–10,000 to study the effect of the *crowd size* on the success (or failure) rate of the mob. This should also help in finding the relationship between the *number of invited people* and *the needed powerful actors* (organizers, e.g., for a given mob with a specific number of invited people how many organizers do we need to make the mob succeed?). We also simulated 10,000 mobs for each case.

We found that the average number of *needed powerful actors* is positively correlated (0.85 PCC using Eq. 1 OR 0.21 PCC using Eq. 2) with the *number of invited people* which means the bigger the *crowd size* the *more* powerful actors we need to make a mob succeed. Also, when we ignore the people who might act against the mob (i.e., using Eq. 2), the correlation becomes less, which means we do not need that many powerful actors (or organizers) to make the mob succeed. In other words, less powerful actors (organizers) are needed when there are no people acting against the mob.

Finally, we found that in both cases (counting or ignoring the participants acting against the mob) there is a positive correlation (0.87 PCC using Eq. 1 OR 0.79 PCC using Eq. 2) between the *number of invited people* and *the mob success rate*. This means as we have more people invited to a mob the chance of participation increases which also increases the chance of having a successful mob. This finding aligns with the findings of Sung-Ha Hwang [21] who stated that larger group sizes favor punishers (in our case those who participate in the mob).

5   Limitation

This paper does not claim that the model we created will be able to predict the success (or failure) of a real-world mob and the number of organizers needed for a real-world mob to succeed with 100% accuracy because this claim needs ground truth data to be measured. However, this theoretically supported model should give us a good estimation. Most of the factors used here have been studied in the literature but have never been used computationally to simulate and study mobs. The model still needs to consider other factors such as the time of the event, the existence of social ties between the mobbers, the location of the events, etc. as all these factors can significantly affect the mobber's decision to act/participate (or not) in a mob. However, building a more accurate model requires interdisciplinary knowledge and collaboration between psychologists, sociologists, computer scientists, and others. This model serves as a proof of concept that factors from the theories of social science can be extracted and computationally used to simulate real-world mobs, or behaviors to understand their effects on society and be prepared when things do not go as expected.

6 Conclusion and Future Research Directions

In this study, we simulated around 760,000 mobs using the Monte Carlo method guided by scenarios (decision rules) build based on factors extracted from the theory of Collective Action. The goal is to build a theoretical model that can help us better understand the mob phenomenon.

We found that the mob success rate, using either Eq. 1 or Eq. 2, has a strong negative correlation with the threshold value. We also found that the average participation rate (regardless of the provided threshold) is around 35.5% when we used Eq. 1 and 48% when we used Eq. 2. This implies that when we have people acting against the mob, less participation should be expected. The participation rate is positively correlated with the number of mobbers who act and negatively correlated with the number of mobbers who act against, withdraw, or do power exchange. This implies that when more people act, the chance of the mob succeeding increases. The number of needed powerful actors has a positive correlation with the number of invited people using either Eq. 1 or Eq. 2 which means the bigger the crowd size the more powerful actors are needed to make a mob succeed. The correlation is also less when we use Eq. 2 which shows the effect of the people who can act against the mob, i.e., if we do not have people act against the mob, we will need fewer powerful actors (mob organizers) for a mob to succeed (and vice versa). Finally, we found that in both cases the more people invited to the mob, the higher the chance of succeeding (i.e., there is a strong positive correlation between the number of invited people and the mob success rate).

As stated in the limitation section, this is a simple model which provides good insights and proof of concept, however, a future model refinement is needed as more factors can be added to the model such as the risk of participation, suitability of the location, etc. Another future research direction could be to compare the results obtained from the model to ground truth data (real-world mobs) as it would serve as a great model validation method. Also, currently, the model is implemented using Python programming language, however creating a web-based tool of the model would better serve non-technical savvy users and could be another future work. Finally, Clark Mcphail et al., [26] stated that purposive individuals in the same gathering can generate similar reference signals that result in varying forms of collective action of varying complexity: (1) *Independently*: no communication between individuals when they decide to act or not, (2) *Interdependently*: individuals communicate with other individuals to figure out what to do, and (3) *Voluntarily or Obediently*: individuals communicate with their bosses (e.g., powerful actors) and do what they are asked to do, i.e., to act the same way as the powerful actors, i.e., act. Our model is analogous to the first form mentioned above, i.e., *Independently*: after individuals are invited to participate in the mob, they decide what to do based on their interest and control. However, in real-world cases, many people change their mind as the mob progress. For example, some of the invited people to a mob might decide not to act at the beginning then once they see many others participating, they change their mind and decide to act (i.e., follow the herd) and vice versa. So, one possible future research direction is to investigate the dynamic nature of such a phenomenon, i.e., giving participants the freedom to change their minds.

Acknowledgments. This material is based upon work supported in part by the Office of the Under Secretary of Defense for Research and Engineering under award number FA9550-22-1-0332, U.S. Office of Naval Research (N00014-10-1-0091, N00014-14-1-0489, N00014-15-P-1187, N00014-16-1-2016, N00014-16-1-2412, N00014-17-1-2675, N00014-17-1-2605, N68335-19-C-0359, N00014-19-1-2336, N68335-20-C-0540, N00014-21-1-2121, N00014-21-1-2765, N00014-22-1-2318), U.S. Air Force Research Laboratory, U.S. Army Research Office (W911NF-20-1-0262, W911NF-16-1-0189), U.S. Defense Advanced Research Projects Agency (W31P4Q-17-C-0059), the U.S. National Science Foundation (OIA-1946391, OIA-1920920, IIS-1636933, ACI-1429160, and IIS-1110868), Arkansas Research Alliance, the Jerry L. Maulden/Entergy Endowment at the University of Arkansas at Little Rock, and the Australian Department of Defense Strategic Policy Grants Program (SPGP) (award number: 2020-106-094). Any opinions, findings, conclusions, or recommendations expressed in this material are those of the author(s) and do not necessarily reflect the views of the U.S. Department of Defense. The researcher(s) gratefully acknowledges the generous support.

References

1. Al-khateeb, S., Agarwal, N.: Cyber flash mobs: a multidisciplinary review. Soc. Netw. Anal. Min. (2021)
2. Al-khateeb, S., Anderson, M., Agarwal, N.: Studying the role of social bots during cyber flash mobs. Presented at the International Conference on Social Computing, Behavioral-Cultural Modeling and Prediction and Behavior Representation in Modeling and Simulation (SBP-BRiMS2021), Washington DC, USA, July 2021
3. Tucker, E., Watkins, T.: More flash mobs gather with criminal intent. NBC News 09 Aug 2011. https://www.nbcnews.com/id/wbna44077826. Accessed 07 Jan 2021
4. Steinblatt, H.: E-Incitement: A Framework for Regulating the Incitement of Criminal Flash Mobs, p. 43 (2011)
5. Staff, W.P.: Woman dies after shooting in U.S. Capitol; D.C. National Guard activated after mob breaches building. Washington Post, 06 January 2021. https://www.washingtonpost.com/dc-md-va/2021/01/06/dc-protests-trump-rally-live-updates/. Acccssed 11 Jan 2021
6. Barry, D., McIntire, M., Rosenberg, M.: Our president wants us here': the mob that stormed the capitol. The New York Times (2021). https://www.nytimes.com/2021/01/09/us/capitol-rioters.html. Accessed 11 Jan 2021
7. Pratley, N.: The Reddit flash mob won't be able to work the GameStop magic on silver," the Guardian, 01 February 2021. http://www.theguardian.com/business/nils-pratley-on-finance/2021/feb/01/reddits-flash-mob-wont-be-able-to-work-the-gamestop-magic-on-silver. Accessed 05 Feb 2021
8. Brignall, M.: How GameStop traders fired the first shots in millennials' war on Wall Street," the Guardian, 30 Janurary 2021. http://www.theguardian.com/business/2021/jan/30/how-gamestop-traders-fired-the-first-shots-in-millenials-war-on-wall-street. Accessed 05 Feb 2021
9. Zelle, J.M.: Python Programming: An Introduction to Computer Science, 3rd edn. Franklin, Beedle & Associates, Inc., USA (2004). https://mcsp.wartburg.edu/zelle/python/ppics3/index.html. Accessed 12 June 2021
10. Kenton, W.: Monte Carlo Simulation. Investopedia, 27 December 2020. https://www.investopedia.com/terms/m/montecarlosimulation.asp. Accessed 12 June 2021
11. Palisade: What is Monte Carlo Simulation?. Monte Carlo Simulation: What is it and How Does it Work? - Palisade. https://www.palisade.com/risk/monte_carlo_simulation.asp. Accessed 12 June 2021

12. Al-Khateeb, S., Agarwal, N.: Modeling flash mobs in cybernetic space: evaluating threats of emerging socio-technical behaviors to human security. In: 2014 IEEE Joint Intelligence and Security Informatics Conference, pp. 328–328 (2014)
13. Al-khateeb, S., Agarwal, N.: Analyzing flash mobs in cybernetic space and the imminent security threats a collective action based theoretical perspective on emerging sociotechnical behaviors. In: 2015 AAAI Spring Symposium Series (2015)
14. Al-Khateeb, S., Agarwal, N.: Developing a conceptual framework for modeling deviant cyber flash mob: a socio-computational approach leveraging hypergraph constructs. J. Digit. Forensics Secur. Law 9(2), 10 (2014)
15. Al-Khateeb, S., Agarwal, N.: Analyzing deviant cyber flash mobs of Isil on Twitter. In: International Conference on Social Computing, Behavioral-Cultural Modeling, and Prediction, pp. 251–257 (2015)
16. Nicholson, J.A.: Flash! Mobs in the Age of Mobile Connectivity, no. 6, p. 15 (2005)
17. Barnes, N.G., MOB IT AND SELL IT: CREATING MARKETING OPPORTUNITY THROUGH THE REPLICATION OF FLASH MOBS. Market. Manag. J. 16(1) (2006)
18. Do Vale, S., Trash mob: Zombie walks and the positivity of monsters in western popular culture. In: The Domination of Fear, Brill Rodopi, pp. 191–202 (2010)
19. Al-khateeb, S., Agarwal, N.: Flash mob: a multidisciplinary review. SNAM 11(1), 97 (2021). https://doi.org/10.1007/s13278-021-00810-7
20. Muralidhar, K.: Monte Carlo simulation. In: Encyclopedia of Information Systems, vol. 3, pp. 193–201. Elsevier, Amsterdam (2003). https://doi.org/10.1016/B0-12-227240-4/00114-3. Accessed 09 Sept 2021
21. Hwang, S.-H.: Larger groups may alleviate collective action problems. In: Working Paper 2009-05, Department of Economics, University of Massachusetts, Amherst, MA (2009). http://hdl.handle.net/10419/64195. Accessed 14 June 2021
22. Lanchester, F.W.: Aircraft in Warfare: The Dawn of the Fourth Arm. Constable Limited (1916)
23. Olson, M.: Logic of Collective Action: Public Goods and the Theory of Groups. Harvard University Press (1965)
24. Coleman, J.S.: Mathematics of Collective Action. Transaction Publishers (2017)
25. Biggart, N.W.: Readings in Economic Sociology, vol. 4. Blackwell, Malden (2002)
26. McPhail, C., Powers, W.T., Tucker, C.W.: Simulating individual and collective action in temporary gatherings. Soc. Sci. Comput. Rev. 10(1), 1–28 (1992)

Dynamic Approach to Modeling Hierarchical Conflict Situations in Small Groups

Ludmila Borisova$^{(\boxtimes)}$ and Mira Fridman

Financial University under the Government of RF, 49, Leningradsky Prospect, Moscow 125993, Russia
lrborisova@fa.ru

Abstract. The paper deals with a dynamic approach to modeling some social conflicts using differential equations. The presence of conflicts in society at different levels has both negative and positive aspects. The negative ones include financial, material, psychological and other losses, up to the loss of participants' lives. However, there is also a certain positive moment - the conflict, like any movement in society, contributes to its development and exit from the state of stagnation.

The dynamic approach proposed by the authors finds application not in global and mass conflicts, but in the interaction of small groups of participants. This model has certain limitations, but its application in some cases allows obtaining results confirming its adequacy.

In this paper a dynamic model (linear and non-linear) is used to study the superior-subordinate (boss-subordinates) conflict. The results obtained allow us to formulate the conditions that the exhaustion of the resources of one of the parties, leading to the end of the confrontation between the participants (players in terms of game theory).

The nonlinear dynamic model leads to interesting results - the independence of the solution from the initial conditions. The solution is determined only by the ratio of the model parameters. The paper analyzes marginal outcomes and their impact on conflict resolution. Conditions are formulated under which the end of the conflict means the complete disappearance of the initiative of workers.

Keywords: Differential equations · System parameters · Simulation

1 Introduction

Achieving maximum results is the ultimate goal of any operating company. Various factors affect the success of the company's activity - financial, managerial, social and others. An important role among them is played by the cohesion of the employments team. Team cohesion is a factor primarily related to small groups in which there are elements of the hierarchy - the boss (manager) and subordinates.

N. Agarwal et al. (Eds.): MSBC 2022, CCIS 1717, pp. 14–26, 2023.
https://doi.org/10.1007/978-3-031-33728-4_2

In case of there is cohesion in every small group and there are no irreconcilable contradictions and insoluble conflicts, then the association of such prosperous groups into a large team is fruitful and improves the operating the whole company. For these reasons the authors consider it important and relevant to study small groups with elements of a hierarchy. One very important aspect of the research of such groups is the conflict situations study. Conflicts can be, for example, personal, emotional, religious, racial, related to lack of tolerance, etc.

Such conflicts have a destructive effect on production activities and are considered a negative factor in its implementation.

However, there are also purely professional conflicts that are an integral part of production activities and in many cases have a positive effect on the result of operation. As a result of such conflicts, optimal ways of solving operational tasks are developed.

Formalization and creation of adequate mathematical models in the study of any psychological problems, including the problem of the emergence and dynamics of the development of conflict situations, is a very difficult task [1]. The process consists, first of all, in the maximum possible level of formalization of the situation without a significant loss of its adequacy, then the construction of a mathematical model, the selection of the most important parameters and the choice of methods for solving the problem.

The authors chose a dynamic model, which has already been used in other areas, and for the first time adapted it to the study of conflict situations in small groups with hierarchical elements. A game-theoretic approach was also applied to solve similar problems.

2 Results

2.1 Deterministic Conflict Models

During the First World War, the English mathematician Frederick William Lanchester (1868–1945) proposed a mathematical model of air combat [2, 3]. During it, the likely losses of the aircraft of the opposing sides will be proportional to the number of possible meetings. With equal success, this model can be used for other types of conflict confrontations between the two sides. The Cauchy problem for a system of two differential equations is the following:

$$\begin{cases} \frac{dN_1}{dt} = -k_1 N_1 N_2, \\[2mm] \frac{dN_2}{dt} = -k_2 N_1 N_2, \\[2mm] N_1(t_0) = N_{10}, N_2(t_0) = N_{20}. \end{cases}$$

The Lanchester model has an analytical solution:

$$\frac{dN_1}{dN_2} = \frac{k_1}{k_2}.$$
$$N_1 k_2 - N_2 k_1 = const.$$

$$N_1 k_2 - N_2 k_1 = N_{10} k_2 - N_{20} k_1.$$

From the analysis of the solution, it is clear at what ratio of parameters one or the other side prevails.

It is worth noting that M.P. Osipov was a year ahead of Lanchester in publishing a model of military conflict. He considered a model of ground combat [4]. Osipov's article was published in 1915, Lanchester's in 1916. For the case of ground combat, when enemy losses occur as a result of direct contact on the front line, Osipov proposed the following model:

$$\begin{cases} \dfrac{dN_1}{dt} = -k_1 N_2, \\ \dfrac{dN_2}{dt} = -k_2 N_1, \\ N_1(t_0) = N_{10}, N_2(t_0) = N_{20}. \end{cases}$$

This system has an analytical solution $k_2 N_{10}^2 - k_1 N_{20}^2 = C, C = const.$

The conclusion from the Osipov model is the following: if it is necessary to overcome an equal opponent, then you need to have twice as many resources as he has. The Lanchester model predicts that it takes as much force as the opponent to contain an equal opponent. Osipov's model is more realistic. The ideas of Osipov and Lanchester were used to create more complex models of conflict that would take into account direct and feedback [5]. As a rule, these more advanced models in the literature were supported by specific historical data or the parameters of such models were selected based on real conflicts [5, 6].

2.2 The Study of Human Relationships Using the Methodology of System Dynamics

A feature of modern conflicts is the sharply increased role of information support for the conflict, since in the global information field, directed information and disinformation are most actively used for ideological, political and economic purposes, which is very difficult for an unprepared person to distinguish from the general background. Previously, the authors used a dynamic approach to the study of paired conflicts arising in the labor collective [7].

When modeling, to begin with, we will limit ourselves to considering pair relationships. Paired relationships between two equal members of the team become especially important when the question arises about the joint implementation of a project that requires long-term communication between employees, and the result of work depends not only on the abilities and qualifications of each of the partners, but also on their ability to work in a team, discuss, make joint decisions. In this case, subjective moments begin to play an important role, which we can conditionally call "liking" and "dislike" [8].

Let's consider two components of any organization – leaders and ordinary members of the organization. We will describe their number by variables x and y, respectively.

The system of equations in this case will take the form:

$$\begin{cases} \dfrac{dx}{dt} = ax + by + f, \\ \dfrac{dy}{dt} = cx + dy + g. \end{cases}$$

If we equate the right-hand sides of these equations to zero, we get a system of two linear algebraic equations:

$$\begin{cases} aA + bB + f = 0, \\ cA + dB + g = 0. \end{cases}$$

By solving this system, one can find stationary values $\overline{A}$ and $\overline{B}$:

$$\overline{A} = \frac{gb - df}{ad - bc}, \quad \overline{B} = \frac{cf - ag}{ad - bc}.$$

Thus, in this system, with a certain set of parameters, an equilibrium stable state is quickly achieved.

Let's write a characteristic equation for these differential equations:

$$\lambda^2 - \lambda(a + d) + ad - bc = 0.$$

The roots of the characteristic equation are the numbers

$$\lambda_{1,2} = \frac{a + d \pm \sqrt{(a + d)^2 - 4(ad - bc)}}{2}.$$

If $(a + d)^2 - 4 \cdot (ad - bc) > 0$, then both roots are valid. In the case $(ad - bc) > 0$ both roots are negative. If $(ad - bc) < 0$ one root is negative, the other is positive.

In the first case, there is a long-term confrontation between the leaders and ordinary members of the organization. In the second case, one of the parties cannot make up for its losses, and the conflict that has arisen between the leaders and ordinary members will be exhausted.

Now let's see how the behavior of the system will change taking into account non-linear interactions. We modify the system of linear equations discussed above. Let the variable x denote the number of leaders, and the variable y – the number of ordinary members of the organization:

$$\begin{cases} \frac{dx}{dt} = \alpha x - \beta xy + \delta y - \varepsilon x, \\ \frac{dy}{dt} = \beta xy - \gamma x. \end{cases}$$

Consider the case when $\alpha - \varepsilon = \gamma$, $\delta = 0$. In this case, under the given initial conditions, it is possible to obtain an exact solution of the system and analyze it.

Let initial conditions are following:

$$x(0) = x_0, \ y(0) = y_0.$$

Over time, the size of the organization does not change, that is

$$x(t) + y(t) = x_0 + y_0.$$

Under these conditions, the Cauchy problem for a system of nonlinear differential equations has a unique solution that is not difficult to find analytically. The system of differential equations with the above parameters will be written as follows:

$$\begin{cases} \frac{dx}{dt} = \gamma x - \beta xy, \\ \frac{dy}{dt} = \beta xy - \gamma x. \end{cases}$$

From the condition of immutability of the size of the organization over time, it follows that

$$y(t) = x_0 + y_0 - x(t).$$

We substitute this relation into the first equation of the system presented above. We obtain an autonomous equation:

$$\frac{dx}{dt} = \gamma x - \beta x(y_0 + x_0 - x).$$

After separating the variables, we obtain the equation

$$\frac{dx}{(\gamma - \beta(y_0 + x_0))x + \beta x^2} = dt.$$

This equation is integrated in quadrature's. After integrating and taking into account the immutability of the number of organizations over time, we obtain a solution to a system of equations:

$$x(t) = \frac{x_0(\gamma - \beta(y_0 + x_0))}{(\gamma - \beta(y_0 + x_0)) \exp(-(\gamma - \beta(y_0 + x_0)t)) + N(t)},$$
$$N(t) = \beta x_0(1 - \exp(-(\gamma - \beta(y_0 + x_0)t))),$$

$$y(t) = y_0 + x_0 - \frac{x_0(\gamma - \beta(y_0 + x_0))}{(\gamma - \beta(y_0 + x_0)) \exp(-(\gamma - \beta(y_0 + x_0)t)) + N(t)}.$$

Dynamics $x(t)$, $y(t)$, calculated at $\gamma = -0.0085$, $\beta = 0.00001$, $x(0) = 30$, $y(0) = 25$ is presented in Fig. 1

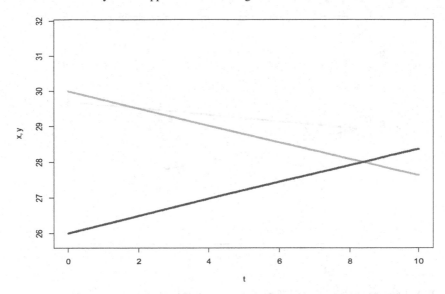

Fig. 1. Solving the model of two nonlinear differential equations in R-Studio.

The analysis of the model shows that the solution does not depend on the initial conditions, but is determined by the parameters of the model. It is possible to achieve that the number of leaders decreases to zero, while the number of ordinary members tends to the total number of members of the organization, which will minimize any initiative in the organization.

Modifying the model. Let's consider a conflict situation in a small team in the presence of a third party – a peacemaker. To simulate such a situation, one can use the apparatus of differential equations to study the main trends in the behavior of the opposing sides. Let's denote these sides by the variables x, y. We will take the peacemaker for z. These variables indicate the information component of the conflicting parties. A system of differential equations describing a generalized industrial conflict situation in this case it can have the form:

$$\begin{cases} \dfrac{dx}{dt} = \alpha x - \beta z - \gamma_1, \\[2mm] \dfrac{dy}{dt} = \alpha y - \beta z - \gamma_2, \\[2mm] \dfrac{dz}{dt} = \delta(x + y). \end{cases}$$

In the first approximation, we neglect nonlinear interactions. In addition, the variables of the model do not describe the number of participants in the conflict, but some information component of the conflict. All the negativity is assumed by the peacemaking side, and the conflict fades away, and it is possible to achieve a state when one of the conflicting parties practically does not get out of balance (see Fig. 2). Dynamics $x(t)$, $y(t)$, $z(t)$ calculated at.

$\alpha = 0.001, \beta = 0.01, \gamma_1 = 0.05, \gamma_2 = 0.01, \delta = 0.0025, x(0) = 20, y(0) = 20, z(0) = 20.$

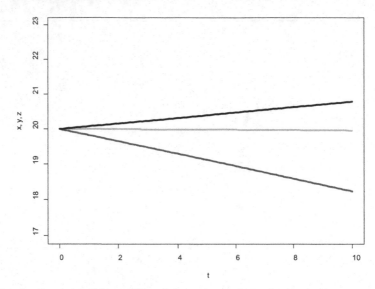

Fig. 2. Solving the model of three differential equations in R-Studio (black colour $-z(t)$, red $-x(t)$, blue $-y(t)$). (Color figure online)

2.3 Using Game Theory Methods to Investigate Conflict

We have considered mathematical models of both the dynamics of the conflict, where two interested parties participate, and models of negotiations involving a third, independent party who will be responsible for decision-making. To describe the results of the activities of a third party, an arbitrator, we introduce a continuous random variable with a known distribution law [9].

A normal distribution (Laplace-Gaussian) is a distribution in which a variable change continuously, with extreme values of the magnitude (largest and smallest) they rarely appear, but the closer the attribute values are to the center (to the arithmetic mean), the more common it is [10].

As is known (in accordance with the Central Limit Theorem), most quantities that can be considered as the sum of independent uniformly distributed random variables have a normal distribution. Such, for example, are the height of a person or the weight of a person. A person's psyche and mental abilities are also, as a rule, influenced by many independent factors. On the other hand, the Italian economist Wilfredo Pareto found out a century ago that in different countries of the world the wealthiest 25% of the population controlled most of the wealth. The consequences of the phenomenon discovered by Pareto are known by many names: the 80/20 rule, Zipf's law, power law distribution, the winner—takes-all principle - but the distribution model is always the same: the richest, most active, most connected participants in the system are responsible for states, actions or the number of connections that are many times higher than the average. For these reasons, it is interesting to analyze the normal distribution of the arbitrator's opinion and the Pareto distribution [11].

2.4 Mathematical Modeling of the Arbitration Procedure in the Normal Distribution of the Arbitrator's Opinion and in the Pareto Distribution

As an example, let's consider the problem of the participation of two conflicting parties in solving some economic dispute (the delivery of the object to the customer, the agreement of the two parties on the contractual salary for the work performed) [12].

The customer offers payment under the contracts – h, and the contractor insists on paying g. The arbiter has his own opinion – x. Let the arbiter's opinion be a random variable having a continuous distribution function $F(x)$ and a distribution density function $f(x)$. Let the cost of work under the contract be $S(h, g)$. Consider the case when a random variable – the arbitrator's opinion on the amount of payment under the contracts – has a normal distribution law with parameters a (mathematical expectation) and σ^2 (variance). 9 Distribution function:

$$F(x) = \frac{1}{2} + \frac{1}{2}\Phi(\frac{x-a}{\sigma}), \quad \Phi(x) = \frac{2}{\sqrt{2\pi}} \int_0^x e^{-\frac{t^2}{2}} dt.$$

We assume that $h < g$. Let the arbitrator, having his opinion on the level of payments under the contract – x – choose the offer from the two available, which is closer to x. Consider

$$S(h, g) = hF\left(\frac{h+g}{2}\right) + g\left(1 - F\left(\frac{h+g}{2}\right)\right).$$

We investigate the equilibrium situation when partial derivatives $\frac{\partial S}{\partial h}$ and $\frac{\partial S}{\partial g}$ are equal to zero:

$$\frac{\partial S}{\partial h} = F(\frac{h+g}{2}) + \frac{h}{2}f(\frac{h+g}{2}) - \frac{g}{2}f(\frac{h+g}{2}) = 0,$$

$$\frac{\partial S}{\partial g} = \frac{h}{2}f(\frac{g+h}{2}) + 1 - F(\frac{h+g}{2}) - \frac{g}{2}f(\frac{g+h}{2}) = 0.$$

Let's solve this system of algebraic equations with respect to F and f:

$$F(\frac{h+g}{2}) = \frac{1}{2}, f(\frac{h+g}{2}) = \frac{1}{g-h}.$$

The point at which the partial derivatives $\frac{\partial S}{\partial h}$ and $\frac{\partial S}{\partial g}$ are zero will be the saddle point corresponding to the Nash equilibrium [13]. It is possible to find an equilibrium situation that is rational for all players.

We got the value of $F(x)$ equal to $\frac{1}{2}$ at value $x = \frac{h+g}{2}$. This means that the average value of a random variable – the number a – coincides with the value $\frac{h+g}{2}$. The value of the probability density function at $x = a$

$$f(a) = \frac{1}{\sigma\sqrt{2\pi}}f(\frac{h+g}{2}) = \frac{1}{g-h}.$$

Solving a system of algebraic equations

$$\begin{cases} g - h = \sigma\sqrt{2\pi}, \\ g + h = 2a \end{cases}$$

we get the equilibrium proposals of the opposing sides.

For the standard normal distribution ($a = 0$, $\sigma^2 = 1$) we have:

$$h = -\sqrt{\tfrac{\pi}{2}} \approx -1,253, \quad g = -\sqrt{\tfrac{\pi}{2}} \approx 1,253.$$

A simple assumption is logically justified that the opinion of the arbitrator is some function of the arithmetic mean of the parties involved in the negotiations. The variance of the random variable describing the arbitrator's decisions mainly determines the difference in the requirements of the two conflicting parties.

By choosing the law of distribution, which obeys the opinion of the arbitrator, we reflect the actual nature of his behavior. The result of solving the problem should be directly related to the choice of the distribution law.

We have made calculations for three more laws of the distribution of the arbitrator's opinion. In the case of another symmetric law, the Laplace distribution, the result practically did not differ from the calculation using the normal distribution law. In this case we have:

$$h = -\frac{\sqrt{2}}{2} \approx -0,7, \quad g = -\frac{\sqrt{2}}{2} \approx 0,7.$$

If the random variable X is subject to a logistic distribution, then for a = 0 and G = 1 (standard lognormal distribution):

$$h = -\frac{2\sqrt{3}}{\pi} \approx -1,103, \quad g = -\frac{2\sqrt{3}}{\pi} \approx 1,103.$$

Note that the lognormal distribution is symmetric with respect to the logarithm of the mean value of the studied quantity. We investigate the case when the random variable under study has an asymmetric distribution law. Let the opinion of the arbitrator be a random variable distributed according to Pareto's law. The Pareto distribution is two–parameter. Let its parameters – x_0 be the minimum possible value and m be the exponent. The probability density function has the form:

$$f(x) = \frac{m}{x_0}\left(\frac{x_0}{x}\right)^{m+1}.$$

Distribution function of Pareto's law: $F(x) = 1 - \left(\frac{x_0}{x}\right)^{m+1}$.

Mathematical expectation of a random variable distributed according to the Pareto law:

$$E(x) = \frac{mx}{m-1}.$$

Variance, unlike mathematical expectation, is a constant value:

$$Var(x) = \frac{m}{m-2}\left(\frac{x_0}{m-1}\right).$$

Consider the case when $x_0 = 1$, $m = 3$ (with these parameters, the variance is Var(x) = 0,75). We obtain (as in the previous two cases) a system of two algebraic equations, from which it follows that

$$h = \sqrt[4]{2} - \frac{1}{3} \approx 0.86, \; g = \sqrt[4]{2} + \frac{1}{3} \approx 1.52.$$

Thus, in the case of a power dependence, the opinions of the disputing parties differ slightly, and since $x > x_0 = 1$, the arbitrator is likely to take the side of the customer, since the value of h is closer to this value x than g.

It is possible to logically predict the behavior of players and, therefore, it is possible to find an equilibrium situation that is rational for all players, if we use game theory. Finding such a balance is possible with some artificial restrictions, for example, that the players do not know about each other's actions or have only a single opportunity to respond, etc.

But in real life, it is difficult to find the right ratio between the degree of simplification of the problem for its manageability and maintaining a sufficient level of complexity for the adequacy of the model. In addition, it is necessary to exclude a situation where the final decision is made without taking into account the initial assumptions in this model, since the result in game theory is very sensitive to the initial conditions.

2.5 Choosing the Best Strategy for Conflict Resolution in Small Teams

In this regard, it seems interesting to develop a model of [14], in which a narrow set of strategic options is first generated. They can be adjusted to take into account changes in various assumptions. Instead of solving a single game, the model automatically includes a sequence of several games, allowing players to adjust their actions after each of them and find the best way for various combinations of factors. As a result, he realistically supports management decisions, presenting managers with the advantages and disadvantages of strategic options that remain at each stage of development. At the second stage, the model finds the "best reliable option", taking into account its growth potential and downside risks under all possible scenarios, assumptions and sensitivity over time. This approach is different from trying to find balance in an artificially simplified world.

Let's consider a possible example of using such a model.

Let's imagine a hypothetical situation where certain funds are allocated to prevent possible competitive actions. Between the various directions of preventive work, there is a need for their optimal distribution. There are mixed strategies for allocating these funds in order to reduce the risk possible in these situations.

From the point of view of unscrupulous competitors, the range of available options can be divided into four main options. Unscrupulous competitors may imitate existing operators by providing similar services. They may offer a more attractive service, for example, cheaper or more active. They could specialize by offering services, probably only during peak hours, which are not designed to compete with existing operators during less active user hours. Finally, they could stand out by providing clearly distinctive services.

Let's consider the possibility of using game theory for the situation of unfair competition described in the previous paragraph. Let's find the optimal mixed strategy of some particular game.

Let Company A (competitor) try to weaken Company B's business. Company A has two ways to attract customers profitably – price liberalization and network advantages. Company B has four operators that provide services. In order to cause economic damage to company B, it is sufficient that at least one of the services usually provided by company B is performed by company A, if it manages to attract buyers to its side. In order to carry out its unscrupulous activity of attracting company B customers, Company A uses one of two directions. Suppose that side A chose strategy A_1, side B chose strategy B_1. If no client uses the services of the company, the winning side is zero ($a_{11} = 0$).

Let the strategies A_1 and B_2 be chosen. In this situation, no matter which two directions side B chooses to place customer orders, the attackers will always have favorable options, and even if only one is losing. Let's assume that when choosing strategies A_1 and B_2, the likely gain of side A is 5/6. If we have complete information on the strategies of players A and B, we will fill in the remaining elements of the payment matrix of this game. Suppose that the payment matrix has the form shown in the Table 1.

Table 1. Payment matrix.

The company	B1	B2	B3	min
A_1	0	5/6	1/2	0
A_2	1	1/2	3/4	1/2
max	1	1/2	3/4	–

The lower price of the game is 1/2, the upper is 3/4. There is no saddle point, the optimal solution lies in the area of mixed strategies.

Let's make an optimization problem. The distribution of company B's efforts should be such that the company's profit in such a counteraction to unfair competitors is the greatest. This distribution is determined by solving a linear programming problem:

$$x_1 + x_2 \rightarrow \min.$$

The restrictions of the optimization problem are as follows:

$$\begin{cases} \dfrac{5}{6}x_1 + \dfrac{1}{2}x_2 \geq 1, \\ \dfrac{1}{2}x_1 + \dfrac{3}{4}x_2 \geq 1, \\ x_1 \geq 0; \quad x_2 \geq 1 \end{cases}$$

The optimal solution to this problem is the following:

$$x_1 = 0, 6; \quad x_2 = 1.$$

We get that it is impractical to use strategy B_3, strategy B_1 is used with probability 1/4, strategy B_2 is used with probability 3/4.

Such a model provides wide opportunities for application in the field of management of various industries, starting from the development of strategies for the operation of extensive networks of aviation and railway transport, the management of restaurant chains in a competitive environment, the management of personnel of the enterprise in order to improve the quality of work and reduce staff turnover.

When considering management problems in real life, it is always possible to find several conditions under which the interests of the players could be considered as consistent and mutually balanced.

You can see that the results depend on the initial assumptions: in other words, with a small modification of one of the parameters, completely different results are obtained. From this point of view, the model is a kind of business simulator, which allows managers to get a clear idea of the likely development of competition in various conditions. This helps companies generate the best option as competitors' actions become apparent.

3   Discussion and Conclusion

The use of various mathematical methods and the construction of adequate models for the analysis of conflict situations is a difficult task due to the high degree of uncertainty in real conditions. The authors present and substantiate a new methodology for processing sociological data in situations of conflict in small groups using dynamic and statistical game models.

Two classical approaches to resolving conflict situations involving a third party are considered. The presence of a sufficient amount of statistical data on the parties to the conflict is necessary to select the opinion of the arbitrator, which is modeled by a continuous distribution function. An interesting result was obtained in the case of a power dependence of the distribution function under study. In this case, it is difficult to choose a solution in favor of one of the parties, since this choice is of the same sign, which is significantly different from the conclusion in the case of symmetric distribution laws.

The use of differential or difference equations for modeling conflict situations in the presence of specific statistical data is also useful for studying the dynamics of industrial conflict. A specific calculation of the attenuation of the conflict for one side (indicated by the variable y) is given, provided that this side shares information with the peacekeeping side.

The dynamic approach proposed by the authors finds application not in global and mass conflicts, but in the interaction of small groups of participants. This model has certain limitations, but its application allows in some cases to obtain results confirming its adequacy. The authors assume in the future, having received the necessary information, to apply this model in real situations.

In conclusion, we note that the combination of managerial experience and intuition with the application of game theory is one of the most important ways to find optimal solutions to complex management problems that modern managers face, especially in conflict teams.

References

1. Simon, H.: A behavioral model of rational choice. In: Models of Man, Social and Rational: Mathematical Essays on Rational Human Behavior in a Social Setting. Wiley, New York (1957)
2. Lanchester, F.W.: Aircraft in Warfare: The Dawn of the Fourth Arm. Constable and Co., London (1916)
3. Shumov, V.V., Korepanov, V.O.: Mathematical models of combat and military operations. Comput. Res. Model. **12**(1), 217–242 (2020)
4. Osipov, M.P.: Vliyanie chislennosti srazhayushchikhsya storon na ikh poteri [The influence of the number of parties fighting on their losses]. Voennyi sbornik, no. 6, pp. 59–74; no. 7, pp. 25–36; no. 8, pp. 31–40; no. 9, pp. 25–37 (in Russian)
5. Novikov, D.A., Chkhartishvili, A.G.: Refleksiyai upravlenie: matematicheskie modeli [Reflection and control: mathematical models]. Moscow: Izd-vo fiziko-matematicheskoi literatury, p. 412 (2013)
6. Kress, M.: Lanchester models for irregular warfare. J. Math. **8**(5), 737 (2020). https://www.mdpi.com/709876
7. Borisova, L., Fridman, M.: Dynamic model of relationships. J. Mod. Math. Concepts Mod. Math. Educ. **1**(1), 51–54 (2015)
8. Wauer, J., Schwarzer, D., Cai, G.O., Lin, Y.K.: Dynamical models of love with time-varying fluctuations. J. Appl. Math. Comput. **188**, 1535–1548 (2007)
9. Myerson, R.B.: Game Theory: Analysis of Conflict. Harvard University Press, Cambridge-Massachusetts, London-England (1997)
10. Lee, M.-Y.: Strategic payoffs of normal distribution bump into Nash equilibrium in 2×2 game. Int. J. Game Theory Technol. **2** (2014)
11. Fonseca-Morales, A., Hernández-Lerma, O.: A note on differential games with Pareto-optimal Nash equilibria: deterministic and stochastic models. J. Dyn. Games **4**(3), 195–203 (2017)
12. Tokareva, Yu.S.: Modified arbitration procedure on the last proposal with the committee. Sci. Notes Petrozavodsk State Univ. **8**, 89–92 (2010)
13. Borisova, L.R., Kremer, N.S., Fridman, M.N.: Some approaches to the application of game theory in management tasks. J. Self-gov. **4**, 251–244 (2022)
14. Lindstädt, H., Müller, J.: Making game theory work for managers. https://www.mckinsey.de/business-functions/strategy-and-corporate-finance/our-insights/making-game-theory-work-for-managers

A Cognitive Simulation Model of a Regional Higher Education System

Olga Gorbaneva$^{(\boxtimes)}$ [ID], Anton Murzin [ID], Guennady Ougolnitsky [ID], and Stanislav Mikhalkovich [ID]

Southern Federal University, Rostov-on-Don, Russian Federation
{oigorbaneva,admurzin,miks}@sfedu.ru, gaougolnitsky@sfedu.com

Abstract. We propose and investigate a difference Stackelberg game with sustainable development requirements based on a cognitive model of a regional higher education system. In this model, the federal administration acts as the Leader, whereas higher education institutions (HEIs) act as Followers. The model is identified on an example of the Rostov region of the Russian Federation. The results of computer simulation with some analytical solution elements are presented. The influence of sustainable development conditions on the choice of control strategies is described. Several recommendations for the upper-level control subject and HEIs are formulated.

Keywords: cognitive model · computer simulation · difference Stackelberg games · higher education · sustainable management

1 Introduction

The cognitive modeling of complex systems is an extensive research area that has been actively developing for several decades. In a broad sense, cognitive modeling is understood as the use of various artificial intelligence (AI) models, e.g., neural networks [1]. A particular decision methodology for weakly structured systems based on cognitive maps was proposed by R. Axelrod [2]. A cognitive map is a signed or weighted oriented graph with the vertices corresponding to system components and the arcs to the relations between them. The paper [3] was among the first publications on the subject; the approach was described in detail in [4]. Fuzzy cognitive map models were surveyed in [5–7].

The methodology of cognitive modeling as the simulation modeling of complex systems based on cognitive maps was developed by N.A. Abramova, Z.K. Avdeeva, et al. (Trapeznikov Institute of Control Sciences RAS) and G.V. Gorelova et al. (Southern Federal University) [8–13]. The paper [8] provided a detailed analysis of the verification problem of cognitive models and an illustrative example of a particular model from this point of view. Some prospects for the development of this research area were outlined in [9, 12].

The work is supported by the Russian Science Foundation, project #23-21-00131.

S.V. Kovriga and V.I. Maximov (Trapeznikov Institute of Control Systems RAS) considered cognitive modeling as a structure-and-goal analysis tool with application to the development problems of Russian regions as well as stated and solved control problems; see [14, 15]. The experience of cognitive modeling of regional socio-economic processes was presented in [16]. The influence of a regional higher education system on the innovative development of the region was studied in [17].

Financial and organizational aspects of the higher education are considered in [18–20]. Budgeting and financial management in universities are studied in those papers.

A. Uspuriene, L. Sakalauskas, and V. Dumskis consider a problem of financial resource allocation in a higher education institution using mathematical modeling [21]. A financial flaw planning model of a university has been created, using multi-stage stochastic programming algorithms, with easily selected education institution's accounting data. The created model has been adapted to solve two-stage and multi-stage financial flaw optimization problems of a branch of university, and the obtained results of two-stage and multi-stage tasks have been compared. The proposed mixed integer programming algorithm can be flexibly adapted for practical needs of financial planning of education institutions [21].

All mentioned works pointed to the very important managerial aspect of cognitive modeling. In our opinion, this aspect should play a key role due to the activity of complex socio-economic and other weakly structured systems [22–25]. It is reasonable to distinguish between dynamic models of optimal control with a single subject [26, 27], conflict control with several competing subjects [28], and hierarchical control with an ordered set of control subjects [29]. Game-theoretic models on cognitive maps [30] are of particular interest. The author's approach to solving complex dynamic control problems using simulation modeling was described in [31].

However, the investigation of higher education institutions by means of cognitive modeling seems to be insufficient. In this paper, we construct and analyze a cognitive hierarchical control model for a regional higher education system. The model is written as a difference Stackelberg game with several lower-level subjects (higher education institutions of a region, HEIs). We find a Stackelberg equilibrium and investigate the model through computer simulation with analytical solution elements. In particular, the upper-level control problem is reduced to a linear programming problem. The model is applied to manage the higher education system of the Rostov region of the Russian Federation. The model parameters are identified, and the simulation results are used to formulate several recommendations for the upper-level control subject and the lower-level controlled subjects (HEIs).

The main novelty of the paper is that it illustrates possibilities of the application of optimal control and game theoretic problems on cognitive maps using real data about specific universities. This approach provides an analytical tool for complex investigation of a regional higher education system and allows for some recommendations on the management.

The remainder of this paper is organized as follows. Section 2 presents the model and its basic assumptions. The general investigation procedure of the model is outlined in Sect. 3. In Sect. 4, we describe in detail the identification methodology of the model based on available data for the Rostov region. In Sect. 5, we find a Stackelberg equilibrium of the model. Section 6 demonstrates the application of the model to universities in the Rostov region. Several control recommendations are provided in Sect. 7. In concluding the paper, Sect. 8 indicates some shortcomings of the approach and ways to overcome them.

2 A Cognitive Hierarchical Control Model of a Regional Higher Education System References

Consider a cognitive hierarchical control model of higher education development. There are an upper-level control subject (the government represented by the Federal Ministry of Education and Science) and lower-level controlled subjects (HEIs) directly subordinate to the upper level. HEIs enroll in M specialties. Students can study in an HEI on state-funded (budgetary) or commercial places. Budgetary places in an HEI are allocated by the upper-level control subject: their number does not directly depend on the HEI management. The number of commercial places for particular specialties can be set by an HEI independently. Also, an HEI determines the price of commercial education for each specialty. The government determines the financial per capita rate, i.e., the amount each HEI receives for each budgetary place. An HEI bears the costs of educating a given number of students (on commercial and budgetary places). Some commercial places provided by an HEI can remain unclaimed by applicants. We assume that the demand for commercial places in a specialty is directly proportional to the future wage of a graduate and inversely proportional to the price of commercial education. Also, the more attractive a specialty is for applicants, the more graduates will be employed. For a chosen planning horizon T, we obtain a mathematical model of the form:

$$J_0 = \sum\nolimits_{t=1}^{T} \sum\nolimits_{i=1}^{N} \sum\nolimits_{j=1}^{M} a_{0j} x_{ij}(t) \to max; \tag{1}$$

$$x_{ij}^B(t) \geq 0, a_{ij}^B(t) \geq 0; \tag{2}$$

$$\sum\nolimits_{i=1}^{N} \sum\nolimits_{j=1}^{M} a_{ij}^B x_{ij}^B(t) \leq B, \tag{3}$$

$$\sum\nolimits_{i=1}^{N} x_{ij}(t) \geq x_j^{min}; \tag{4}$$

$$J_i = \sum\nolimits_{t=1}^{T} \sum\nolimits_{j=1}^{M} \left[a_{ij}^B x_{ij}^B(t) + a_{ij}^C x_{ij}^C(t) - c_{ij} \left(\sum\nolimits_{j=1}^{M} x_{ij}(t) \right)^2 \right] \to max; \tag{5}$$

$$x_{ij}^C(t) \geq 0, a_{ij}^C(t) \geq 0; \tag{6}$$

$$x_{ij}(t+1) = x_{ij}^B(t+1) + min\{x_{ij}^C(t+1), (\gamma_j - a_{ij}^C(t)/4)^{\alpha_j} y_{ij}(t)\}, \ x_{ij}(0) = x_{ij0} \tag{7}$$

$$y_{ij}(t+1) = (1 - \kappa_{ij}) x_{ij}(t), \ y_{ij}(0) = y_{ij0}, \ i = 1, ..., N, \ j = 1, ..., M, \ t = 1, ..., T. \tag{8}$$

This model is a difference hierarchical game of the upper-level control subject (the Principal) and N HEIs (a difference Stackelberg game of $(N + 1)$ persons) with the following notations: N is the number of HEIs in a given region; M is the number of specialties; T is the planning horizon (game length); B is the annual budget of the upper-level control subject; $x_{ij}(t)$ is the number of students for the j-th specialty in the i-th HEI in year t; $x_{ij}^B(t)$ is the number of budgetary places for the j-th specialty in the i-th HEI in year t; $x_{ij}^C(t)$ is the number of commercial places for the j-th specialty in the i-th HEI in year t; x_{ij}^{min} is the minimum permissible number of graduates with the j-th specialty; a_{0j} is the social utility of one graduate with the j-th specialty; $a_{ij}^B(t)$ is the budget subsidy per one student for the j-th specialty in the i-th HEI in year t; $a_{ij}^C(t)$ is the price of commercial education for the j-th specialty in the i-th HEI in year t; γ_{ij} is the influence coefficient of potential employment on applying to the j-th specialty in the i-th HEI; κ_{ij} is the share of unemployed graduates with the j-th specialty in the i-th HEI; finally, c_i is the education cost coefficient of the i-th HEI depending on the total number of students in year t, and $y_{ij}(t)$ is the number of employed graduates with the j-th specialty of i-th university in year t.

Formula (1) defines the Principal's control goal, interpreted as the maximum social utility. Constraint (4) is treated as a sustainable development condition controlled by the Principal. According to this condition, the number of students in each specialty has a lower bound.

The model is reflected in a cognitive map (Fig. 1).

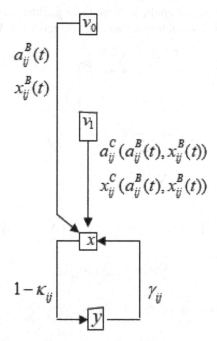

Fig. 1. The cognitive map of regional higher education control

The demand of applicants for commercial places in the j-th specialty (see the function (6)) is given by the term $(\gamma_j - a_j^C(t)/4)^{\alpha_j} y_j(t)$. The expression in parentheses can be explained as follows. By some estimates [32], long-term investments in higher education in Russia have an average payback period of 10 years: the price of commercial education is covered by future wages in a specialty at the rate of at least 10% annually. According to the Tabiturient portal (https://tabiturient.ru/vuzcost/), the average price of higher education in Russia in 2022 is 174533 rubles per year (about 17453 rubles per month). As discovered by the analytical center of Synergy University (https://ria.ru/20210914/zarplata-1749940260.html), the average desired wage is about 50–70 thousand rubles per month, which provides a sufficient level of comfortable life. Thus, for an effective return on investment in higher education in Russia, the future wage of a graduate should be at least three times higher than the monthly expenditures on education.

Let us introduce two simplifying assumptions:

1) All budgetary places allocated are filled.
2) There is no expulsion, i.e., all applicants are graduates of the HEI.

Thus, at each time instant, an HEI is informed by the Principal about the number of budgetary places allocated for each specialty. This is important for HEIs since education costs depend on the total number of students. After the HEI receives information on budgetary places, it decides on the maximum possible enrollment of commercial students and determines the price of commercial education in each specialty.

3 Description of the Study

Let us investigate model (1)–(8) by computer simulation. The uncontrolled parameters of the model, i.e., the vector

$$\left(\{\gamma_j\}_{j=1}^M, \left\{ \{\kappa_{ij}\}_{i=1}^N \right\}_{j=1}^M, \left\{ \{c_{ij}\}_{i=1}^N \right\}_{j=1}^M, \left\{ \{x_{ij0}\}_{i=1}^N \right\}_{j=1}^M, \right.$$
$$\left. \left\{ \{y_{ij0}\}_{i=1}^N \right\}_{j=1}^M, \{\alpha_j\}_{j=1}^M, \{a_{0j}\}_{j=1}^M \right),$$

are identified, and then different control scenarios are analyzed. Each scenario consists in specifying:

- the vector of exogenous variables

$$\left\{ a_{ij}^B(t), x_{ij}^B(t) \right\}, i = 1, \ldots, N, \, j = 1, \ldots, M, \, t = 0, \ldots, T-1,$$

- the vector of control actions

$$\left\{ a_{ij}^C(t), x_{ij}^C(t) \right\}, i = 1, \ldots, N, \, j = 1, \ldots, M, \, t = 0, \ldots, T-1,$$

for the HEI.

Six enlarged groups of specialties were taken for the study as the most important ones: pedagogy, medicine, economics, engineering, construction, and agriculture. Then the key HEIs of the Rostov region with the corresponding specialties were selected: Rostov State Medical University (RostSMU), Don State Technical University (DSTU), and Southern Federal University (SFedU).

Table 1 shows the specialties of these HEIs.

Table 1. The specialties of HEIs in the Rostov region

	RostSMU	DSTU	SFedU
Pedagogy		+	+
Medicine	+		
Economics		+	+
Engineering		+	+
Construction		+	+
Agriculture		+	

4 Parameter Identification

The components of the vector

$$\left(\{\gamma_j\}_{j=1}^{M}, \left\{ \{\kappa_{ij}\}_{i=1}^{N} \right\}_{j=1}^{M}, \left\{ \{c_{ij}\}_{i=1}^{N} \right\}_{j=1}^{M}, \left\{ \{x_{ij0}\}_{i=1}^{N} \right\}_{j=1}^{M}, \right.$$

$$\left. \left\{ \{y_{ij0}\}_{j=1}^{N} \right\}_{j=1}^{M}, \{\alpha_j\}_{j=1}^{M}, \{a_{0j}\}_{j=1}^{M} \right),$$

which form the uncontrolled parameters of the model, were to be identified. We discuss them in detail.

1) The parameter γ_j is the influence coefficient of potential employment on applying to the j-th specialty. As this parameter, we took the average wage of the corresponding profession in the Rostov region. Note that its value does not depend on a particular HEI. The data were provided by the territorial body of the Federal State Statistics Service in the Rostov region (Rostovstat; see https://rostov.gks.ru). For each industry and specialty, the average wages were calculated for several years. The data for 2020 were taken as the parameter γ_j (Table 2).

Table 2. Identification of the parameter γ_j for the Rostov region

Specialty	Parameter	Value, in rubles
Pedagogy	γ_1	28550
Medicine	γ_2	35849
Economics	γ_3	35000
Engineering	γ_4	53000
Construction	γ_5	47000
Agriculture	γ_6	23726

2) The parameter x_{ij0} is the number of graduates for the j-th specialty in the i-th HEI in the initial year of the planning horizon. The data were taken from public documents (self-evaluation reports, enrollment orders, and enrollment statistics by year) on the official portals of RostSMU, DSTU, and SFedU. The number of graduates and enrolled students for 2020 was considered (Table 3).

Table 3. Identification of the parameter x_{ij0} for the Rostov region

	Parameter	RostSMU	DSTU	SFedU
Pedagogy	x_{i10}	–	40	666
Medicine	x_{i20}	165	–	–
Economics	x_{i30}	–	319	296
Engineering	x_{i40}	–	675	895
Construction	x_{i50}	–	586	150
Agriculture	x_{i60}	–	138	–

3) The parameter κ_{ij} is the share of unemployed graduates with the j-th specialty in the i-th HEI. This parameter was calculated based on public documents on the official portals of the HEIs (Table 4).

Table 4. Identification of the parameter κ_{ij} for the Rostov region

	Parameter	RostSMU	DSTU	SFedU
Pedagogy	κ_{i1}	–	0.45	0.45
Medicine	κ_{i2}	0.16	–	–
Economics	κ_{i3}	–	0.45	0.18
Engineering	κ_{i4}	–	0.45	0.18
Construction	κ_{i5}	–	0.45	0.07
Agriculture	κ_{i6}	–	0.45	–

For the calculations, this parameter was set equal to 1 for the HEIs without appropriate specialties.

4) The parameter y_{ij0} is the number of employed graduates with the j-th specialty in the initial year of the planning horizon. It was calculated (see Table 5) through the parameters x_{ij0} and κ_{ij} by the formula $y_{ij0} = \left(1 - \kappa_{ij}\right) \cdot x_{ij0}$.

5) The parameter c_{ij} is the education cost coefficient for the j-th specialty of the i-th HEI depending on the total number of students in year t. It is directly related to the prime

Table 5. Identification of the parameter y_{ij0} for the Rostov region

	Parameter	RostSMU	DSTU	SFedU
Pedagogy	y_{i10}	–	22	366
Medicine	y_{i20}	139	–	–
Economics	y_{i30}	–	171	213
Engineering	y_{i40}	–	371	644
Construction	y_{i50}	–	323	144
Agriculture	y_{i60}	–	76	–

cost of tutoring in this specialty. The prime cost of tutoring is not open information. Therefore, this parameter was assigned through expertise as 80% of the price of commercial education available from public sources: the official portals of SFedU (https://sfedu.ru), DSTU (https://donstu.ru), and RostSMU (http://rostgmu.ru). See Table 6 below.

Table 6. Identification of the prime cost of tutoring for the Rostov region

	RostSMU	DSTU	SFedU
Pedagogy	–	86000	88000
Medicine	125000	–	–
Economics	–	86000	107000
Engineering	–	100000	104000
Construction	–	100000	113000
Agriculture	–	100000	–

The data from this table were used for identifying the parameter c_{ij}. Due to the quadratic costs, the value c_{ij} is given by the following formula (Table 7)

$$c_{ij} = \frac{prime\ cost\ of\ tutoring}{x_{ij0}}.$$

For the calculations, this parameter was set equal to almost infinity for the HEIs without appropriate specialties.

6) The parameter α_j is the elasticity of demand for commercial places in the j-th specialty. It characterizes demand variations under changing the future wage or the price of commercial education. The data were taken from https://iq.hse.ru/news/177671083.html: the cited source indicates the relative variation *pov* under increasing the demand

Table 7. Identification of the parameter c_{ij} for the Rostov region

	Parameter	RostSMU	DSTU	SFedU
Pedagogy	c_{i1}	–	2150	132
Medicine	c_{i2}	758	–	–
Economics	c_{i3}	–	270	361
Engineering	c_{i4}	–	148	116
Construction	c_{i5}	–	171	753
Agriculture	c_{i6}	–	725	–

of applicants for a specialty with a 40% increase in graduate wages. Therefore, we calculated the parameter α_j (see Table 8) by the formula

$$\alpha_j = \log_{1.4}(1 + pov/100).$$

Table 8. Identification of the parameter α_j for the Rostov region

Specialty	Pov	α_j
Pedagogy	76	$\alpha_1 = \log_{1.4} 1.76 = 1.68$
Medicine	131	$\alpha_2 = \log_{1.4} 2.31 = 2.48$
Economics	77	$\alpha_3 = \log_{1.4} 1.77 = 1.70$
Engineering	42	$\alpha_4 = \log_{1.4} 1.42 = 1.04$
Construction	51	$\alpha_5 = \log_{1.4} 1.51 = 1.22$
Agriculture	41	$\alpha_6 = \log_{1.4} 1.41 = 1.02$

This parameter does not depend on the HEI as well.

7) The parameter a_{0j} is a weight coefficient that characterizes the social utility of the j-th specialty. It was calculated using the data from [32] (the forecasted needs of the Rostov region in different employees). The resulting values were normalized (Table 9). From all enlarged groups of specialties, we selected those with weights exceeding 5%.

Table 9. Identification of the parameter a_{0j} for the Rostov region

	Parameter	a_{0j}
Pedagogy	a_{01}	0.39
Medicine	a_{02}	0.23
Economics	a_{03}	0.16
Engineering	a_{04}	0.09
Construction	a_{05}	0.065
Agriculture	a_{06}	0.065

Even at the identification stage, we arrive at the following conclusion: it is unprofitable for applicants to study medicine and agriculture on commercial places. Really, the expression $\gamma_{ij} - \frac{a_{ij}^C(t)}{4}$ (the basis for calculating the demand) is negative even at the prime cost of tutoring. For agriculture, it can be explained by low wages; in the case of medicine, the reason is the high prime cost of tutoring. Engineering and construction attract applicants for commercial places with high future wages. Economics and pedagogy lie at the borderline: the future wages are commensurate with the price of commercial education.

For the prices $a_{ij}^C(t) > 4\gamma_{ij}$, there is no demand for commercial education: see medicine and agriculture as examples. Therefore, the problem for RostSMU has a trivial solution and will not be considered below.

In view of (7), HEIs need not enroll commercial students above the demand $(\gamma_{ij} - a_{ij}^C(t)/4)^{\alpha_j} y_{ij}(t)$. (Although HEIs incur no losses from the excessive commercial enrollment.) When increasing the number of students, the costs grow faster than the income (5). Hence, there exists a finite optimal number of commercial students for an HEI: for this number, the goal function (5) achieves maximum. The HEI should enroll precisely this number of commercial students.

5 Stackelberg Equilibrium

In the hierarchical game under consideration, a Stackelberg equilibrium is found in two stages as follows.

1) Calculation of the HEI's optimal response to the Principal's control strategy.

The HEI problem is solved in two stages.

1. For each specialty, it is required to determine the maximum number of commercial students

$\left\{x_{ij}^C(t)\right\}$, $i = 1, \ldots, N, j = 1, \ldots, M, t = 0, \ldots, T - 1$, profitable for the HEI considering the goal function (5) and the demand for commercial places (7).

2. For each specialty, it is required to select the maximum price of commercial education

$\left\{a_{ij}^C(t)\right\}$, $i = 1, \ldots, N, j = 1, \ldots, M, t = 0, \ldots, T - 1$, that maximizes the function (5). The price is determined as a markup to the prime cost of tutoring.

We give examples of model calculations for two cases: no budgetary places and some budgetary places allocated to the HEI. The planning horizon is $T = 3$ years.

Case 1. If the HEI does not receive any budgetary places, the model takes the following form:

$$J_i = \sum_{t=1}^{T} \sum_{j=1}^{M} \left(a_{ij}^C x_{ij}(t) - c_{ij}\left(x_{ij}(t)^2\right) \right) \to max;$$

$$x_{ij}^C(t) \geq 0, a_{ij}^C(t) \geq 0;$$

$$x_{ij}(t+1) = min\{x_{ij}^C(t+1), \left(\gamma_{ij} - a_{ij}^C(t)/4\right)^{\alpha_j} y_{ij}(t)\}, \ x_{ij}(0) = x_{ij0};$$

$$y_{ij}(t+1) = (1 - \kappa_{ij})x_{ij}(t), \ y_{ij}(0) = y_{ij0}, \ j = 1, \ldots, M, \ t = 1, \ldots, T - 1.$$

The calculation results for DSTU are combined in Table 10. (There is no information about agriculture due to no demand for this specialty.)

Table 10. Calculation results for DSTU (no budgetary places)

Specialty	First year		Second year		Third year	
	Commercial enrollment	Markup, %	Commercial enrollment	Markup, %	Commercial enrollment	Markup, %
Pedagogy	100	3	38	3	95	3
Engineering	56	30	63	30	5	30
Construction	67	19	65	19	8	19
Economics	130	9	85	9	35	9

Table 11. Calculation results for SFedU (no budgetary places)

Specialty	First year		Second year		Third year	
	Commercial enrollment	Markup, %	Commercial enrollment	Markup, %	Commercial enrollment	Markup, %
Pedagogy	250	11	250	11	250	11
Engineering	86	18	98	18	9	18
Construction	28	1	27	1	5	1
Economics	250	8	250	8	250	8

The calculation results for SFedU are combined in Table 11.

At SFedU, admission to pedagogy and economics is limited by the university's capacity and does not exceed 250 places. The demand for commercial places for these specialties is above 250.

Note that generally, the demand for commercial places decreases over time due to the rational search for budgetary ones. Consequently, HEIs have to reduce the price of commercial education.

2) Calculation of the Principal's optimal strategy.

The problem has the form

$$J_0 = \sum_{t=1}^{T} \sum_{i=1}^{N} \sum_{j=1}^{M} a_{0j} x_{ij}^B(t) + \sum_{t=1}^{T} \sum_{i=1}^{N} \sum_{j=1}^{M} a_{0j} \min\{x_{ij}^C(t+1),$$
$$(\gamma_j - a_{ij}^C(t)/4)^{\alpha_j} y_{ij}(t)\} \to max;$$

$$x_{ij}^B(t) \ge 0, a_{ij}^B(t) \ge 0;$$

$$\sum_{i=1}^{N} \sum_{j=1}^{M} a_{ij}^B x_{ij}^B(t) \le B,$$

$$\sum_{i=1}^{N} x_{ij}^B(t) + \sum_{i=1}^{N} \min\{x_{ij}^C(t+1), (\gamma_j - a_{ij}^C(t)/4)^{\alpha_j} y_{ij}(t)\} \ge x_j^{min};$$

$$J_i = \sum_{t=1}^{T} \sum_{j=1}^{M} \left[a_{ij}^B x_{ij}^B(t) + a_{ij}^C x_{ij}^C(t) - c_{ij} \left(\sum_{j=1}^{M} x_{ij}(t) \right)^2 \right] \to max;$$

$$x_{ij}^C(t) \ge 0, a_{ij}^C(t) \ge 0;$$

$$x_{ij}(t+1) = x_{ij}^B(t+1) + \min\{x_{ij}^C(t+1), (\gamma_j - a_{ij}^C(t)/4)^{\alpha_j} y_{ij}(t)\}, \ x_{ij}(0) = x_{ij0}$$

$$y_{ij}(t+1) = (1 - \kappa_{ij}) x_{ij}(t), \ y_{ij}(0) = y_{ij0}, \ i = 1, ..., N, \ j = 1, ..., M, \ t = 1, ..., T.$$

The HEIs have no right to give up budgetary places. Therefore, the Principal can neglect the linear terms corresponding to commercial places when solving its problem (and consider them to be constant). Hence, the Principal's problem reduces to the following one:

$$J_0 = \sum_{t=1}^{T} \sum_{i=1}^{N} \sum_{j=1}^{M} a_{0j} x_{ij}^{B}(t) + const \rightarrow max;$$

$$x_{ij}^{B}(t) \geq 0, \, a_{ij}^{B}(t) \geq 0;$$

$$\sum_{i=1}^{N} \sum_{j=1}^{M} a_{ij}^{B} x_{ij}^{B}(t) \leq B,$$

$$\sum_{i=1}^{N} x_{ij}^{B}(t) + const \geq x_{j}^{min}.$$

From the budget condition it follows that the coefficients a_{ij}^{B} should be minimal. In other words, the per capita subsidy of budgetary places should be at the prime cost level: $a_{ij}^{B}(t) = c_{ij}$. (This fact explains the reluctance to disclose this information.) As a result, the Principal's problem turns into the linear programming problem (LPP)

$$J_0 = \sum_{t=1}^{T} \sum_{i=1}^{N} \sum_{j=1}^{M} a_{0j} x_{ij}^{B}(t) \rightarrow max;$$

$$x_{ij}^{B}(t) \geq 0;$$

$$\sum_{i=1}^{N} \sum_{j=1}^{M} c_{ij} x_{ij}^{B}(t) \leq B,$$

$$\sum_{i=1}^{N} x_{ij}^{B}(t) + const \geq x_{j}^{min}.$$

Now we study the Principal's behavior without the sustainable development condition. Since the constraints on t do not depend on other time points, we can reduce the dynamic problem to the T static problems:

$$J_0 = \sum_{i=1}^{N} \sum_{j=1}^{M} a_{0j} x_{ij}^{B} \rightarrow max; \tag{9}$$

$$x_{ij}^{B} \geq 0; \tag{10}$$

$$\sum_{i=1}^{N} \sum_{j=1}^{M} c_{ij} x_{ij}^{B} \leq B, \tag{11}$$

$$\sum_{i=1}^{N} x_{ij}^{B} + const \geq x_{j}^{min}. \tag{12}$$

For this purpose, it is required to solve the LPP (9)–(11), e.g., by the simplex method. At first, we write the problem (9)–(11) in canonical form. For this purpose we introduce a variable x_0:

$$J_0 = \sum_{i=1}^{N} \sum_{j=1}^{M} a_{0j} x_{ij}^{B} \rightarrow max;$$

Table 12. The first simplex table of LPP (9)–(11)

	$x_{11}^B x_{12}^B$ ... $x_{1m}^B x_{21}^B x_{22}^B$ ... x_{2m}^B ... $x_{n1}^B x_{n2}^B$ ... $x_{nm}^B x_0$	Free term
x_0	$c_{11} c_{12}$ ... $c_{1m} c_{21} c_{22}$ ... c_{2m} ... $c_{n1} c_{n2}$ ... c_{nm} 1	B
-F	$-a_{01}$ $-a_{02}$ ... $-a_{0m}$ $-a_{01}$ $-a_{02}$ ... $-a_{0m}$ ... $-a_{01}$ $-a_{02}$ ... - a_{0m} 0	0

Table 13. The next simplex table of LPP (9)–(11)

	$x_{11}^B x_{12}^B$ ... $x_{1m}^B x_{l1}^B x_{l2}^B$ ... x_{lk}^B ... x_{lm}^B ... $x_{n1}^B x_{n2}^B$ ... x_{nm}^B x_0	Free term	Val ue
x_0	$c_{11} c_{12}$ ... $c_{1m} c_{l1} c_{l2}$ ... $\mathbf{c_{lk}}$ ... c_{lm} ... $c_{n1} c_{n2}$ ... c_{nm} 1	B	B/c_{lk}
-F	$-a_{01}$ $-a_{02}$ ... $-a_{0m}$ $-a_{01}$ $-a_{02}$ ... $\mathbf{-a_{0k}}$... $-a_{0m}$ ... - a_{01} $-a_{02}$ ... $-a_{0m}$ 0	0	

$x_{ij}^B \geq 0; x_0 \geq 0; \sum_{i=1}^{N}\sum_{j=1}^{M} c_{ij}x_{ij}^B + x_0 = B$.

The first simplex table contains one line with the base variable x_0 (Table 12):

Let us introduce the notations k $= Arg \ \max_j a_{0j}$ (the specialty with the highest social utility) and l $= Arg \ \min_i c_{ik}$ (the HEI with the lowest prime cost of tutoring in this specialty). We go to the next basic variable $x_{lk}^B(t)$ (Table 13):

The second simplex table is presented in the Table 14.

Table 14. The second simplex table of LPP (9)–(11)

	$x_{11}^B x_{12}^B$ ... $x_{1m}^B x_{l1}^B x_{l2}^B$ ... x_{lk}^B ... x_{lm}^B ... $x_{n1}^B x_{n2}^B$ ... x_{nm}^B x_0	Free term
x_{lk}^B	$\frac{c_{11}}{c_{lk}} \frac{c_{12}}{c_{lk}}$ ... $\frac{c_{1m}}{c_{lk}} \frac{c_{l1}}{c_{lk}} \frac{c_{l2}}{c_{lk}}$ ... 1 ... $\frac{c_{lm}}{c_{lk}}$ ... $\frac{c_{n1}}{c_{lk}} \frac{c_{n2}}{c_{lk}}$ ... $\frac{c_{nm}}{c_{lk}} \frac{1}{c_{lk}}$	$\dfrac{B}{c_{lk}}$
-F	$z_{11} z_{12}$ ... $z_{1m} z_{l1} z_{l2}$... 0...z_{lm} ... $z_{n1} z_{n2}$ ... $z_{nm} \frac{a_{0k}}{c_{lk}}$	$\dfrac{Ba_{0k}}{c_{lk}}$

Here $z_{ij} = -a_{0j} + \frac{c_{ij}}{c_{lk}}a_{0k}$. Note that $\frac{c_{ij}}{c_{lk}} \geq 1$ for all $i = 1,...,n$, j $= 1,...,$m. That is why $z_{ij} = -a_{0j} + \frac{c_{ij}}{c_{lk}}a_{0k} \geq -a_{0j} + a_{0k} \geq 0$. Hence, there are no negative elements in the last line. The solution is optimal.

We write the solution as

$$x_{lk}^B(t) = \frac{B}{c_{lk}},$$

$$x^B_{ij}(t) = 0.$$
$$i \neq l \vee j \neq k$$

A possible interpretation is as follows: all budgetary places are allocated to the specialty with the highest social utility and to the HEI with the lowest prime cost of tutoring in this specialty. As applied to the Rostov region, this means that all budgetary places should be allocated to DSTU and only to pedagogy.

However, ignoring other specialties with not the highest but significant social utility (medicine, economics, and construction) will not meet the sustainable development condition.

Therefore, we analyze changes in the solution of (9)–(11) under condition (12). Let us solve the LPP (9)–(12) by the simplex method. Introducing the notation $l_j = Arg\ \max\limits_{i} c_{ij}$ (the HEI with the lowest prime cost of tutoring in the j-th specialty), we write the solution as

$$x^B_{l_j j, j \neq k}(t) = x^{min}_j,$$

$$x^B_{l_k k}(t) = \frac{B - \sum_{j \neq k} x^{min}_j}{c_{l_k k}},$$

$$x^B_{ij, i \neq l_j}(t) = 0.$$

Thus, first of all, it is necessary to allocate the minimum number of budgetary places stipulated by the sustainable development condition to all specialties, except the one with the highest social utility, to the HEIs with the lowest prime cost of tutoring in these specialties. The residual budgetary places are allocated to the specialty with the highest social utility.

In the Rostov region, this means that all budgetary places in all specialties, except medicine, should be allocated primarily to DSTU. After distributing the minimum number of budgetary places among all specialties, the residual budgetary places should be allocated to pedagogy to different HEIs, particularly DSTU.

But the natural question is: who and how should determine in practice the minimal number of budgetary places for all specialties? (The Principal is not interested in this activity!).

Let us modify the Principal's objective function: replace the linear convolution by the minimum convolution. Such an approach will stabilize budgetary places for all specialties with different social utilities. In this case, the Principal's problem takes the form:

$$J_0 = \sum_{t=1}^{T} \min_{1 \leq j \leq n} \left\{ \frac{\sum_{i=1}^{N} x^B_{ij}(t)}{a_{0j}} \right\} \rightarrow max;$$

$$x^B_{ij}(t) \geq 0;$$

$$\sum_{i=1}^{N} \sum_{j=1}^{M} c_{ij} x^B_{ij}(t) \leq B.$$

Using the change of variables $z = \min\limits_{1 \leq j \leq n} \left\{ \dfrac{\sum_{i=1}^{N} x_{ij}^{B}(t)}{a_{0j}} \right\}$ and the equivalent transforma-

tions $\sum_{i=1}^{N} x_{ij}^{B}(t) = z \cdot a_{0j}$ and $x_{ij}^{B}(t) = z \cdot a_{0j} - \sum_{i=2}^{N} x_{ij}^{B}(t)$, we reduce this problem
to:

$$J_0 = \sum\nolimits_{t=1}^{T} z \to max;$$

$$z, x_{ij}^{B}(t) \geq 0;\ i = 2, \ldots, N, j = 1, \ldots, M,$$

$$\sum\nolimits_{j=1}^{M} c_{1j}(z \cdot a_{0j} - \sum\nolimits_{i=2}^{N} x_{ij}^{B}(t)) + \sum\nolimits_{2=1}^{N} \sum\nolimits_{j=1}^{M} c_{ij} x_{ij}^{B}(t) \leq B.$$

This condition can be expressed as

$$z \cdot \sum\nolimits_{j=1}^{M} c_{1j} a_{0j} + \sum\nolimits_{2=1}^{N} \sum\nolimits_{j=1}^{M} (c_{ij} - c_{1j}) x_{ij}^{B}(t) \leq B.$$

Since the constraints on t does not depend on other time points, we can reduce the
dynamic problem to the T static problems:

$$J_0 = z \to max;$$

$$z, x_{ij}^{B} \geq 0;\ i = 2, \ldots, N, j = 1, \ldots, M,$$

$$z \cdot \sum\nolimits_{j=1}^{M} c_{1j} a_{0j} + \sum\nolimits_{2=1}^{N} \sum\nolimits_{j=1}^{M} (c_{ij} - c_{1j}) x_{ij}^{B} \leq B.$$

The resulting problem is a linear programming problem as well. It can be solved by
the simplex method. We introduce the variable x0. Then the canonical form is.
$J_0 = z \to max;$

$$z, x_{ij}^{B} \geq 0;\ i = 2, \ldots, N, j = 1, \ldots, M,$$

$$z \cdot \sum\nolimits_{j=1}^{M} c_{1j} a_{0j} + \sum\nolimits_{2=1}^{N} \sum\nolimits_{j=1}^{M} (c_{ij} - c_{1j}) x_{ij}^{B}(t) + x_0 = B.$$

The first simplex table contains one line with the base variable x_0 (Table 15):

Table 15. The first simplex table of LPP with minimum convolution

	z $\quad x_{21}^B \ldots x_{2m}^B \qquad \ldots x_{ij}^B \ldots x_{nm}^B x_0$	Free term
x_0	$\sum_{j=1}^M c_{1j} a_{0j} (c_{21} - c_{11}) \ldots \qquad (c_{2m} - c_{1m}) \ldots (c_{ij} - c_{1j}) \ldots$ $(c_{nm} - c_{1m})1$	B
-F	-1 0 $\qquad \ldots \qquad$ 0 0 00	0

We introduce to the basis the variable z. To reduce the bulkiness of the table we write here only the general case x_{ij}^B. The second simplex method is in the Table 16.

Table 16. The second simplex table of LPP with minimum convolution

	z $\qquad x_{21}^B$ $\qquad \ldots \qquad x_{2m}^B \qquad \ldots \qquad x_{ij}^B \qquad \ldots$ $x_{nm}^B x_0$	Free term
z	$1 \dfrac{(c_{21}-c_{11})}{\sum_{j=1}^M c_{1j} a_{0j}} \quad \ldots \dfrac{(c_{2m}-c_{1m})}{\sum_{j=1}^M c_{1j} a_{0j}} \cdots \dfrac{(c_{ij}-c_{1j})}{\sum_{j=1}^M c_{1j} a_{0j}} \quad \ldots$ $\dfrac{(c_{nm}-c_{1m})}{\sum_{j=1}^M c_{1j} a_{0j}} \dfrac{1}{\sum_{j=1}^M c_{1j} a_{0j}}$	$\dfrac{B}{\sum_{j=1}^M c_{1j} a_{0j}}$
F	$0 \dfrac{(c_{21}-c_{11})}{\sum_{j=1}^M c_{1j} a_{0j}} \quad \ldots \dfrac{(c_{2m}-c_{1m})}{\sum_{j=1}^M c_{1j} a_{0j}} \quad \ldots \dfrac{(c_{ij}-c_{1j})}{\sum_{j=1}^M c_{1j} a_{0j}} \quad \ldots$ $\dfrac{(c_{nm}-c_{1m})}{\sum_{j=1}^M c_{1j} a_{0j}} \dfrac{1}{\sum_{j=1}^M c_{1j} a_{0j}}$	$\dfrac{B}{\sum_{j=1}^M c_{1j} a_{0j}}$

If all coefficients of the last line are positive, then the first university has the least prime cost at all specialties. Then all budgetary places are allocated to the first university. If exists a university $l \neq 1$ which has the lowest prime cost at the specialty k, then we add to the basis a variable c_{lk}^B, and the next simplex table is presented in the Table 17.

Table 17. The next simplex table of LPP with minimum convolution

	z $\quad x_{21}^B \qquad \ldots \qquad x_{ij}^B \quad \ldots x_{lk}^B \ldots \quad x_{nm}^B x_0$	Free term
x_{lk}^B	$\dfrac{\sum_{j=1}^M c_{1j} a_{0j} (c_{21}-c_{11})}{(c_{lk}-c_{1k})} \dfrac{(c_{ij}-c_{1j})}{(c_{lk}-c_{1k})} \cdots \quad \ldots \quad 1$ $\dfrac{(c_{nm}-c_{1m})}{(c_{lk}-c_{1k})} \dfrac{1}{(c_{lk}-c_{1k})}$	$\dfrac{B}{(c_{lk} - c_{1k})}$
F	$\dfrac{c_{1k}-c_{lk}}{\sum_{j=1}^M c_{1j} a_{0j}} \dfrac{c_{21}-c_{11}+c_{1k}-c_{lk}}{\sum_{j=1}^M c_{1j} a_{0j}} \quad \ldots \dfrac{c_{ij}-c_{1j}+c_{1k}-c_{lk}}{\sum_{j=1}^M c_{1j} a_{0j}} \quad \ldots 0 \quad \ldots$ $\dfrac{c_{nm}-c_{1m}+c_{1k}-c_{lk}}{\sum_{j=1}^M c_{1j} a_{0j}} \quad \ldots \dfrac{1+c_{1k}-c_{lk}}{\sum_{j=1}^M c_{1j} a_{0j}}$	$\dfrac{B + c_{1k} - c_{lk}}{\sum_{j=1}^M c_{1j} a_{0j}}$

If there are other universities which have the least prime on some specialty then one must add the corresponding variable to the basis. And so on until all specialties will be correspond to the HEI with the lowest prime of education. The solution will no longer be trivial for specialties but remain trivial for HEIs: the budgetary places in each specialty should be allocated to the HEI with the lowest prime cost of education.

6   Application to HEIs of the Rostov Region

Let us solve the problem for the HEIs of the Rostov region under the budget B = 5 billion rubles. The resulting distribution of the budgetary places by specialties (Table 18) corresponds to the maximum value of the Principal's objective function.

Table 18. The optimal number of budgetary places by specialties

Specialty	Budgetary places
Pedagogy	1988
Medicine	1173
Economics	816
Engineering	459
Construction	331
Agriculture	331

All these places should be allocated to the HEIs with the lowest prime cost of tutoring in the corresponding specialty (i.e., DSTU and RostSMU).

Now we analyze the effect of budgetary places on commercial enrollment. DSTU receives many budgetary places from the government, so the university has no capabilities to tutor commercial students. On the other hand, Southern Federal University can afford any commercial enrollment it benefits from: this university does not receive any budgetary places.

7   Recommendations

Within the model, if an HEI is allocated budgetary places in a specialty, it has no resources left for commercial enrollment. In this case, commercial places in excess of the budgetary ones incur losses. (The model does not allow HEI's refusal from the allocated budgetary places.) A large number of commercial places remains economically justified only in case of no budgetary enrollment (SFedU).

Allocating a small number of budgetary places has economic advantages: the HEI provides the maximum of commercial places within the resource potential and gains higher income.

HEIs are recommended to choose the priority of enrollment (budgetary or commercial). If budgetary places are the priority, HEIs should agree with each other on the distribution of specialties and establish a clear specialization to avoid enrollment intersections. On the other hand, the Principal benefits from allocating all budgetary places in the specialty to the HEI with the lowest prime cost of tutoring.

8 Conclusions

In this paper, we have constructed and analyzed a cognitive model to control the higher education system of a region. The model is a Stackelberg difference game. The Stackelberg equilibrium has been found using analytical and computer simulation methods. The model has been applied to control higher education in the Rostov region of the Russian Federation. The model parameters have been identified, the resulting model has been studied, and several recommendations have been formulated for the upper-level control subject and HEIs.

Due to the significantly simplified assumptions of the model, the results of this study are often extreme and do not fully reflect the reality. We can enumerate the following limitations of the model: (1) the objective functions are quite simple and not completely comprehensive; (2) not all real factors of influence are considered; (3) budgeting procedures are oversimplified.

In the future, it is expected to modify the objective functions of the players to describe other decision factors arising in practice. For example, even with full budgetary enrollment, HEIs should still be able to accept commercial students. It seems reasonable to consider other dependencies of the demand for commercial education on potential employment. Also, a university rating should be considered.

Besides the economic aspects, socio-political requirements for tutoring should be investigated. However, formalization difficulties will arise along this way. This study has shown the importance of sustainable development requirements at the level of society. This line of research should be continued.

References

1. Thad, A. (ed.): Cognitive Modeling. Polk and Colleen M. Seifert, 1291 p. MIT Press, Cambridge (2002)
2. Axelrod, R.: The Structure of Decision: Cognitive Maps of Political Elites. Princeton University Press, Princeton (1976)
3. Maruyama, M.: The second cybernetics: deviation-amplifying mutual causal processes. Am. Sci. 51(2), 164–179 (1963)
4. Roberts, F.: Discrete Mathematical Models with Applications to Social, Biological and Ecological Problems, 560 p. Pearson (1976)
5. Papageorgiou, E.: Review study on fuzzy cognitive maps and their applications during the last decade. In: Glykas, M. (ed.) Business Process Management. SCI, vol. 444, pp. 281–298. Springer, Heidelberg (2013). https://doi.org/10.1007/978-3-642-28409-0_11
6. Groumpos, P.: Modelling and analyzing manufacturing systems using advanced methods of fuzzy cognitive maps. J. Comput. Intell. Electron. Syst. 3(2), 143–150 (2014)
7. Felix, G., Nápoles, G., Falcon, R., Froelich, W., Vanhoof, K., Bello, R.: A review on methods and software for fuzzy cognitive maps. Artif. Intell. Rev. 52(3), 1707–1737 (2017). https://doi.org/10.1007/s10462-017-9575-1

8. Abramova, N.A.: Expert verification in formal cognitive map application. Approaches and practices. Large-Scale Syst. Control **30**(1), 371–410 (2010). (in Russian)
9. Abramova, N.A.: On the prospects of the modern paradigm of cognitive modelling. In: Proceedings of the 13th All-Russian Meeting on Control Problems (AMCP-2019), pp. 1858–1863. Trapeznikov Institute of Control Sciences RAS (2019). (in Russian)
10. Avdeeva, Z.K., Kovriga, S.V.: On the statement of control problems of the situation with many active stakeholders with use of cognitive maps. Large-Scale Syst. Control **68**, 74–99 (2017)
11. Avdeeva, Z.K., Kovriga, S.V.: Some principles and approaches to construction of group cognitive maps. Large-Scale Syst. Control **52**, 37–68 (2014). (in Russian)
12. Gorelova, G.V.: Cognitive modeling of complex systems: state and prospects. In: Proceedings of the 25th International Scientific and Practical Conference "System Analysis in Design and Management", St. Petersburg, pp. 224–248 (2021). (in Russian)
13. Gorelova, G.V.: Cognitive approach to simulation of large systems. Izvestiya SFedU. Eng. Sci. **103**(40), 239–250 (2013). (in Russian)
14. Maksimov, V.I.: Structure and goal analysis of the development of socio-economic situations. Control Sci. **3**, 30–38 (2005)
15. Maksimov, V.I., Kovriga, S.V.: Application of structure and goal analysis of the development of socio-economic situations. Control Sci. **3**, 39–44 (2005)
16. Arzhenovskiy, I.V., Dakhin, A.V.: Cognitive regionology: the experience of modeling regional socio-economic processes. Russ. J. Region. Stud. **28**(3), 470–489 (2020). (in Russian)
17. Makarova, E.L., Firsova, A.A.: Cognitive modeling the impact of a regional system of higher education in the innovative development of the region. Izv. Saratov University. Econ. Manag. Law **5**(4), 411–416 (2015). (in Russian)
18. Lepori, B., Usher, J., Montauti, M.: Budgetary allocation and organizational characteristics of higher education institutions: a review of existing studies and a framework for future research. High. Educ. **65**(1), 59–78 (2013)
19. Liefner, I.: Funding, resource allocation, and performance in higher education systems. High. Educ. **46**, 469–489 (2003)
20. Raudla, R., Karo, E., Valdmaa, K., Kattel, R.: Implications of project-based funding of research on budgeting and financial management in public universities. High. Educ. **70**(6), 957–971 (2015)
21. Uspuriene, A., Sakalauskas, L., Dumskis, V.: Financial resource allocation in higher education. Inform. Educ. **16**(2), 289–300 (2017)
22. Novikov, D. (ed.): Mechanism Design and Management: Mathematical Methods for Smart Organizations, 163 p. Nova Science Publishers, New York (2013)
23. Novikov, D.A.: Theory of Control in Organizations, 341 p. Nova Science Publishers, New York (2013)
24. Laffont, J.-J., Martimort, D.: The Theory of Incentives: The Principal-Agent Model, 421 p. Princeton University Press, Princeton (2002)
25. Ougolnitsky, G.A.: Sustainable Management, 288 p. Nova Science Publishers, New York (2011)
26. Pontryagin, L.S., Boltyansky, V.G., Gamkrelidze, R.V., Mischenko, E.F.: Mathematical Theory of Optimal Processes, 360 p. Interscience Publishers–Wiley, New York–London (1962)
27. Grass, D., Caulkins, J.P., Feichtinger, G., Tragler, G., Behrens, D.A.: Optimal Control of Nonlinear Processes (with Applications to Drugs, Corruption, and Terror), 529 p. Springer, Heidelberg (2008). https://doi.org/10.1007/978-3-540-77647-5
28. Dockner, E., Jorgensen, S., Long, N.V., Sorger, G.: Differential Games in Economics and Management Science, 382 p. Cambridge University Press, Cambridge (2000)
29. Gorelov, M.A., Kononenko, A.F.: Dynamic models of conflicts. III. Hierarchical games. Autom. Remote Control **76**(2), 264–277 (2015)

30. Novikov, D.A.: Cognitive games: a linear impulse model. Autom. Remote Control **71**(2), 718–730 (2010)
31. Ougolnitsky, G.A., Usov, A.B.: Computer simulations as a solution method for differential games. In: Pfeffer, M.D., Bachmaier, E. (eds.) Computer Simulations: Advances in Research and Applications, pp. 63–106. Nova Science Publishers, New York (2018)
32. Forecast of the needs of the regional labor market of the Rostov region for enlarged groups of higher education specialties for 2021–2027. https://invest-don.ru/ru/prognoz_potrebnosti. (in Russian)

Behavioral Model of Interaction Between Economic Agents and the Institutional Environment

George Kleiner[1,2] , Maxim Rybachuk[1,2(✉)] , and Dmitry Ushakov[3]

[1] Central Economics and Mathematics Institute of the Russian Academy of Sciences,
47 Nakhimovsky Ave., 117418 Moscow, Russia
{kleiner,rybachuk}@cemi.rssi.ru
[2] State University of Management, 99 Ryazansky Ave., 109542 Moscow, Russia
[3] Institute of Psychology of the Russian Academy of Sciences, 13b1 Yaroslavskaya Str., 129366
Moscow, Russia
UshakovDV@ipran.ru

Abstract. This article creates and analyzes an agent-based simulation model that reflects the interaction between economic agents and the institutional environment surrounding them. Special attention is paid to changing the agents' mentality under the influence of the institutional structure of society and the transformation of the institutional environment under the influence of agents' mental values. Computational experiments are carried out with the model, and the possibilities of achieving equilibrium by the system are calculated depending on the minimum labor productivity in society. An equilibrium state of the system is one in which the agents' mentality and public institutions are in harmony and do not contradict each other. It has been revealed that agents' mentality significantly influences their attitude to public institutions and their behavior in situations of economic choice. It has been established that the higher the labor productivity of agents and the more developed and prosperous the society is, the faster the system goes into harmony.

Keywords: Agent-Based Model · Computational Experiment · Economic Behavior · Economic Choice · Economic Psychology · Public Institutions · Mentality

1 Introduction

Approaches to defining a model of a human as a participant in economic activity, identifying decision-making mechanisms by individuals, and searching for factors influencing agents' behavior in economics are constantly evolving [see, e.g., 1, 2 and others]. Researchers are increasingly criticizing and abandoning the idealized model of *homo economicus*, a person who has perfect rationality and maximizes his benefit, in favor of more complex interdisciplinary models [3–6 and others]. In our opinion, one of the most promising areas is the consideration of psychological characteristics in the economic behavior of agents [7–12].

N. Agarwal et al. (Eds.): MSBC 2022, CCIS 1717, pp. 48–62, 2023.
https://doi.org/10.1007/978-3-031-33728-4_4

The perception of reality by economic agents, their actions, and deeds are determined by the *mentality*, which is the subject of psychology study and is a unique set of socio-psychological characteristics and goals of the individual. The agent's mentality is formed cumulatively under the influence of the external environment (social institutions, cultural patterns, information about the actions and decisions of other agents and others) based on the experience gained by a person in various life situations. From this, we can conclude that the decisions made by the agent at the current moment reflect the effect of "path dependence" [13–15], i.e., dependence on the previous path of development.

In general, two main groups of factors have a decisive influence on the behavior of an agent: his psychology, primarily mentality, and the external environment, primarily social institutions. Between these factors, there is a non-linear bilateral dynamic relationship, the implementation of which leads to the variability in the mentality of economic agents influenced by the dynamics of the institutional system of society. On the other hand, changes in the institutional system of society are influenced by the restructuring of a significant group of agents' mentalities. These changes occur iteratively and, as a rule, take a significant amount of time.

The issues of studying the above dependencies between the mentality and public institutions are challenging due to their insufficient research and high significance both for the competitiveness of the economy and for the sustainability of the development of society [16–18].

In an ideal society, the mentality of economic agents and social institutions are dynamically close to equilibrium, and society itself has the antifragility property [19–21 and others]. In this case, there is harmony, consistency, and the absence of long-term contradictions between the mentality of economic agents and public institutions that influence individuals' decision-making. In such a situation, economic agents do not experience psychological discomfort and pressure from the institutional system. In turn, the institutional system does not take corrective actions concerning agents' actions.

This equilibrium should not be confused with market or commodity-money equilibrium, which has been repeatedly studied in the economic literature [22–25 and others]. At the same time, the "mentality of agents – public institutions" system is closely related to the concepts of institutional equilibrium [26, 27] and the market of institutions [28, 29]. On the one side, the presented link reflects the demand on the part of economic agents for some social institutions, which is formed under the influence of the mentality of agents. On the other side, it demonstrates the proposal of institutions that influence the actions of individuals. At the same time, in an equilibrium situation, the supply of institutions corresponds to agents' mental needs (demand). Otherwise, the system is in a non-equilibrium state, and the mechanisms of mental and institutional changes begin to operate, pushing the system to gain balance. At each stage, the economic agent compares the price that he will have to pay for the corresponding institutional changes with the price of mental changes and chooses to favor one or another option. An economic agent's refusal to change negatively affects his satisfaction with life generally.

The socio-psychological characteristics of agents play an essential role in mental and institutional adaptation. Thus, conservatives prefer established traditions, and innovators seek to support innovations; individualists are guided by their own opinion and view of the world, while collectivists make decisions based on the opinion of their environment;

introverts, as a rule, share their thoughts only with a close circle of people, and extroverts try to spread their ideas as widely as possible, and so forth.

In this paper, we develop a conceptual agent-based model of interaction between economic agents and the institutional environment, as well as a series of experiments based on conditional synthetic data that allow us to evaluate the process of achieving an equilibrium in the "mentality of economic agents – public institutions" system, depending on the minimum labor productivity of agents. Note that agent-based modeling solves numerous problems in studying complex systems, analyzing and optimizing their functioning [see, e.g., 30], including describing the psychological factors of agents' behavior [31, 32].

2 Structuring the Internal Filling of Socio-economic Systems and the Institutional Structure of Society

The functioning of the socio-economic system, regardless of the characteristics of the economy to which it belongs, is primarily determined by the behavior of its constituent agents. At the same time, the socio-economic system influences the behavior, actions, and decision-making of such agents and, accordingly, the formation and change of their mentality.

Based on the system paradigm in the internal space of each socio-economic system (country, region, enterprise, and others), seven subsystems can be distinguished that reflect the processes of formation of the main factors of its behavior. Note that any economic agent can also be considered a socio-economic system. Let us briefly describe the subsystems that determine the agent's identity in terms of groups of factors of his behavior.

The first subsystem is "Worldview", which determines a person's life position, ideals, attitude toward the world around him, and place within it. These principles directly influence the agent's economic decisions. The second subsystem – "Culture", reflects the features of human interaction with other people and artifacts, assessing such relationships, especially the language of communications. The cultural subsystem also influences the subjectivity or objectivity of an individual's decision-making. The third subsystem – "Rules and Regulations", includes formal and informal settings that affect the agent's life. The fourth subsystem – "Knowledge", is responsible for a human's selection, perception, and processing of information. It combines all the mechanisms and results of cognition used by the individual. The fifth subsystem – "Infrastructure", is the artifacts of the material world, providing the vital needs of a person. The sixth subsystem – "Benchmarking", reflects a person's orientation to other people's experiences and includes various behavioral patterns, patterns, and cases transplanted from the outside world. The seventh subsystem – "Archive", contains the life history of the agent, his own experience of interaction with other people, the experience of independent decision-making, appropriate assessments, experiences, emotional upheavals, and others.

The mentioned subsystems form the agent's mentality; in most cases, one of the subsystems can be singled out, which dominates the rest.

Schematically, the structure of an agent as a socio-economic system can be represented as a pyramid, which includes the seven indicated subsystems (layers), see Fig. 1.

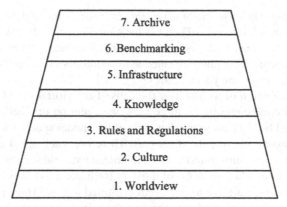

Fig. 1. Typical structure of an agent as a set of subsystems that form the agent's mentality.

The shape of the pyramid representing the socio-economic system reflects the difficulty in changing and managing the lower layers of the pyramid compared to changing and managing its upper layers. The lower levels are less manageable and less specific compared to the upper levels of the socio-economic system and, to a greater extent, determine its distinctive features and individuality.

A particular group of socio-economic institutions in the structure of society carries out institutional support for each subsystem. Thus, the functioning of the subsystem "Worldview" is supported by the institutions of communication and institutions of religion, the subsystem "Culture" – by socio-cultural institutions, the subsystem "Rules and Regulations" – by normative-sanctioning institutions and institutions of political parties, the subsystem "Knowledge" – by education, the subsystem "Infrastructure" – by the institutions of property rights, the "Benchmarking" subsystem – by the institutes of statistics, the "Archive" subsystem – by the institutions of strategic planning and corporate citizenship.

Note that this approach significantly simplifies the variety of existing institutional forms affecting agents' behavior to seven enlarged groups.

3   Model Space as a Field of Interaction Between Economic Agents and Public Institutions

The analysis of the "mentality of economic agents – public institutions" system is carried out on the ground of the activity model of a predetermined community of agents, so their number, as well as the number of groups of institutions that affect the activities of agents, does not change.

The model space (virtual world), following the traditions of agent-based modeling, can be imagined as a limited area on a plane covered with a grid. At the grid nodes, cells are placed, a peculiar niche for the agents to conduct economic activities. Occupying such a niche, the agent focuses on a specific type of activity and performs it in a particular geographical location. Each cell, therefore, has two coordinates on the plane, interpreted as one of the types of activity (abscissa axis) and the territorial location of an economic agent (ordinate axis). The ordering of activities can be implemented, for example, using the indicator of research intensity. Then the location along the abscissa axis will show the level of research intensity of this type of activity. Similarly, it is possible to arrange a set of locations according to their distance to the conditional center of the geographic space, for example, the country's capital.

The initial distribution of agents over the cells of the virtual world is set randomly in the model, while there can be no more than one agent on one cell. The cell where the agent is located borders on four other cells of the model space, some of which are free, while other agents occupy the other part. Therefore, each agent can have from 0 to 2 "neighbors" close to him in terms of economic activity (abscissa axis) and from 0 to 2 "neighbors" close to him in terms of territory (ordinate axis). It is assumed that the number of connections available to one agent is limited to four. Thus, a kind of limited horizon of the agent is manifested, i.e., the agent can, in its behavior, focus only on the two nearest "neighbors" in technology and only on the two closest "neighbors" in the territory.

4 Economic Agents and Their Model Characteristics: Mentality, Performance, Satisfaction

Economic agents have a mentality determined by the dominant (dominant feature, super value) that affects the agent's behavior in various economic situations and his perception of the world around him. The dominant role in this model is played by one of the seven types of subsystems considered in Sect. 1 (see Fig. 1).

It is also assumed that different groups of public institutions regulate economic activity in different market niches. At the same time, depending on the position in a particular market niche, the agent's mentality will either be supported by the corresponding group of regulatory institutions or resist it.

The agent's mentality and the social institution that regulates the market niche occupied by the agent are initially assigned randomly. At the same time, in market niches where there are no agents, there are no institutions. If there is no agent, then there is no economic activity; accordingly, there is no subject to institutional regulation.

The functioning of the "mentality of economic agents – public institutions" model is considered in discrete time. Each time step, the agent achieves particular economic activity results in the occupied market niche (*result*). These results depend on the following factors: 1) the minimum labor productivity of each agent in society; 2) the intensity of the efforts invested by the agent in production activities; 3) the experience and knowledge accumulated by the agent; 4) the conditions of the agent's activity.

The minimum labor productivity of each agent in the society for a one time step (*productivity*) is set exogenously in the model (by default, from 1 to 30 units). The intensity of the efforts invested by the agent in production activity (*individuality*) is determined randomly in the range from 0.5 to 2; it is believed that there are always agents working half-heartedly, and there are agents who, on the contrary, demonstrate double labor productivity. Before the start of the first time step, agents do not have experience (*experience*), but for each step of work in the same market niche, they receive an increase of 1 unit of experience due to their increasing skills. The accumulated experience has a positive effect on labor productivity (*experience_coefficient*). It is assumed that in the case of 10 units up to 19 units of experience, the agent receives an increase in labor productivity equal to 10%; in the case of 20 units up to 29 units of experience – 20%; in the case of more than 30 units of experience – 30%.

It is believed that the conditions for the agent's activity are favorable if: a) an institution operating in the niche occupied by the agent supports his mentality; b) at least one of the adjacent niches is occupied by some agent; c) in adjacent niches, some institutions support the mentality of the agent. The fulfillment of these conditions is characterized by a vector consisting of Boolean variables. The variable takes the value "+" if the condition is met and the value "−" if the condition is not met. The coordinates of this vector are aggregated into a generalized variable *environment_coefficient* following Table. 1.

Table 1. Generalized characteristics of the conditions for the agent's activity.

Conditions of the agent's activity	Combination of Boolean variables				
	1	2	3	4	5
The institution operating in the niche occupied by the agent supports his mentality	–	–	+	+	+
At least one of the adjacent niches is occupied by some agent	–	+	–	+	+
In adjacent niches, some institutions support the mentality of the agent	–	–	–	–	+
The final value of the *environment_coefficient*	0.8	0.9	0.9	1.0	1.1

In general, the production results of an economic agent achieved in a one time step are formed as follows: $\sum_{t=1}^{n} result = productivity \cdot individuality \cdot experience\_coefficient_t \cdot environment\_coefficient_t$, where n – number of time steps of the model, t – time step number, $t = 1, \ldots n$.

The *satisfaction* parameter reflects the agent's satisfaction with acting in the occupied market niche, and the initial value is set randomly in the range from 0.5 to 1.5. After that, when all the conditions are documented in Table 1 (the vector of Boolean variables contains only "+" values), the value of the parameter *satisfaction* increases by 0.1 every time step. If at least one of these conditions is not met, then the *satisfaction* parameter's value decreases by 0.1 every time step.

5 Mechanisms for Finding Equilibrium in the System "Mentality of Economic Agents – Public Institutions"

The model implements a number of mechanisms, the use of which allows the "mentality of economic agents – public institutions" system to achieve equilibrium. At each time step, the agent decides to move to a new market niche for doing business or stay in the same place. The agent's goal is to occupy a market niche where he can achieve the maximum efficiency of his production activities if this niche meets the conditions indicated in Table 1. In this case, if all agents occupy such niches, it is considered that the system has reached equilibrium, and the simulation ends. The second condition for the completion of the simulation is its duration – no more than 200 time steps. Below is a description of these mechanisms.

1. A direct change in the institution that regulates activities in the market niche occupied by the agent or a change in the market niche and/or territorial location to get out of the institution's influence. If an agent occupies a market niche regulated by an institution that does not support his mentality, then the agent has two options. The first option is to change the institutional structure of this market niche to strengthen the position and establish the dominant position of another institution that corresponds to the mentality of the agent. The second option is to change the economic activity/territorial location type by moving to another market niche. In this case, the first option is preferable for the agent. However, if it is impossible to perform the specified changes in the current time step, then the agent implements the second option.

In the first case, the agent needs to be paid for changing the institutional structure of the market niche he occupied (*change_price*). The price of such a change depends on the nature of the agent's environment and on the price of occupying this niche (*buy_price*), which, in turn, does not depend on the agent and the number of the time cycle, is constant and is set randomly on the set of niches in the range from 50 to 250 units. If the same institution regulates activity in adjacent market niches, the price of changing the institutional structure in this market niche is equal to *buy_price · k*. The coefficient *k* takes the value of 1.25 if there is one adjacent niche; 1.5 if there are two adjacent niches; 1.75 – three adjacent niches, and 2 – in the presence of four adjacent niches from the agent's environment, regulated by the same institution. This condition reflects the assumption that the higher the cost of changing the institutional structure, the more widespread this institution is in the agent's environment.

Thus, if the funds accumulated by the agent since the beginning of the simulation are more than the cost of changing the institutional structure $\sum_{t=1}^{n} result > change\_price$, this structure is successfully changed. At the same time, the value $\sum_{t=1}^{n} result$ decreases by the price of changes paid by the agent. The agent's experience is reset to zero. In case of negative satisfaction with functioning in the market niche, the value of the agent's *satisfaction* parameter reset to zero too. Here and below, the agent's adaptation to new conditions is similarly reflected.

In the second case, the agent needs to be paid for occupying a new market niche (*buy_price*). At the same time, this niche must satisfy the following conditions: 1) the market niche is free; 2) at least one of the four adjacent niches is dominated by an institution that corresponds to the mentality of the agent; 3) the agent must have the funding resources to overcome the entry barrier to occupy the chosen niche. The sufficiency of funds *enough_money* necessary to move the agent to a new market niche is determined by the amount spent by him to overcome the entry barrier when occupying the *buy_price* niche he leaves, and the funds accumulated since the beginning of the simulation $\sum_{t=1}^{n} result$. Moving to a new market niche passes if *enough_money* $\geq$ *buy_price* of this market niche. If the agent has more funds than necessary to occupy a new market niche, the remainder is added to the *result = enough_money – buy_price*. After moving to a new market niche, the agent's *satisfaction*, *experience*, and *experience_coefficient* parameters change accordingly.

2. Satisfying a need in society and the agent's search for an institutional environment that matches his mentality. The agent seeks to become part of the community, to find "neighbor" agents operating in adjacent market niches to receive environmental support. To do this, the agent is looking for a free market niche, where at least one niche adjacent to it is occupied by some agent.

The best solution for the agent is to find a niche where he will not only stop being "lonely", but will also be able to function in an institutional environment that corresponds to his mentality. This problem is solved by searching for a free niche, where at least two of the four niches adjacent to it, the activity of agents is regulated by an institution that supports the mentality of this agent. Moving to a new market niche and changing the agent's parameters in both the first and second cases takes place considering adaptation to new conditions.

3. Finding an exemplary group and changing the agent's mentality. In case of a decrease in satisfaction with the conditions of activity in the market niche, *satisfaction* ≤ 0.5, the agent pays attention to popular activities and strives to become part of some exemplary group of other agents. To do this, the agent searches for a free niche, where at least three niches adjacent to it are occupied by other agents. The condition for moving to a market niche is the agent's ability to pay the price of changing the institutional structure in it *enough_money* $\geq$ *change_price*. If the agent succeeds in occupying this market niche, he chooses one of the new "neighbors" with the highest total result $\sum_{t=1}^{n}$ *result* and, focusing on this agent as the most successful in the group, adopts his mentality. Then, as in the mechanisms discussed above, the agent's *satisfaction*, *satisfaction*, and *experience_coefficient* parameters are changed in the established order.

We also note that the mechanism 3 is used when an agent searches for an institutional environment that supports his mentality when there are no market niches with the required parameters in the model space and the agent has already moved more than twice to new market niches *number_of_moves* > 2.

4. Removal (retirement) of an agent from the virtual world. Some economic agents may not find a suitable market niche for functioning and, accordingly, cease to carry out economic activities. The model provides two scenarios for removing an agent from the "mentality of economic agents – public institutions" system, developed specifically for such cases. The first scenario is triggered in case of decreasing the agent's satisfaction with the conditions of his activity *satisfaction* ≤ -2.5. The second scenario is implemented in the case of many attempts to conduct activities in various market niches by the agent, expressed in movements in them *number_of_moves* > 3.

5. Checking the current status of agents and public institutions, redefining the total economic results of the agent. At the end of each time step, after the agent uses one of the above mechanisms 1–4, the value $\sum_{t=1}^{n}$ *result* is updated, and the agent's characteristics *experience_coefficient* and *institution_coefficient* are re-evaluated, which will affect the agent's production results in the next time step. The current state of public institutions that regulate activities in market niches occupied by agents is ralso monitored. Additionally, for all market niches, the *change_price* parameter of the change price of the institution is redefined because the placement of agents in market niches and the composition of the institutions regulating their activities change every time step.

6   Software Implementation of the Model and Analysis of the Results of Experiments

For the software implementation of the agent-based model of the "mentality of economic agents – public institutions" system, the basic conditions and mechanisms of which are described above, the NetLogo platform was used, which has proven itself as an environment for modeling and conducting experiments with various multi-agent systems [see, e.g., 33–37 and others].

The virtual world, implemented on the NetLogo platform, is a limited area marked into cells. On Fig. 2 shows the primary distribution of agents and public institutions in the model space.

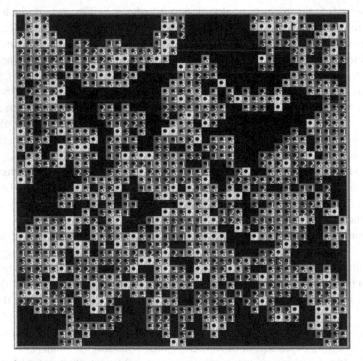

Fig. 2. Primary distribution of agents and public institutions in the model space.

Free cells are black, and cells with public institutions are marked with grayscale and numbers 1,…, 7, depending on the group of institutions that affect them. Agents in equilibrium are marked with black flags. If at least one condition of the agent's activity, from those presented in Table 1, is failed, agents are marked with black circles. Agents can only move within the virtual world and cannot go beyond it.

Note that the simulation ends when the system reaches equilibrium, at which all agents occupy market niches and achieve maximum performance, or when the simulation duration is more than 200 time steps. An example of the experiment's results of finding an equilibrium in the "mentality of economic agents – public institutions" system on the NetLogo platform is shown in Fig. 3.

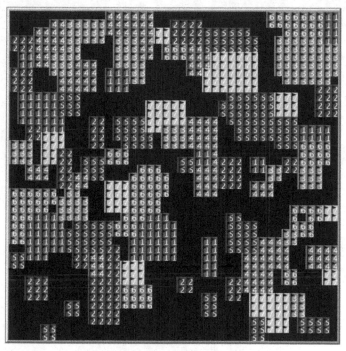

Fig. 3. The results of the experiment of finding equilibrium in the "mentality of economic agents – public institutions" system on the NetLogo platform.

The NetLogo platform and the R programming language were used to analyze the results of experiments, as in our previous work [38]. However, before that, we used the *RNetLogo* package [39, 40]; now, we use the *nlrx* [41, 42], a more modern package (set of functions) for R.

In order to simulate the process of achieving equilibrium in the "mentality of economic agents – public institutions" system, the following conditions for simulations were established. The number of simulations is 100; the number of agents in the virtual world is 1000; the minimum labor productivity of agents during the experiment varies from 1 to 30, with the change step being 1.

Based on the calculated data obtained from simulations, we study the dependence of the time the system reaches equilibrium and the number of retired agents on their minimum labor productivity. To do this, we will build an appropriate multi-panel plot, see Fig. 4.

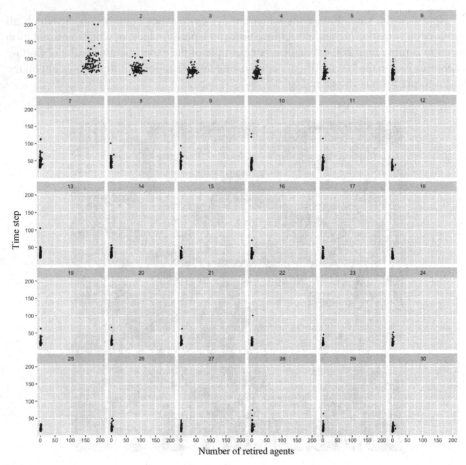

Fig. 4. The multi-panel plot of the dependence of the time the system reaches an equilibrium and the number of retired agents on their minimum labor productivity.

In each panel in Fig. 4, there are 100 points characterizing the results of the experiments conducted at various levels of the minimum labor productivity of agents. With an increase in the minimum labor productivity of agents, the scatter of points gradually decreases. This fact indicates a decrease in the time for the system to reach equilibrium and a decrease in the number of economic agents retiring from the system.

Furthermore, we construct a graph of the average values of the time the system reaches equilibrium and the number of retired agents, depending on the agents' minimum labor productivity in the community. The results are presented in Fig. 5.

According to Fig. 5, with an increase in the minimum labor productivity of agents, the average time for the system to reach equilibrium decreases from 90 to 17 time steps, i.e., about 5 times, as well as the average number of agents who left the system from 173 (with a minimum labor productivity of 1) to 1 (with a minimum labor productivity of 9 to 30).

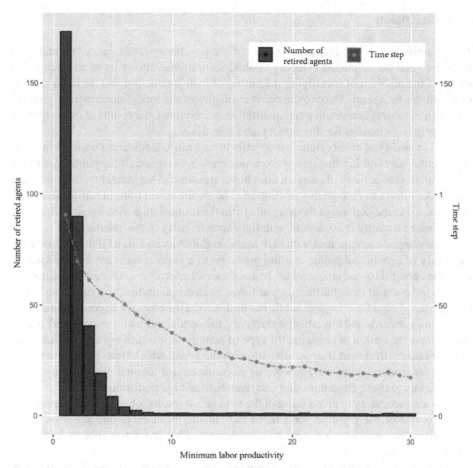

Fig. 5. Graph of the dynamics of the average values of the time the system reaches equilibrium and the number of retired agents depending on the minimum labor productivity of agents in the community.

Thus, we can conclude that the more developed, prosperous, and attentive to traditions a society is, the faster the balance in the "mentality of economic agents – public institutions" system comes, and a smaller number of agents fail in the process of finding and occupying of market niches for the most effective economic activity. Let us also focus on the effects of grouping agents at the end of the experiment, shown in Fig. 3. We see that economic agents gather into "institutional blocks" or groups of agents that occupy adjacent market niches, regulated by the same institutions. This effect is reminiscent of the results obtained in the Tiebout model [43], in which consumers seeking to obtain the necessary public goods for a certain fee change their residence and join one of the preferable territorial communities – "vote with their feet". In our situation, agents "vote with their mentality" for particular groups of public institutions.

7 Conclusion

The combination in one functional model of the psychological category "mentality of an agent" and the economic category "public institutions" allows us to advance in the study of the problem of identifying the nature of their interaction and decision-making mechanisms by agents. Despite the conventionality of the model constructions and the adoption of several quantitative and qualitative assumptions, the results allow us to draw meaningful conclusions for this subject area's analysis.

The mentality of agents significantly affects their attitude towards public institutions and agents' behavior in situations of economic choice. Moreover, if the public institution that regulates the activity of an agent does not correspond to his mentality, then the agent will make efforts to change this institution. The public institution, in turn, resists such changes, using the support of those agents from the immediate environment of the given one, whose mentality is consistent with the characteristics of this institution.

In developed communities with high labor productivity and high GDP per capita, the mentality of agents and public institutions come to a state of harmony because agents have the opportunity and resources to change their niche location and/or adapt institutions even in the event of disequilibrium conditions. Such communities, as a rule, also have a transparent system for changing public institutions. On the contrary, in communities with low living standards and low labor productivity, the opposite situation is observed: agents do not have the option of changing the type of activity or institutional environment, and the external environment is aggressive towards the agent, which leads to the emergence of various shadow schemes, allowing to circumvent institutional norms. Only a few agents adapt to these conditions and can demonstrate high performance.

It is also necessary to give a sense of the simulation results' objectivity. The proposed model is one of the possible versions of the "mentality of economic agents – public institutions" system, which should be complemented by alternative models to achieve objectivity of knowledge.

In the future, it is planned to continue work in this direction to model the transformation of the institutional structure of society depending on various initial configurations of the mentality of economic agents and public institutions.

References

1. Thaler, R.H.: From homo economicus to homo sapiens. J. Econ. Perspect. **14**(1), 133–141 (2000)
2. Kapeliushnikov, R.I.: Who is homo oeconomicus? Ekonomicheskaya Politika **15**(1), 8–39 (2020). (In Russian)
3. Hodgson, G.M.: The evolution of morality and the end of economic man. J. Evol. Econ. **24**(1), 83–106 (2013). https://doi.org/10.1007/s00191-013-0306-8
4. Belianin, A.V.: Homo Oeconomicus and Homo Postoeconomicus. Zhournal Novoi Ekonomicheskoi Associacii **33**(1), 157–161 (2017). (in Russian)
5. Taffler, R.J., Spence, C., Eshraghi, A.: Emotional economic man: Calculation and anxiety in fund management. Acc. Organ. Soc. **61**, 53–67 (2017)
6. Urbina, D.A., Ruiz-Villaverde A.: A critical review of homo economicus from five approaches. Am. J. Econ. Soc. **78**(1), 63–93 (2019)

7. Kahneman, D.: Maps of bounded rationality: psychology for behavioral economics. Am. Econ. Rev. **93**(5), 1449–1475 (2003)
8. Newell, B.R., Lagnado, D.A., Shanks, D.R.: Straight Choices: The Psychology of Decision Making, p. 318. Psychology Press (2015)
9. Schiliro, D.: Economics and psychology. The framing of decisions. J. Math. Econ. Financ. **II**(2(3)), 77–88 (2016)
10. Kumacheva, S., Gubar, E., Zhitkova, E., Tomilina, G.: Modeling the behaviour of economic agents as a response to information on tax audits. In: Agarwal, N., Sakalauskas, L., Weber, G.-W. (eds.) MSBC 2019. CCIS, vol. 1079, pp. 96–111. Springer, Cham (2019). https://doi.org/10.1007/978-3-030-29862-3_8
11. Kleiner, G.B., Rybachuk, M.A., Ushakov, D.V.: Psychological factors of economic behavior: a systemic view. Terra Economicus **16**(1), 20–37 (2018). (in Russian)
12. Plikynas, D., Miliauskas, A., Laužikas, R., Dulskis, V., Sakalauskas, L.: The cultural impact on social cohesion: an agent-based modeling approach. Qual. Quant. **56**, 4161–4192 (2021). https://doi.org/10.1007/s11135-021-01293-6
13. Koch, J., Eisend, M., Petermann, A.: Path dependence in decision-making processes: exploring the impact of complexity under increasing returns. BuR Bus. Res. J. **2**(1) (2009)
14. Bednar, J., Page, S.E.: When order affects performance: culture, behavioral spillovers, and institutional path dependence. Am. Polit. Sci. Rev. **112**(1), 82–98 (2018)
15. Bednar, J., Jones-Rooy, A., Page, S.E.: Choosing a future based on the past: institutions, behavior, and path dependence. Eur. J. Polit. Econ. **40**, 312–332 (2015)
16. Zhuravlev, A.L., Ushakov D.V., Yurevich, A.V.: Prospects of psychology on Russian society problems' solving. Part III. Interaction between social institutes and mentality: the ways of optimization. Psikhologicheskii Zhurnal **34**(6), 5–25 (2013). (in Russian)
17. Zhuravlev, A.L., Ushakov, D.V., Yurevich, A.V.: Mentality, society and "homo psychosocial-is" (response to the participants of the discussion). Psikhologicheskii Zhurnal **38**(1), 107–112 (2017). (in Russian)
18. Ushakov, D.V.: Mentality and the socioeconomic achievements of countries. Her. Russ. Acad. Sci. **90**(2), 142–148 (2020)
19. Taleb, N.N.: Antifragile: Things that Gain from Disorder, p. 521. Random House, New York (2012)
20. Markey-Towler, B.: antifragility, the black swan and psychology. Evol. Inst. Econ. Rev. **15**(2), 367–384 (2018)
21. de Bruijn, H., Größler, A., Videira, N.: Antifragility as a design criterion for modelling dynamic systems. Syst. Res. Behav. Sci. **37**(1), 23–37 (2020)
22. Von Neumann, J.: A model of general economic equilibrium. In: Readings in the Theory of Growth, pp. 1–9. Palgrave Macmillan, London (1971)
23. Arrow, K.J.: General economic equilibrium: purpose, analytic techniques, collective choice. Am. Econ. Rev. **64**(3), 253–272 (1974)
24. Hicks, J.: IS-LM: an explanation. J. Post Keynesian Econ. **3**(2), 139–154 (1980)
25. King, R.G.: The new IS-LM model: language, logic, and limits. FRB Richmond Econ. Q. **86**(3), 45–104 (2000)
26. Wilkin, J.: Institutional equilibrium. What is it about and what is its role in the economy? Ekonomia **15**, 26–37 (2011)
27. Shepsle, K.A.: Institutional arrangements and equilibrium in multidimensional voting models. Am. J. Polit. Sci. **23**(1), 27–59 (1979)
28. Shepsle, K.A.: Institutional equilibrium and equilibrium institutions. In: Weisberg, H. (ed.) Political Science: The Science of Politics, pp. 51–82. Agathon, New York (1986)
29. Ross, S.A.: Institutional markets, financial marketing, and financial innovation. J. Financ. **44**(3), 541–556 (1989)

30. Akopov, A.S., Beklaryan, L.A., Saghatelyan, A.K.: Agent-based modelling of interactions between air pollutants and greenery using a case study of Yerevan, Armenia. Environ. Model. Softw. **116**, 7–25 (2019)
31. Jackson, J.C., Rand, D., Lewis, K., Norton, M.I., Gray, K.: Agent-based modeling: a guide for social psychologists. Soc. Psychol. Personal. Sci. **8**(4), 387–395 (2017)
32. Yin, X., Wang, H., Yin, P., Zhu, H.: Agent-based opinion formation modeling in social network: a perspective of social psychology. Physica A **532**, 121786 (2019)
33. Chiacchio, F., Pennisi, M., Russo, G., Motta, S., Pappalardo, F:. Agent-based modeling of the immune system: NetLogo, a promising framework. BioMed Res. Int. **2014**, 907171 (2014)
34. Wilensky, U., Rand, W.: An Introduction to Agent-Based Modeling: Modeling Natural, Social, and Engineered Complex Systems with NetLogo, p. 504. The MIT Press, Cambridge. London (2015)
35. Carbo, J., Sanchez-Pi, N., Molina, J.M.: Agent-based simulation with NetLogo to evaluate ambient intelligence scenarios. J. Simul. **12**(1), 42–52 (2018)
36. Jaxa-Rozen, M., Kwakkel, J.H., Bloemendal, M.: A coupled simulation architecture for agent-based/geohydrological modelling with NetLogo and MODFLOW. Environ. Model. Softw. **115**, 19–37 (2019)
37. Sulis, E., Tambuscio, M.: Simulation of misinformation spreading processes in social networks: an application with NetLogo. In: IEEE 7th International Conference on Data Science and Advanced Analytics (DSAA), pp. 614–618. IEEE (2020)
38. Kleiner, G.B., Rybachuk, M.A., Ushakov, D.V.: Agent-oriented model of professional expertise and decision making on individual public significant initiatives support. Terra Economicus **17**(2), 23–39 (2019). (in Russian)
39. Thiele, J.C.: R marries NetLogo: introduction to the RNetLogo package. J. Stat. Softw. **58**(2), 1–41 (2014)
40. Thiele, J.C., Kurth, W., Grimm, V.: RNetLogo: an R package for running and exploring individual-based models implemented in NetLogo. Methods Ecol. Evol. **3**(3), 480–483 (2012)
41. Salecker, J., Sciaini, M., Meyer, K.M., Wiegand, K.: The nlrx r package: a next-generation framework for reproducible NetLogo model analyses. Methods Ecol. Evol. **10**(11), 1854–1863 (2019)
42. Kleiner, G.B., Rybachuk, M.A., Ushakov, D.V.: The mentality of economic agents and institutional change: in search of an equilibrium model. Terra Economicus **19**(4), 6–20 (2021)
43. Tiebout, C.M.: A pure theory of local expenditures. J. Polit. Econ. **64**(5), 416–424 (1956)

Attitudes to Vaccination: How the Opinion Dynamics Affects the Influenza Epidemic Process

Suriya Kumacheva[1]([✉])[iD], Ekaterina Zhitkova[1][iD], and Galina Tomilina[2][iD]

[1] St. Petersburg State University, 7/9 Universitetskaya nab., St. Petersburg 199034, Russia
{s.kumacheva,e.zhitkova}@spbu.ru
[2] EPAM Systems, Spain S.L., Avd. Imperio Argentina 19–21, 2 planta, Malaga, 29004 Andalucia, Spain
g.tomilina@yandex.ru
http://www.spbu.ru, https://www.epam.com/

Abstract. A hypothesis about the influence of the opinion dynamics on the subsequent epidemic process is considered. The existence of relation between the population's attitude to vaccination and the dynamics of the influenza epidemic is assumed. Emphasis is placed on the spectrum of opinions of the population: from extremely negative to super-positive. Along with persons who are firmly confident in their point of view and propagandize it, there are doubting agents who make their choice to vaccinate or not under the influence of others' opinions. Their decisions have an impact on the formation of their personal immunity and of the collective immunity of entire population. Opinion dynamics is assumed to be completed before the seasonal influenza rising incidence starts, and each individuum has decided to vaccinate or not until this moment.

The purpose of this study is to identify the relationship between the parameters that characterize the opinions' influence in the population and the number of people who have been infected (vaccinated and unvaccinated) at the beginning of influenza epidemic.

Simulation modeling of the dynamics of opinions is carried out using a network model for graphs of various configuration (grid, strongly connected graph, weakly connected graph). Modeling is carried out in a closed population using statistical data on morbidity and annual vaccination campaigns in Russia. The epidemic (SIR) process is represented by modification of the classical Kermack-McKendrick model (1927). A series of repeated simulations was carried out, a numerical experiment based on statistical data and scenario analysis were performed.

Keywords: Vaccination · Anti-vaccine propaganda · Epidemic model · Network model · Opinion dynamics

---

Supported by Saint Petersburg State University grant "Improvement of Insurance Coverage of the Population under Biological Threat", Pure ID: 92423789.

N. Agarwal et al. (Eds.): MSBC 2022, CCIS 1717, pp. 63–77, 2023.
https://doi.org/10.1007/978-3-031-33728-4_5

1   Introduction

Epidemics have always been one of the major biological threats to humanity. In recent decades, modeling of epidemic processes has occupied one of the leading positions in scientific research. This is due to many reasons, among which it is impossible not to mention the rapid increase in the number of viral diseases, some of which are especially dangerous for humans. On the other hand, an important role is played by the fact that the number of routes and movements of the population around the planet has also increased significantly. Under such conditions, it is quite difficult to control the spread of disease and isolate the population in certain cities and regions in order to prevent the further spread of the epidemic.

At the same time, it must be taken into account that any epidemic has a detrimental effect on many areas of human life [19]. First of all, a heavy and uneven burden falls on the medical sector, sometimes leading to a blockage of the capacity of medical workers and institutions. It is also worth noting that, even if temporary, an increase in the incidence, the number of disabled workers and overdue works in any industry has a bad effect on the economic situation in total. If we are talking about a sudden onset of a pandemic of a new unknown disease, it is very difficult to select tools to counteract the spread of such a situation. In this case, mathematical modeling of epidemic processes can help predict the course of a pandemic, its peaks and troughs [12,18]. But it is technically difficult and requires a large number of assumptions and clarifications.

However, if we are talking about a seasonal rise in the incidence of a known virus, there is a very realistic alternative to the negative phenomena described above, leading to an increase in morbidity, mortality and a worsening economic situation. It is about vaccine prevention, its implementation and distribution [1–3]. And the modeling of the epidemic process in this case should include such a factor as vaccination of the population [9,19]. But what is the real attitude towards vaccines in society? Recent studies, as well as the pandemic COVID-19 [12,18], have shown an ambiguous attitude towards this medical tool, the stratification of society, and the heterogeneity of its views on the problem.

In the base of the current research is an assumption that there is a relation between the population's attitude to vaccination and the dynamics of the influenza epidemic. In our study we focused on the study of influenza epidemic according to the following reasons. First of all, influenza remains one of the most widespread viruses in the world, included in the top 10 most dangerous infections on the planet. On August 30, 2022, the World Health Organization (WHO) announced an increased risk of resurgence of the influenza virus after the decline of the COVID-19 pandemic [25], and strongly recommended the combined use of vaccination against two infections at once on October 12. On the other hand, numerous influenza vaccines have been developed in various laboratories around the world [5]. Finally, regular outbreaks of seasonal influenza in various countries of the world and ongoing vaccination have made it possible to collect extensive statistics [2,3,9,19]. We suppose that there exist two opposing groups in their attitude to vaccination. We also assume that there are doubting agents in the population who make decisions about vaccination under the influence of others' opinions. Therefore, we consider the opinion dynamics [6,14], which is completed before the seasonal rising incidence starts, each agent is assumed to decide to vaccinate or not until this moment. After the phase of their decision, the epidemic rising, which is supposed to be described by modification of the classical Kermack-McKendrick model (1927) [9], starts. General idea of the presented research is to verify a hypothesis about the influence of the opinion dynamics on the subsequent development of the epidemic process.

The paper is organized as follows. In Sect. 1, we discuss the features of the current attitude towards vaccination among the population. Section 2 presents the model of the dynamics of opinion and Sect. 3 describes numerical simulation we conducted to support our assumptions. Section 4 is devoted to the modelling of the epidemic process. In Sect. 4.1, we present the numerical experiments which illustrate how the epidemic model works. In Sect. 5, we formulate main conclusions of our study and discuss its future prospects.

2 Attitude to Vaccination

As noted above, the attitude towards vaccination in society is very different. It can be classified into three gradations, let's formally name them as follows: extremely negative, rational and totally positive.

In [1–3,13], a detailed analysis of the statistics of refusals to vaccinate and the motives influencing the attitude to this problem in society was carried out. Among the basic groups of people who have formed an extremely negative attitude towards vaccination (let's call it *attitude A*), the authors of these works distinguish the following groups:

– medics and scientists who consider insufficient evidence for the effectiveness of a given vaccine (or vaccination against a given disease);
– those, who believe (often erroneously) that they or their relatives are immune to the disease;
– those, who believe that a healthy lifestyle is enough without any vaccination;
– those, who have a negative experience of vaccination in the past (side effects, disease after vaccination, etc.);
– parents of little children who actively oppose their vaccination, considering it as an unnecessary burden on the immune system of babies and underestimating the seriousness of the diseases for which this vaccination is carried out;
– others (any particular personal reasons).

In the framework of our research we consider these groups as forming the antivax community. In Cambridge Dictionary [23] the word **antivaxxer** (also anti-vaxxer, anti vaxxer) is defined as follows: "someone who does not agree with vaccinating people (= giving them injections to prevent disease) and spreads and encourages opinions against vaccines". Therefore, in the current study we assume the influence of this community on the opinion of another part of population.

Continuing the analysis of the above-mentioned research, we can distinguish the following groups of individuals among those who have a totally positive attitude towards vaccination (*attitude B*):

- medics and scientists – once again – because in most cases, adherents of the scientific approach to disease prevention recognize the effectiveness and importance of vaccination;
- those who have benefited from vaccination in the past;
- others (mainly those who are subject to tangible influence of representatives of the first two groups).

These groups are supposed to form pro-vax community. In real life from the available opinions (attitude A and attitude B), the following combinations can be added (Fig. 1):

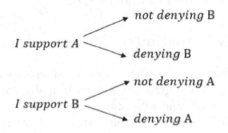

Fig. 1. Formation of the distribution of opinions in society.

Formally, **anti-vaxxers** attitude can be described by the scheme {Support A | denying B}. At the same time, **pro-vaxxers** are those who obey to the opposite scheme {Support B | denying A}. Any other person who is inclined to rationally perceive the opposing points of view presented by anti-vaxxers and pro-vaxxers ({Support A | not denying B} and {Support B | not denying B}), will adjust their strategy according to the dynamics of opinion in society.

3   Opinion Dynamics

Consider the problem of the dynamics of opinion in society [6,7,14,15]. In the current study, we construct a model of this dynamics, similar to the process of dissemination of information in the population of economic agent [15], represented by networks of various modifications.

In the future research a limited small population consists of 30 – 50 agents will be considered. Such a limitation is justified by the realistic interpretation: it is worth starting to study the dynamics of opinions not from the exchange of information in a large population, but from small teams, for example, one small office or parents of children from the same class at school or one group in kindergarten.

Following the approach explored earlier in [7], we represent the dynamics of opinions in the network as a Markov process [6,14] and understand the stabilization of such a system as the reaching a consensus in the sense of the De Groot model [4].

In the following study we suppose that there are n agents of three types – anti-vaxxers, pro-vaxxers and undecided agents, rationally responding to available information. As initial assumptions we use the results of psychological research on risk-propensity [16]: the number of risk-loving agents from the general population is 18%, risk-neutral agents are 65%, risk-avoidants are 17%. These results gave us an assumption of possible initial distribution of attitudes among the population: 17% of pro-vaxxers, 65% of rational deciders and 18% of anti-vaxxers.

As it was mentioned previously, in our work the studied population is represented as a network $G = (N, P)$, where N is the set of agents, P is a stochastic matrix of connections p_{ij}, $i, j = \overline{1, N}$, between agents. The matrix P can have various modifications that determine the appropriate variants of the network structure. The most representative network modifications for further research are the random sparse graph and random connected graph. Therefore we focus our attention on them. The players are considered in pairs. Applying the Erdős-Rényi model [8,17], the connection between them is formed with probability $\frac{1}{k}$, where k is a natural number.

At the initial time moment each agent $i = \overline{1, N}$ has his/her characteristics. Among them there is an agent's type or risk-status (in our model they are anti-vaxxer, pro-vaxxer or rational agent) and his/her certain belief f_i^0, which characterises his/her own attitude and decision (do not vaccinate / vaccinate).

Before the information exchange process begins, all agents have some "natural" perception of the necessity of vaccination. Based on the type definition, the agents against vaccination rate it at 0 and keep this representation, and the agents in favor of vaccination rate it at 1 and either do not change their opinion. Among risk-neutral agents the information is initially distributed normally with the fixed parameters. Various options for distributing agents of different types over the network are considered.

The algorithm based on the Markov process [4] is used: not only connection between agents is indicated, but also the measure of confidence of agents to each other (opinion weight). At each iteration, each agent i updates the estimates f_i^t of their attitude to the problem based on the average estimates of the neighbors, taking into account the weights from the matrix of connections:

$$f_i^t = \sum_{j=1}^{n} p_{ij} f_j^{t-1}$$

The interaction continues until 10^3 iterations reached or until the moment T when the following conditions are satisfied for all i:

$$\sqrt{\sum_{t=1}^{T} (f_i^t - f_i^{t-1})^2} < 10^{-3}.$$

After the process is stopped (the system reached its steady state), the final strategies of the agents are determined. It means that at this moment each agent made his/her vaccination decision. In accordance of the previous assumptions of the studied model, anti-vaxxers remain non-vaccinated regardless of their estimates, pro-vaxxers remain vaccinated regardless of their estimates and only rational agents make their decision depending on a critical value: if their estimates is higher than it, they are vaccinated.

3.1 Numerical Simulation of Opinion Dynamics

In order to study the dynamics of opinions about vaccination in the network, we conducted a series of repeated simulations using the algorithm described above, implemented in the program code in Python on the platform Jupyter Notebook. To represent the results of simulation graphically first we need to visualize the network.

To initialise the random sparse graph and random connected graph the program forms the connections between nodes of the network with probability $\frac{1}{k}$, where k is a natural number given at the start of the program. In our experiment the parameter $\frac{1}{15}$ is used to simulate a graph with conditionally "weak" connectivity, to simulate a graph with "strong" connectivity we used $\frac{1}{5}$.

Each agent is represented by a node with the following characteristics:

1. the propensity to vaccination, which is visualized as the form of the node:
   - positive attitude – triangles;
   - neutral (rational) – squares;
   - negative attitude – circles;
2. the agents' current decision on vaccination is represented by the node's color:
   - decided to vaccinate – yellow;
   - decided not to vaccinate – blue.

To represent the distribution of information among risk-neutral agents we assume that this information is initially distributed normally with the following parameters: expectation is 0.5, standard deviation is 0.4. The critical value for decision making for such agents is assumed to be 0.5. With further development of the model in the experiments, the level of this threshold may change.

The results of the simulation are studied in the following examples.

Example 1. In the considered example the number of nodes is 30. As a network we consider a random connected graph. The distribution of initial propensities to risk, or, in the terms of our model, attitudes to vaccination, is following: extremely negative attitude is represented by 8 nodes, number of agents with totally positive attitude is 3, and the number of neutral agents is 19. At the same time, the initial distribution of opinions is following: there are 14 agents who are going to vaccinate and 16 who are not going at the initial state of population.

Simulating the process of opinion dynamics we get that the process converges, formally, after 11 iterations, but informally, after 3 iterations. It means that, starting from the 4-th state, the process does not change the behavior of the system. Finally, we obtained 22 agents who decided to vaccinate and 8 who decided not to vaccinate.

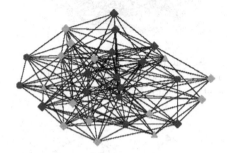

Fig. 2. Initial state of population, before opinion dynamics (Color figure online)

Fig. 3. Population after the first iteration (Color figure online)

Comparing networks in the Fig. 2 and Fig. 3, we can see that after the first iteration the number of those who are going to vaccinate (represented by yellow nodes) is increasing.

Comparing the states of population after the second iteration (Fig. 4) and the resulting state after the third iteration (Fig. 5), we understand that here we get the case of dynamics which is positive in the following meaning: the number of those who are going to vaccinate increases and becomes bigger than the number of those who are not going to vaccinate. Among the possible reasons of this effect, we can name the large number of agents with neutral attitude in the initial state of the network and the location of such agents: they are located throughout the network with a large number of connections. As the final result of this dynamics, we get the state when only persons with initially negative attitude will not vaccinate.

Example 2. In this example we still consider the network which consists of 30 nodes but has the modification of the random sparse graph. Distribution of initial attitudes to vaccination is following: negative attitude is represented by 5 nodes, positive – also by 5 nodes, neutral – by 20. There are 14 agents who are going to vaccinate and 16 who are not going to vaccinate in the network at its initial state (Figs. 6, 7, 8 and 9).

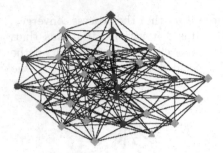

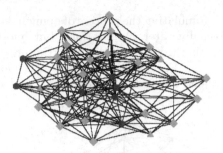

Fig. 4. Population after the second iteration (Color figure online)

Fig. 5. The result of opinion dynamics: final state of population after the third iteration (Color figure online)

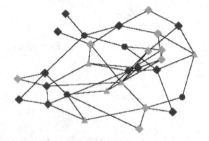

Fig. 6. Initial state of population, before opinion dynamics (Color figure online)

Fig. 7. Population after the first iteration (Color figure online)

Process formally converges after 43 iterations and informally – after 3 iterations. In the final state we get 25 agents who decided to get vaccination and 5 who decided not to vaccinate.

This example is also a case of "positive" dynamics: the number of those who are going to vaccinate increases and becomes bigger than the number of those who are not going to vaccinate. Along with the reasons mentioned earlier, it is also worth noting the impact of that the first agent who changed the opinion had a positive attitude: in the similar case with another type of agent at this position we got another type of dynamics. The final result is similar to the previous example's one.

Example 3. In the current example we simulate the studied process in the random connected graph with 30 nodes. Distribution we analyze is following: 8 nodes with negative attitude, 3 nodes – with positive and 19 – with neutral. Among them there are 15 who are initially going to vaccinate and 15 who are not going to vaccinate (Figs. 10 and 11).

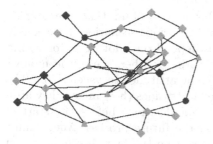

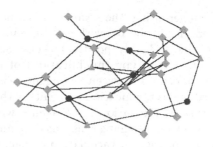

Fig. 8. Population after the second iteration (Color figure online)

Fig. 9. The result of opinion dynamics: final state of population after the third iteration (Color figure online)

Fig. 10. Initial state of population, before opinion dynamics (Color figure online)

Fig. 11. The result opinion dynamics: final state of population after the second iteration (Color figure online)

Process formally converges after 9 iterations, informally – after 2 iterations. At the final state there are 16 who decided to get vaccination and 14 who decided not to get vaccination.

In this example, we are facing "negative" dynamics: the number of those agents who are going to vaccinate finally increases but not significantly (only one added). Analyzing this fact, we find the following reasons: agents with different predispositions are highly mixed in the network; at the same time, the agents with a negative attitude have a large number of connections. Taking into account these facts, we can formulate that in such types of examples there is no effect from opinion dynamics. The final state of the system does not differ much from the initial one.

Generalizing the examples discussed above, we obtain that the opinion dynamics in the network can be represented by various scenarios (from highly negative to highly positive). These scenarios depend on a lot of factors. First of all, it is a type (modification) of the network. Another one is the number of connections between the agents with different attitudes to vaccination. The third one is the location of agents with different attitudes (how mixed they are). Naturally, the ratio of the agents with different decisions before the start of the opinions exchange also has an impact on the future process. And, finally, the propensity to vaccination of agents, who will be the first disseminators of opinion in the network, also influences on the result of the dynamics.

4   Epidemic Process

When forming the model, we assume that the opinion dynamics is completed and the agents made their decisions about vaccination (and were vaccinated or not in accordance with it) before the start of the seasonal epidemic rise.

So far, we have considered isolated limited teams, studying the circulation of opinions and the exchange of information in them. But the epidemic rise is a process that concerns not individual groups, but society as a whole. Therefore, to simulate a population, it is natural to consider the union of modeled teams into one set. Speaking about the interpretation of this approach, in everyday life it can be the union of different rooms into one open space office, of groups in a kindergarten, classes in a school, various departments in a large corporation, and many others. And these unions can consist of subpopulations simulated by the networks of various configurations.

We assume that the season epidemic rise can be described by a SIR-like model [10]. Let's make the following notations. Let H be the total number of agents in the population (cardinality of the mentioned union of subpopulations), P is the number of those who did not receive immune protection among the total number of vaccinated, P^- is the number of those who did not receive immune protection among the total number of unvaccinated, I is the number of infected, R is the number of immunized. P, P^-, I, R are the dynamic functions.

Now we can apply the classic SIR model [10] in epidemic modeling, following the studies described in works [11,22]. According to their results, the epidemic process can be represented by the following system of equations:

$$\begin{cases} \dot{P} = -a\,P\,I \\ \dot{P^-} = -a^-\,P^-\,I \\ \dot{I} = a\,P\,I + a^-\,P^-\,I - \beta I \\ \dot{R} = \beta I \end{cases} \tag{1}$$

In this system a, a^- and β are the parameters of the model. The parameters have their epidemic meaning. For example, β is recovery rate $\beta = 1/T_b$, where T_b is a characteristic duration of illness; for the vast majority of influenza strains it is assumed to be $T_b = 15$ days [10,11,22]. Along with T_b let's consider the parameter T, named the duration of the seasonal rise ($T = 90$ days). The parameters a and a^- are found in accordance with real data on vaccination in Russia [9,22].

Continuing to describe the notation used, let's denote by V the number of vaccinated, and the number of unvaccinated by V^-. In the framework of our model V and V^- can be defined as the results of opinion dynamics.

We assume that there are those who did not receive immune protection among those who were vaccinated. Similarly, there exist those who were not vaccinated but have their immune protection. In accordance with Pareto principle, we suppose that initially $P(0) = 0.2\,V$; $P^-(0) = 0.8\,V^-$ (20% and 80% correspondingly). At the initial time moment: $I(0) = 1$, $R(0) = H - P(0) - P^-(0) - I(0)$.

Along with the initial condition, we should take into account the epidemic start conditions:

$$a\,P(0)\,I(0) + a^-\,P^-(0)\,I(0) - \beta\,I(0) > 0.$$

Two basic goals of such research are to find the values of the number L of recovered patients among the vaccinated and the number L^- of recovered patients among those unvaccinated:

$$L = \int_0^\tau a\,P\,I\,dt, \qquad L^- = \int_0^\tau a^-\,P^-\,I\,dt, \tag{2}$$

where τ is length of intervals by months; it can take values $\{30, 60, 90\}$.

4.1 Numerical Simulations of Epidemic Process

To study the differences between scenario of epidemic processes depending on the result of the previous dynamics of opinions, consider the following experimental examples.

Example 4. In the considered example the model has the following parameters: the total number of agents in the population is $H = 180$, $\beta = 0.067$, $a = 0.001$ and $a^- = 0.003$. Using a specially implemented program application, we obtain experimental dynamics of the number of agents in groups P (blue curve), P^- (orange curve) and I (green curve) correspondingly. For the given set of parameters we will get the following results.

In this example we can see that after the opinion dynamics, the number of those going to be vaccinated increased from 116 to 160. At the same time the number of susceptible among the vaccinated has decreased. The maximum number of cases decreases 11 times (Fig. 12, 13).

Example 5. Here we will use the same set of the epidemic model parameters: $H = 180$, $\beta = 0.067$, $a = 0.001$ and $a^- = 0.003$. But the epidemic process, fixed by such parameter values, will be superimposed on a network with another initial distribution of opinions and another result of their dynamics. The results in this case will be following.

This example represents the case of "negative dynamics" of opinions; most part of the studied population is not going to get vaccinated. Thus, there is a rapid rise in the number of infected, on the 20th day a maximum is reached; all of P and P^- will get sick. Without opinion dynamics there is an increase in the number of infected by 42 days, and the maximum will be no more than 18 people per a day (Fig. 14, 15).

Example 6. Here we are analyzing another set of the model parameters: the bigger population is considered, $H = 240$, $\beta = 0.067$, $a = 0.01$ and $a^- = 0.001$. For these parameters we obtained the following results.

This example represents the case of "negative dynamics" of opinions; most part of the studied population is not going to get vaccinated. Thus, there is a rapid rise in the number of infected, on the 20th day a maximum is reached; all of P and P^- will get sick. Without opinion dynamics there is an increase in the number of infected by 42 days, and the maximum will be no more than 18 people per a day (Fig. 16, 17).

Analyzing the digital information we possess and the obtained plots of dynamics, we can see that after the opinions dynamics, the number of those who are going to vaccinate increased. At the same time, the number of unvaccinated people who recovered from the disease decreased by almost half, but the maximum number of infected people is approximately the same. It is worth noting that t_{max} shifts to the left. Most likely this is due to the fact that the parameter $a > a^-$, that is, the rate of disease among vaccinated people is higher.

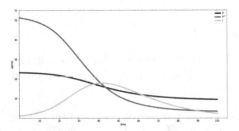 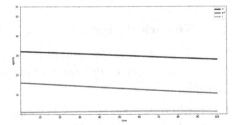

Fig. 12. Epidemic process with initial distribution of opinions ($V = 116$, $V^- = 64$; $P(0) = 23.2$, $P^-(0) = 51.2$; $L = 13.54$, $L^- = 47.505$, $I_{max}(42) = 17.83$) (Color figure online)

Fig. 13. Epidemic process after opinion dynamics ($V = 160$, $V^- = 20$; $P(0) = 32$, $P^-(0) = 16$; $L = 3.77$, $L^- = 5.012$, $I_{max}(62.8) = 1.54$) (Color figure online)

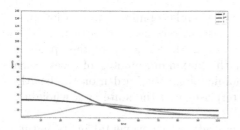

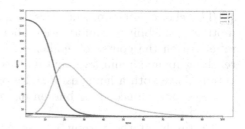

Fig. 14. Epidemic process with initial distribution of opinions ($V = 116$, $V^- = 64$; $P(0) = 23.2$, $P^-(0) = 51.2$; $L = 13.54$, $L^- = 47.51$, $I_{max}(42) = 17.83$) (Color figure online)

Fig. 15. Epidemic process after opinion dynamics ($V = 20$, $V^- = 160$; $P(0) = 4$, $P^-(0) = 128$; $L = 3.44$, $L^- = 127.64$, $I_{max}(20.4) = 69.64$) (Color figure online)

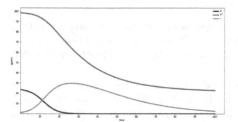

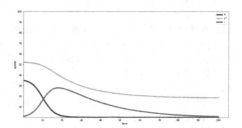

Fig. 16. Epidemic process with initial distribution of opinions ($V = 117$, $V^- = 123$; $P(0) = 23.4$, $P^-(0) = 98.4$; $L = 23.4$, $L^- = 74.82$, $I_{max}(26.6) = 29.81$) (Color figure online)

Fig. 17. Epidemic process after opinion dynamics ($V = 175$, $V^- = 65$; $P(0) = 35$, $P^-(0) = 52$; $L = 34.99$, $L^- = 33.18$, $I_{max}(18) = 27.97$) (Color figure online)

5   Conclusions and Future Discussion

The main object of the current research is the limited population which is heterogeneous in terms of risk propensity, or, in the framework of our model, in terms of attitude to vaccination. As a part of the study, many scenarios of the dynamics of opinions in small teams were simulated. The implementation of each scenario leads to different results, which are considered as initial conditions for modeling the epidemic. The main conclusions from the study are listed below.

The dynamics of opinion about vaccination can have both positive and negative effects on the subsequent course of the epidemic in the population. These effects depend on many factors such as modification of the network we are modelling, on how well the persons with different propensities is mixed in the considered population, the initial distribution of attitudes and opinions at the initial state of the network. From this fact the second one follows.

The choice of competent ways to manage public opinion (vaccination promotion, availability of information about existing vaccines, etc.) can positively influence on the course of epidemics, increasing the duration of the epidemic reaching its maximum level and reducing the maximum number of cases. Such actions have both a humanistic and economic effect: the burden on the healthcare system, the economic burden on enterprises and the state as a whole are reduced.

Certainly, at the current moment the study is experimental in its nature and the model needs further improvement. In future, it is planned to pay more attention to the study of negative scenarios of the dynamics of opinions. By the other hand, we are going to take into account mortality and describe it in the framework of our model.

References

1. Antonova N., Yeritsyan K.: The systematic review of empirical research of factors of refusal from vaccination. Gigiena i Sanitaria (Hygiene and Sanitation, Russian journal) 97(7), 664–670 (2018). (in Russian) https://doi.org/10.18821/0016-9900-2018-97-7-664-670

2. Briko, N., Mindlina, A., et al.: Assessment of attitudes towards immunization in different groups of population of the Russian Federation. Zh. Mikrobiol. Epidemiol. Immunobiol. **2**, 98–103 (2017). https://doi.org/10.36233/0372-9311-2017-2-98-103

3. Briko, N., Feldblyum, I.: The modern concept of development of vaccine prevention in Russia. Epidemiol. Vaccinal Prev. **18**(5), 4–13 (2019). https://doi.org/10.31631/2073-3046-2019-18-5-4-13. (in Russian)

4. De Groot, M.H.: Reaching a consensus. J. Am. Stat. Assoc. **69**(345), 118–121 (1974)

5. Gao S., Teng Z., Nieto J., Torres A.: Analysis of an SIR epidemic model with pulse vaccination and distributed time delay. Journal of Biomedicine and Biotechnology, vol. 2007, Article ID 64870, pp. 1–10. Hindawi Publishing Corporation (2007). https://doi.org/10.1155/2007/64870

6. Gubanov, D., Novikov, D., Chkhartishvili, A.: Social Networks: Models of Informational Influence. Control and Confrontation. Fizmatlit, Moscow (2010). (in Russian)

7. Gubar E., Kumacheva S., Zhitkova E., Tomilina G.: Modeling of the Impact of Information on Tax Audits on the Risk Statuses and Evasions of Individuals. Vestnik SPbGU, series 10, 15, 245–258 (2019). https://doi.org/10.21638/11702/spbu10.2019.208

8. Erdős, P., Rényi, A.: On the evolution of random graphs. Publ. Math. Inst. Hungarian Acad. Sci. **15**, 17–60 (1960)

9. Erofeeva, M., Stukova, M., Shakhlanskaya, E., et al.: Evaluation of the preventive effect of influenza vaccines during the epidemic season 2019–2020 in St. Petersburg. Epidemiol. Vaccinal Prev. **20**(5), 52–60 (2021). https://doi.org/10.31631/2073-3046-2021-20-5-52-60-52-60. (in Russian)

10. Kermack, W.O., McKendrick, A.G.: Contributions to the mathematical theory of epidemics. Proceedings of the Royal Society of London. Series A, Containing Papers of a Math. Phys. Character **115**(772), 700–721 (1927) https://doi.org/10.1098/rspa.1927.0118

11. Kolesin, I., Gubar, E., Zhitkova, E.: Management strategies in medical and social systems. SPbSU, St. Petersburg (in Russian) (2014)
12. Kreps, S.E., Kriner, D.L.: Factors influencing Covid-19 vaccine acceptance across subgroups in the United States: Evidence from a conjoint experiment. Vaccine **39**(24), 3250–3258 (2021). https://doi.org/10.1016/j.vaccine.2021.04.044
13. Matz A.: The modern origins of anti-vaccination insinuations and ideology. Epidemiol. Vaccinal Prev. **3**(70) (2013). (in Russian)
14. Mazalov V.V., Dorofeeva Y.A., Parilina E.M.: Opinion control in a team with complete and incomplete communication. Contributions to Game Theory and Management, vol. XIII, pp. 324–334. St. Petersburg State University, St. Petersburg (2020). https://doi.org/10.21638/11701/spbu31.2020.17
15. Nekovee A., Moreno, Y., Bianconi, G., Marsili, M.: Theory of rumor spreading in complex social networks Phys. A **374**, 457–470 (2007)
16. Niazashvili, A.: Individual differences in risk propensity in different social situations of personal development. Moscow University for the Humanities, Moscow (2007)
17. Raigorodsky, A.M.: Models of Random Graphs. ICNMO Publishers, Moscow (2011). (in Russian)
18. Rosenthal, S., Cummings, C.L.: Influence of rapid COVID-19 vaccine development on vaccine hesitancy. Vaccine **39**(52), 7625–7632 (2021). https://doi.org/10.1016/j.vaccine.2021.11.014
19. Sandmann, F.G., van Leeuwen, E., Bernard-Stoecklin, S., et al.: Health and economic impact of seasonal influenza mass vaccination strategies in European settings: a mathematical modelling and cost-effectiveness analysis. Vaccine **40**, 1306–1315 (2022). https://doi.org/10.1016/j.vaccine.2022.01.015
20. Saperkin, N., Kukunova, V.: Vaccination issues and Internet space. Medical Almanah **2**(26), 75–78 (2013). (in Russian)
21. Wolff, G.G.: Influenza vaccination and respiratory virus interference among Department of Defense personnel during the 2017–2018 influenza season. Vaccine **38**(2), 350–354 (2020). https://doi.org/10.1016/j.vaccine.2019.10.005Vaccine
22. Zhumartova, B.O., Ysmagul, R.S.: Application of the SIR model in epidemic modeling. Int. J. Hum. Natural Sci. **12**–**2**(63), 6–9 (2021). https://doi.org/10.24412/2500-1000-2021-12-2-6-9. (in Russian)
23. The Web-site of the Cambridge Dictionary. https://dictionary.cambridge.org/
24. The web-site of the Russian Federation State Statistics Service. http://www.gks.ru
25. The web-site of the World Health Organization. https://www.who.int

Free-Rider Problem: Simulating of System Convergence to Stable Equilibrium State by Means of Finite Markov Chain Models

Olga Pyrkina[1]([✉]) and Andrey Yudanov[2]

[1] Department of Mathematics, Financial University under the Government of Russian Federation, Moscow, Russia
OPyrkina@fa.ru
[2] Department of Economic Theory, Financial University under the Government of Russian Federation, Moscow, Russia

Abstract. The paper suggests a new approach to classic economic problem – "the problem of free-rider". This well – known problem deals with a process of unrequited consumption of collective goods, and it can be considered as a problem of unfailing interest for economy of each frame of a society. The authors put forward and idea of spontaneous process self-regulation by means of economic instruments and give a description of possible problem solution. The approach suggested includes the control of "free-rider" activity by economic and social agents directly interacting with him. In spite of non-rivalry in consumption, the case when "free-rider" disserves the interests of his nearest surrounding, will results in increasing antagonism and suppression of "free-rider" activity spreading. A mathematical model reflecting authors view is based on Markov chains with absorbing states, created on the base of graph depicting an interaction of "free-rider" with his neighborhood. The simulation represents system convergence from arbitrary initial state to a stable final distribution for Markov chain, demonstrating an opportunity of system self-adjustment.

Keywords: Free Rider problem · Public Good Consumption · Markov Chain with Absorbing State

1 Introduction

The present paper is concerned with study of classic economic "free-rider" problem, analyzing a chance of its solubility by means of economic instruments with the help of model based on finite Markov chain mathematical tools.

"Free-rider" activity is broadly defined in advanced economic theory as consumption of public goods without bearing the costs of its production in a share proportional to propensity to consume. Economic matter of the heart for this problem lies in nonrival and nonexcludable consumption of public goods, that necessitates an opportunity of its exploitation without relevant repayments. As consequence each society has skin in this game and tries to restrict such unpaid consumption.

© The Author(s), under exclusive license to Springer Nature Switzerland AG 2023
N. Agarwal et al. (Eds.): MSBC 2022, CCIS 1717, pp. 78–93, 2023.
https://doi.org/10.1007/978-3-031-33728-4_6

This problem is traditionally discussed in scientific literature as intractable challenge or as a problem feasible by means of government regulation only; but this government intervention can be realized most commonly with the aid of methods of non-economic character so it can't be efficient.

The paper deals with a process of self- regulating for public goods unpaid consumption due to application of economic leverages. The control of "free-rider" activity at the hands of economic and social agents directly interacting with him is demonstrated to become effective, because in this situation, in spite of non - rivalry in consumption, the "free-rider" activity will violate their immediate interests. These economic agents contradict "free-rider' behavior the more active the greater he hurts their interests. Such approach demonstrates the possibility in principle to solve the "free-rider" problem for an important particular case of disservice by "free-rider" action for proximate economic agents.

The mathematical model of a problem is based on Markov chain with absorbing state. The simulation demonstrates system convergence from arbitrary starting state to a stable final distribution of Markov chain, creating a possibility of effective system self – regulation and obtaining a stable solution through economic leverages.

2   Economic Kernel of "Free-Rider" Problem

2.1   Wide Occurrence of "Free-Rider" Problem and Attempts at Solution

A well-known in classic economic literature "free-rider" problem can be regarded to set of system failings of market economy. Difficulties of such kind appear in a range of scopes of activity and parts of the economy and are widely described in literature. So, a "problem of shirking" noted in corporate management theory can be reduced to "free-rider" problem. In a public choice theory one and the same problem is referred to as "group action problem". If we turn to problems of management of natural resources and ecology, we will be faced with problem of "tragedy of commons" [1]. Especially often in recent years, the free rider problem has been addressed as part of the fashionable search for a carbon footprint in the economy. As one paper emphatically states, "In the context of climate mitigation—at its core a global public good—we are all victims of an unchecked free rider problem" [2]. Moreover, the failure of the most ambitious international climate agreements from the high Nobel rostrum was associated precisely with the free rider problem: «Why have landmark agreements such as the Kyoto Protocol and the Paris Accord failed to make a dent on emissions trends? The reason is free riding» [3].

Moreover, a "free-rider" problem touches on not only economy questions; as it was demonstrated in recent research, the similar problems also appear in a broader social sphere. Manifestations of this problem may be found in a number of areas such as politico-military strategy (a choice in favor of defensive warfare or aggression) [4], social revolution in the present-day Ibero America [5], cribbing during exams in institutes of higher education [6], realization of medical insurance reforms carried out by the President of the US Barack Obama [7], ecological activity of international institutions [8], free blood donation. A maximum discussion even unfolded on the subject of whether the stubborn unwillingness of the countless army of Wikipedia readers to do in its favor soliciting donations is a manifestation of "free-riding" [9, 10].

Even in a recent coronavirus pandemic one can see a manifestation of "free-riding", it is non-observance of general rules of safe social behavior by persons. While popular majority stay at home and use masks and gloves in public spaces, a risk of contamination is not so high for persons who don't want to restrict himself and fail to meet the general requirements of safe behavior (in doing so pose a danger for the wider public).

All the situations listed above are joined by the same "free-riding" mechanism: individuals stand to benefit from collective efforts without incurring proportional expenses [11]. Correspondingly we will consider as a "free-rider" a person who uses advantages of some object or situation, product or service without covering of expenses. It should be mentioned immediately that a great majority of cases listed above is badly amenable by legal regulations. A "free-rider" is not a criminal juridically, because access to amenities consumed is free (non-exclusivity in consumption). Besides, the problem can't be solved by administrative measures, fines and other penalties. The difficulties of regulation intensify self-seeking character of "free-rider" behavior: straining after his interests he violates the interests of his social surrounding with impunity! The classic "free-rider" question at issue is in public goods falsely getting, which is made from egoistical motives.

2.2 Boundaries of Non-rivalry in Consumption, or How a "Free-Rider" Violates the Interests of His Immediate Circle

The problem of "free-rider" in general seems as unsolvable one, as many other classic economic problems do. The weak conjunction of well-known property of market self-regulation ("invisible hand" of Adam Smith) with a nature of public goods results in a complete market failure in this sphere. Usually the phenomenon of "free-rider" is deduced from unrestricted character of access to public goods. If the city is illuminated at night, it is impossible to prohibit even deliberate tax dodger to see everything in night-time. However, the non-rivalry in consumption is also essential. Even a lot of tax dodgers walking at night will never interfere bona fide taxpayer who get outside simultaneously with them. Consequently, there is no reasons usually to countercheck "free-rider" activity for the most people.

But at the same time the character of damage from "free-rider" to its immediate circle is underexplored. The authors believe that this damage can be subdivided into two components: public and private. The public damage for society lies in impairment of interests for those who consume public goods, paying for this right by their dues. So, a tax-dodging of part of society results in insufficient funding of public goods production, for example, reduces the funding of state health care system. Similarly, entrepreneurs who don't want to spend money on environmental compliance in manufacturing, can also be considered as "free-rider". Their "free-rider" activity results, for example, in decreasing water quality, or in increasing a level of polluting emissions and so on. It is a common detriment!

However, there is not only the public damage, but as well a private damage for "free-rider" immediate circle. So, the people who live in surroundings of unsustainable enterprise suffer from river pollution considerably larger than the society as a whole!

We can consider as another example an illegal compensation of employees in a form of off-the-book wages. If any employer doesn't pay pension contributions from hidden wages, this behavior pattern naturally results in decrease of pension fund budget.

We should emphasize here that a public good "pension coverage" remains noncompetitive. The fact, that somebody pay less than required into pension capital fund, doesn't decrease personal pension of his/her entourage and so doesn't generate opposition from the majority of pensioners. But the detriment wreaked to employees of the firm with off-the-book wages grows in importance essentially! Such form of payment decreases the size of their future pensions, restricts their ability to draw upon a credit and so on. And it is easy to understand that employees will scarcely be agreeable to it if they have even one possibility of fighting back (we understand that in this situation a possibility of fighting back is restricted by rivalry in labor market, often people are push to the wall and are constrained to agree to every job).

Classification of possible situations appearing in "free-riding" is given at Table 1.

Table 1. Subjects of oppositions to "free-riding" at different levels of public and private detriment.

	High private detriment	Low private detriment
High public detriment	**A**. Olson's small groups /Immediate circle	**B**. State
Low public detriment	**C**. Immediate circle	**D**. Absent/State

The source: compiled by authors

The part of Table 1 corresponding to the situation when the private detriment from "free-rider" activity is not high, describes the situation with tolerant public perception. This position is stipulated by the fact that in non-competitive public good consumption nobody will afflict with "free-riding" activity. Even though the general detriment is high (sector B, for example, if the producing units of a transnational corporation, transferred abroad, are not environmentally acceptable), it weekly affects the interests of individuals inside the country. The authors believe that "free-riding" problem is considered as unsolvable one (if you don't take into account state interference) exactly in such situations with a low level of private detriment. When no one private individual is impinged upon "free-rider" activity, nobody will try to restrict him, and so "free-riding" will continue to thrive on if there are no any counterstand of opposition. Another way for society to solve the problem of free-riding is to vest a state with power to act against free-riding by heavy-handed methods with ineluctable low efficiency.

But in the situation with high level of private detriment we meet an opposite scheme of social behavior. As soon as private interests are prejudiced, the people leave their passive position and begin to push back against "free-rider". Moreover, these countermeasures become more and more strong as far as the detriment is increased.

2.3 The Main Principles of Model Construction

We consider the situation with low public and high private detriment, specifically sector C of Table 1, to construct the mathematical model of this problem and to obtain some quantitative estimates. This model is aimed at demonstration of possibility in principle to restrict "free-riding" in the situation which can be created synthetically in the presence of necessary institutional capabilities. We simulate for such restriction an increase of counterstanding of society under conditions of increased private harm resulting in reduction of time necessary to stop the process of "free - riding" or to decrease it to an acceptable level. The model is based on Markov chains with absorbing states, and we investigate an evolution of system states' distribution in time.

The simulation gives a possibility to estimate necessary number of time step for "free-rider" activity restriction due to counterstand of surroundings and also estimate the values of parameters which make "free-rider" activity unprofitable. An influence on these parameters (for example, by arrangement of institutional conditions) gives an opportunity to manage this process. It should be mentioned that virtually the same approach can be applied for all the manifestations of "free-riding": in analysis of ecological problems, appearing in manufacture process without due account of environmental requirements, and in many other similar situations which can be characterized by the high private detriment of "free-rider" immediate circle.

It is essential for model construction that in all the cases the systems under consideration possess so-called Markov property. This property can be defined from a formal point of view by the following: the conditional probability of system transition into some state at every time step depends only on current system state only and doesn't depend on the system prehistory (that means, on all the previous system states). The process possessing Markov property can be considered through the lens of economics as memoryless process without any type of previous information (path) dependence, the process without long-time memory.

To illustrate our approach to this problem analysis we have carried out a consideration on the base of two concrete shining examples of "free-riding": we develop Markov models for situations of counterfeiting and paying under-the-table wages. In both cases we deal with low public and high private harm. Issue of counterfeit banknotes and implementing them into money turnover disrupts the public good "stability of the state monetary system", but essentially greater damage is inflicted on individuals with these counterfeit banknotes in the wallets. Payment off-the-book wages decreases pension funding, but essentially more strongly endamages the individuals who receive such salaries, depressing their opportunities.

We choose for these models the names "the problem of counterfeiter" and "the problem of off-the-book wages", in both cases we consider the model of process possessing Markov property. Really, it is difficult to reconstruct a prehistory of paper circulation for the banknote in a wallet. Similarly, when a person wants to obtain a credit, only the current value of officially shown salary is important, not the previous one. This Markov property gives an opportunity to construct the model for the process on the base of stationary Markov processes techniques [12].

It should be mentioned that previously a quantitative simulation in investigations of "free-rider" problem was carried out with the help of game theory tools, for example, as it was done in [13]. The problem was considered from the point of view of interacting gamers – participants of public goods creating process, the possibilities of their transforming into "free-riders" were discussed as well as the possibilities to create coalitions with some or other functions and so on. Dynamic models of "free-riding" [14] were discussed from the point of view of infinitely long living economic agents, bringing into action the choice between private consumption and long-term non-refundable investment into material benefits of public usage (bridges, roads and so on). But the method suggested in this paper provides for solution of a problem from outside, by efforts not of public goods makers and not by the choice of behavior strategy but by efforts of "free-rider" immediate circle.

3   Numerical Aspect: Markov Models of a Process

3.1   The Problem of Counterfeiter

If we want to create a Markov model for counterfeiter banknote circulation it is necessary to formalize the problem. We suggest for such formalization that this false banknote was successfully introduced into money turnover by swindlers, and now let's consider what happens with this counterfeit note in further circulation. We give prominence to four possible locations for this banknote ("repositories" of banknote in cash of four conditional types), between which in general case it circulates. These "repositories" form a set of monetary circulation system conditional states (below – system) $S = \{1, 2, 3, 4\}$; they are classified by difference in technological infrastructure levels for input control of banknote authenticity. According to these system states the graph of counterfeit banknote circulation was constructed; it is presented at Fig. 1 (More detailed description of this model is given by authors in [15], in Russian). The state "Junk" is considered as absorbing one.

The transition probabilities p_{ij} for Markov chain are given at the corresponding graph links. Really, they are the probabilities of banknote transitions from one "repository" to another, that means, the probabilities of system transition from the state with number i to another state with number j, and these probabilities do not depend on the way by which the banknote appears in "repository". The system Markov property is manifested in this fact!

We suggest in our model that false banknotes are introduced into turnover at the least level of technological infrastructure, that means at entrance into a "wallet", where it is difficult to identify banknote authenticity. In further banknote turnover that means in money movement from individuals' "Wallet" to "Cash register" or to "Bank" the probabilities of counterfeit banknote not to be detected are d or D (these ones are probabilities to take counterfeit banknote as authentic one). So, the products $p_{ij}d$ and $p_{ij}D$ are the probabilities of false banknote entering into "cash register" or "bank" under failure of input control. And if the false banknote is detected in the entrance it is annihilated, that means the system transit into absorbing state "Junk". An influence of counterfeit banknote concentration q on probabilities of false note "non-detecting" is described as exponential decay by formulae $d = e^{-\gamma q}$ and $D = e^{-\Gamma q}$ (where γ and Γ are some positive coefficients). We base our consideration on the real suggestion that efforts and successes of cash turnover participants increase as fast as the concentration of counterfeit banknotes increases. And it is quite natural, the greater the number of false notes, which are included in circulation, the greater the danger to suffer heavy losses, when anybody takes these false notes as authentic ones. So, the greater the value q, the less the probabilities are d or D of counterfeit banknote not to be detected.

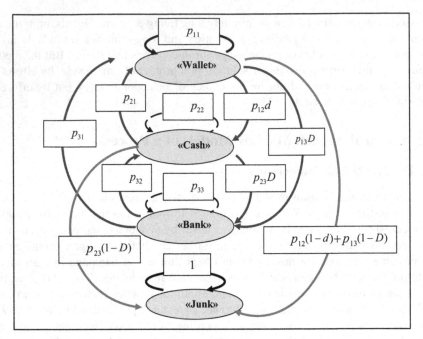

Fig. 1. The graph of possible movements of counterfeit banknote.

The matrix of transition probabilities for the single time step for the system of cash money turnover given that counterfeit banknote (false banknote, so we use the notation $F(1)$ for this matrix) is included into circulation looks like

$$F(1) = \begin{pmatrix} p_{11} & p_{12}\,d & p_{13}\,D & | & p_{12}(1-d) + p_{13}(1-D) \\ p_{21} & p_{22} & p_{23}\,D & | & p_{23}(1-D) \\ p_{31} & p_{32} & p_{33} & | & 0 \\ \overline{0} & \overline{0} & \overline{0} & | & \overline{1} \end{pmatrix} \qquad (1)$$

Let's mention that the state 4 "junk" is an absorbing state of Markov chain; we do not consider an occurrence of legal implications and suggest than counterfeit note is utilized when detected and further does not take part into money turnover.

Now let's create a fundamental matrix N for our Markov chain; the elements of this matrix are unequivocally determined by transition probabilities. For this purpose, we decompound initial matrix $F(1)$ of transition probabilities into 4 blocks (this decomposition is presented by dashed lines into formula (1)):

$$F(1) = \begin{pmatrix} Q & R \\ O & I \end{pmatrix} \qquad (2)$$

Here Q is 3×3 matrix, which elements determine transitions from nonabsorbing states into another nonabsorbing ones. Further, R is 3×1 matrix, which elements describes transitions from nonabsorbing states into absorbing ones. O is 1×3 matrix, consisting of zero elements (its elements are probabilities of "output" from absorbing state). And finally, $I = (1)$ is unit 1×1 matrix describing sojourn time in absorbing state. An inverse matrix $N = (I - Q)^{-1}$ [12] exists for such initial matrix, and this particular matrix is a fundamental matrix for Markov chain with absorbing states. A row sum $\sum_{j=1}^{3} n_{ij}$ of this matrix gives an average time to reach the absorbing state, provided that at the initial moment the chain was in the state i. But in the absence of real statistical information it is not relevant to analyze it.

We also suggest, as it was mentioned above, that initial implementation of counterfeit banknotes into money turnover is carried out in operations of "wallet" - "wallet" type, for example, in cash payments in the marketplace; "cash register" or "bank" are not so attractive for swindlers due to its' better technological infrastructure. The initial state distribution for the system is chosen in such a way that all the false banknotes are concentrate in "wallets", that means in the state 1. Such distribution will take a form of vector $\vec{x}(0) = \{1, 0, 0, 0\}$. Furter we are interested in an evolution of random vector $\vec{x}(t) = \{ x_1(t), x_2(t), x_3(t), x_4(t) \}$ in time. Here each of the probabilities $x_i(t)$ is probability $P\{ X(t) = i \mid \vec{x}(0) \}$ of the event: a system is in the state i at time moment t, given that initially at moment $t = 0$ it have had a distribution $\vec{x} = \vec{x}(0)$. Dynamics of such vector is described by equation [12]

$$\vec{x}(t + \Delta t) = \vec{x}(t) \, P(\Delta t) \tag{3}$$

Getting the final distribution of the form $\vec{x}(t*) = \{0, 0, 0, 1\}$ will mean that all the counterfeit banknotes are detected, eliminated, and successfully utilized. This evolution can be also described by standard equation for Markov chains[1] for n time steps [12]:

$$\vec{x}(n) = \vec{x}(0) \, P^n \tag{4}$$

A simulation of false banknotes transition was carried out for different values of decay parameters γ and Γ as well as for various matrices of transition probabilities $P = F(1)$. We believe that that absorbing state of a system is achieved when the initial distribution $\vec{x}(0) = \{1, 0, 0, 0\}$ is transformed into a final one of a form $X = \{\leq 0.01, \leq 0.01, \leq 0.01, \geq 0.99\}$, that means that is more than 99% of counterfeit banknotes is detected and utilized. This state is considered as a final one, corresponding to the case when "free-riding" is decreased to an acceptable level. When we achieve this distribution, we stop the process and take an average value of time steps n for 50 such cycles as a typical one for a concrete value of q used in this cycle of simulation. So an algorithm of simulation is rather simple: me multiply the initial distribution by the transition probabilities matrix until we obtain a final acceptable distribution $X = \{\leq 0.01, \leq 0.01, \leq 0.01, \geq 0.99\}$.

The data of Table 2 illustrate the results of simulation for values $\gamma = 1$, $\Gamma = 2$ and one among many of the transition probabilities matrixes used in our simulation, which reflect the subjective view of authors on the structure of money circulation.

---

[1] We write this equation in its traditional form, taking a notation P for transition probability matrix, but we have in mind that really it is matrix $F(1)$ of transition probabilities for the counterfeit banknote.

Table 2. Dependence of a number n of time steps before the system achieves an absorbing state on the concentration q of counterfeit banknotes in circulation.

q	0.02	0.05	0.1	0.2	0.3
n	> 300	143	83	40	29

The results obtained demonstrate that the system transfers to final distribution state $\vec{x}(t*) = \{0, 0, 0, 1\}$ during more and more decreasing amount of time steps with increase of concentration q of counterfeit banknote in circulation. It is an indicator of presence of negative feedback in the system and confirms a possibility of system regulation by constructing corresponding institutional conditions (in particular, the case of false banknotes withdrawing from bona fide banknote holder, even without legal consequences). The more "constipated" by counterfeit banknote is currency in circulation, the more quickly the process of "cleaning" is realized. As a result, this "free-rider" activity is restricted due to market surroundings efforts but not due to the government actions and is constantly kept in subdued state.

In other words, a social self-adjustment, if not eliminates counterfeiting completely, maintains this negative phenomenon at a low level, acceptable to society. Really, according to estimates, made by Arkady V. Trachuk, General Director of Goznak (leading Russian banknotes, passports and other security papers producer), there are less than 7 counterfeit banknotes per million in Russia now. It is a very good level, approximately two times less than in the Euro region[2].

3.2   The Problem of Off-the-Book Wages

The similar model on the base of Markov chain with absorbing states was developed for yet one analysis of "free-riding" trait – avoiding taxes by means of envelope wages payment for employee of non-governmental enterprise.

In this situation we distinguish 5 levels – categories of employee, these categories differ from each other in possibility to obtain access to material benefits, such as obtaining credits, tourist trips in which it is necessary to obtain a visa to remain in the country, a perspective of affluent old age with sufficient pension and so on. Correspondingly the set of employment system states $S = \{1, 2, 3, 4, 5\}$ is determined.

The graph of possible system states and transitions between these states is given at Fig. 2.

The main reason for negative response of active employee to employer performance (this employer tries to avoid taxes by means of envelope wages payment) is considered by authors as concrete private harm bringing about a decreasing level of current consumption possibilities for such professional employee. Specifically, on the base of Russian practice we believe, that employee confront this "free-rider" entrepreneur not only thinking about their future pensions but passing constant crack-down on current consumer status. An obtaining of such off-the-book wages gives no chance to buy houseroom mortgaged, to

---

[2] Rossiyskaya Gazeta, 05.07.2022, https://rg.ru/2022/07/05/v-goznake-nazvali-naibolee-chasto-poddelyvaemye-kupiury.html, last accessed 2023/01/10.

buy a car on credit, to pretend to big sum of consumer loan, to obtain a touristic visa in foreign embassy, to get consent to adoption of child and so on. To short the notation, we denote the state in which an access to all these benefits is open as "Credit accessibility".

The matrix of transition probabilities for the graph, presented at Fig. 2, is denoted $P(1)$, and it corresponds to the system with 2 absorbing states, these are the state 4 "Pension" and the state 5 «Accessibility of credits».

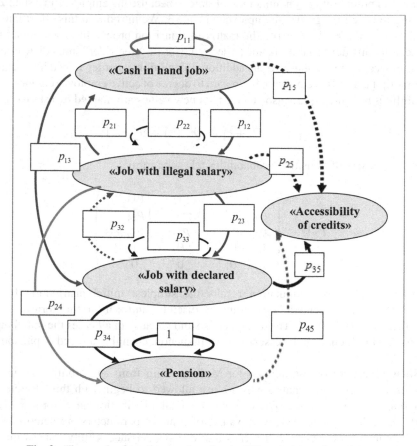

Fig. 2. The graph of employee relocation to different states of employment

In our model under consideration the most interesting is a probability p_{23} of transition from state 2 «Job with off-the book wages» to state 3 «Job with declared salary» (for details look at [16]). This value of this probability should be increased when the pressure of employee on entrepreneur grows; we take this effect into account it in the model in a form

$$p_{23} = c\left(1 - e^{-\alpha L}\right) \tag{5}$$

Here α is some positive coefficient and L is a factor describing the level of concealment for wages ("under the table" part of salary), the expression for L is

$$L = \frac{market\ declared\ salary\ for\ position}{"declared"\ part\ of\ "off-the-book"\ salary} \qquad (6)$$

It is quite evident that the growth of transition probability p_{23} in our model results in reduction of probability p_{22} maintaining of state 2, because the employee in a state 2 are warming to bench for grows of employee in state 3. We introduced this effect into our model as $p_{22} = c\,e^{-\alpha L}$. To write the matrix of transition probabilities we should take into account this depreciating factor (a decay factor of "free-rider" immediate circle – the employee activity) and also an additional condition in order to retain stochastic property (as far as this decay factor has regard to degree of active employee countercheck, probabilities p_{21} and p_{24} are also changed, its new values are marked by asterisk $*$)

$$p_{21}^* + ce^{-\alpha L} + c\left(1 - e^{-\alpha L}\right) + p_{24}^* = 1 \qquad (7)$$

So, the matrix of transition probabilities takes the form

$$P(1) = \begin{pmatrix} p_{11} & p_{12} & p_{13} & p_{14} & 0 \\ p_{21}^* & ce^{-\alpha L} & c\left(1 - e^{-\alpha L}\right) & p_{24}^* & 0 \\ p_{31} & p_{32} & p_{33} & p_{34} & p_{35} \\ 0 & 0 & 0 & 1 & 0 \\ 0 & 0 & 0 & 0 & 1 \end{pmatrix} \qquad (8)$$

For illustration of our simulation results the simplest initial distribution for the system states is presented here, being a discrete uniform in the form $\vec{x}(0) = \{0.2,\ 0.2,\ 0.2,\ 0.2,\ 0.2\}^3$. This approach is valid because in all cases the initial distributions can't influence on the essence of phenomenon, changing a speed of phenomena only.

So we can start our simulation for Markov chain from any arbitrary initial distribution in general, and that is why we are allowed to begin with this discrete uniform one, presented above. Discovering the final distribution in a form $\vec{x}(t*) = \{0,\ 0,\ 0,\ a,\ b\}$, $a + b = 1$, were values of a and b parameters are determined by the age structure of society will means that our system successfully transits into the final state, where all the employee receive either "Officially shown salary" or "Pension". Conditionally all employee in this system state have access to material benefit (that means that transition into legal employment or pension is followed by the state "Credit accessibility").

---

[3] We have also considered the initial distribution in another forms, like $\vec{x}(0) = \{0.4,\ 0.4,\ 0.2,\ 0,\ 0\}$, which approximately corresponds the situation in Russia at the turn of the century; at this time official salaries were paid to employees of state and employees of foreign firms only, pensions were negligibly small and so couldn't motivate anybody, and lending to individuals was absent (there is no any exact statistical data about this distribution, there are only estimates obtained by research structures of commercial firms).

Such structure of society, consisting of well-heeled middle class, which bona fide pays taxes and has access to material benefits, and well-heeled pensioners, received in our model the name "ideal society".

A numerical simulation based on insights given above was carried out for various values of c and L parameters and for different matrixes of Markov chain transition probabilities $P(1)$. Table 3 presents as an example for illustration the results of such simulation for value $c = 0.5$ and one of transition probability matrix. We have used for simulation an Eq. (4) described above. It was taken that the system transits into the final state if the initial uniform distribution $X = \{0.2, \ 0.2, \ 0.2, \ 0.2, \ 0.2\}$ is transformed into the distribution of form $X = \{\leq 0.01, \ \leq 0.01, \ \leq 0.01, \ \geq a, \ \geq b\}$, $a+b = 0, 99$, that means that system achieves a state in which more than 99% of people are in categories, determining the state "ideal society". So, like above in the "problem of counterfeiter", an algorithm of simulation is rather simple: me multiply the initial distribution by the transition probabilities matrix until we obtain a final acceptable distribution.

Table 3. Dependence of a number n of time steps before the system achieves an absorbing state on the value of governing parameter L.

L	2	5	10	20	30
n	> 300	120	72	17	6

The results of simulation show demonstratively that when the proportion of wages concealment (a gap between the completely declared salary and officially paid declared part of illegal off-the-book salary) is increased, the system transits to the state "ideal society" during ever-more dwindling number of time steps. This effect opens the opportunity to restrict the activity of "free-rider", preferring not to spend money on taxes and paying off-the-book wages, and to control the system due to self-regulating mechanism with the help of economic leverages. This also allows to create a system self-regularity provided corresponding institutional conditions. These conditions should give the access to significant welfare to employee with high declared salary only.

Actually, the "ideal" state of society for contemporary Russia is almost achieved for only small social stratum, which is very attractive for employer. This is a group of young (30–40 years old) specialists with extraordinary level of professional qualifications, determining their great competitive advantages at labor market. Due to the high social demands of this group (the requirement of houseroom, car and so on) in Russia it is unprofitable for employer to be a "free-rider" toward such employee. When choosing working conditions, these people have an opportunity to insist on increase of off-the-book salary to such a level that will compensate them all the restrictions caused by its illegal status.

Nevertheless, evidence of "free-riding" depreciation effect, caused by influence of immediate circle of "free-rider", can be manifested in some statistical data. We could consider for illustration an increase of proportion of total mortgage volume in GDP of Russian Federation [22], which is presented at the diagram Fig. 3A. It demonstrates constantly growing requirements in credit on property among the public. And the authors believe, that one of the results of this growth is an increasing number of self-employed citizens, who decided to "step out of the shade" and go legit, so decided to pay all the taxes and obtain all the advantages of "officially declared salary", as soon as such opportunity was opened in beginning of 2020. The diagram of number of self-employed citizens who have fixed their status and apply the special tax regime "Tax on professional income" [23], depending on time, is given at Fig. 3B. The second graph (B) corresponds to the last short time interval of the first one (A), but the corresponding Federal law №422-FZ from 27.11.2018 was put in practice as an experiment in the beginning of 2020 only [24]. And it immediately stimulated decreasing of "free-riding".

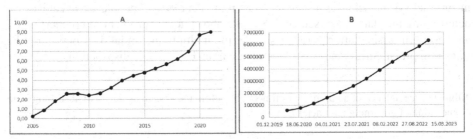

Fig. 3. A) Proportion of total mortgage volume in GDP of Russia and B) Number of self-employed citizens who have fixed their status. Source: compiled by the authors on the base of official data [22, 23]

Naturally, the parameter L in our model reflects the entire set of motives forcing employee to oppose off-the book payment schemes and is not limited to their desire to get a mortgage loan. The identification of other motives is a separate, very complex problem, and difficult, both in terms of theory and in the sense of the possibility of their approximation by statistically measurable indicators. In this article, we did not set ourselves such an ambitious task.

Let's mention as well that in two examples of "free-rider' problems considered above, the general scheme of simulation is of the same kind, although from formal point of view ergodic set of Markov chain consists of various numbers of absorbing states.

4   Conclusion and Discussion

The Markov model, presented in this paper, was developed for illustration of the effect of "free-riding" suppression only. Such opportunity of suppression can appear when "free-rider" activity violates the interests of its' nearest circle. The factor of natural increase of negative reaction of "free-rider" immediate surrounding was introduced in the model as exponential decay of corresponding probabilities in transition matrix of Markov chain. The model is not based on concrete statistical data now, so it can not be used for any kinds of prediction, nevertheless it shows demonstratively that the effect of such required type may exist. Now the problem is in creating of institutional conditions for "switching-on" this effect, as it was done as an experiment by Federal law №422-FZ [24], and this experiment demonstrates good results.

An investigation of "free-rider" immediate circle as a main factor, suppressing this negative phenomenon, now only scratch the surface [16]. It will be very interesting and significant to supplement model information, suggested in this paper, by concrete real statistic data. It would give the possibility to obtain essentially more exact estimation of a lot of process characteristics and stages; in particular, it would be very useful to estimate an average time of system standing in one or another state by means of calculation of inverse matrix for transition probabilities matrix of Markov chain.

It is worth pointing out that results and conclusions obtained by simulation and discussed in this paper, are confirm by empirical data, observed in artificial sociological modelling of "free-riding' situations [17]. It was shown in this investigation that manifestations of "free-riding" decrease with activation and coordination of action of the people directly interacting with "free-rider".

The authors also make good sense to frame differently a classic statement "cui prodest" and formulate the problem as "look for those for whom it is unprofitable". Authors believe that an approach suggested may be applied in any situation of 'free-riding" and may be thought-starter on the way of global problem solution of the hole set of situations.

Besides, the real experiments are more significant. In the current moment a high efficiency of activity for the nearest surrounding of "free-rider" becomes more and more clear for the society. One has only to think about massive protest against building activity for land fill in railway station Shies in the Arkhangelsk Region. Bringing such land fill into being (instead of expensive building and construction work of refuse disposal works) would inflict irreparable harm and damage on ecology and people health. It was successfully shut down by the actions of people striving to prevent ecological catastrophe at their small motherland.

Extremely interesting in terms of the approach outlined in this article are the latest attempts to solve the free rider problem at the international level, in particular, the latest projects to combat global warming. Since the pioneering paper by William Nordhaus [18], attention has focused on the idea of creating a so-called climate club. The essence of the proposal is that in order to stop global warming, it is necessary to move away from the practice of agreeing and voluntarily assuming obligations to reduce greenhouse gas emissions by as many countries as possible.

It is argued that the ambitious international agreements Kyoto Protocol and the Paris Accord failed precisely because they followed this logic. Instead, it is proposed to create a climate club from among the most interested countries and, through the efforts of its members, influence the rest. "The best hope for effective coordination is a Climate Club— a coalition of nations that commit to strong steps to reduce emissions and mechanisms to penalize countries that do not participate" [19]. For example, members of the club should introduce a special environmental tax on imports from non-aligned countries. It is easy to see that we are talking about the formation and institutionalization of the free rider's inner circle. It is it, and not the world community as a whole, that is called upon to punish "environmentally irresponsible countries" with import duties.

By now, the implementation of the climate club project has made significant theoretical progress. For example, there are dedicated studies on how to identify a free rider country, see [20]. But practical efforts to implement the project are especially important.

Extremely reminiscent of the climate club, the final text of the Carbon Border Adjustment Mechanism (CBAM) approved by the European Commission on July 14, 2021, which provides for the introduction of import duties on products of countries that do not comply with EU decarbonization rules by 2026 [21].

Whether it is really correct to equate countries that do not comply with EU environmental rules with free riders is very debatable. On the other hand, there is no doubt that the traditional way of solving the problem of a free rider (for example, with the help of the state or international agreements) in this case is replaced by the mechanism described in this article for using energy against a free rider (or against someone who is declared a free rider) a narrow group of the most interested actors.

References

1. Ostrom, E.: How types of goods and property rights jointly affect collective action. J. Theor. Polit. **15**(3), 239–270 (2003)
2. Roy, N.M.: Climate Change's Free Rider Problem: Why We Must Relinquish Freedom to Become Free, 45 Wm. & Mary Envtl. L. & Pol'y Rev. **45**(3), 821–857 (2021), https://scholarship.law.wm.edu/wmelpr/vol45/iss3/7. Accessed 23 Nov 2022
3. Nordhaus, W.D.: Climate change: The Ultimate Challenge for Economics, Nobel Prize Lecture, December 8 (2018). https://www.nobelprize.org/uploads/2018/10/nordhaus-lecture.pdf. Accessed 23 Nov 2022
4. Leeson, P.T., Coyne, C.J., Duncan, T.K.: A note on the market provision of national defense. J. Private Enterp. **29**(2), 51–55 (2014)
5. Weismuller, J.P.: Social movements and free riders: examining resource mobilization theory through the Bolivian Water War. The Macalester Revie **2**(2/4) (2012)
6. http://www.dailymail.co.uk/femail/article-3137339/Writing-answers-tampon-using-MORSE-CODE-bizarre-ingenious-ways-British-students-cheated-exams-revealed.html. Accessed 23 Nov 2022
7. Kahn, D. A., Kahn, J. H.: Free rider: a justification for mandatory medical insurance under health care reform? Michigan Law Review First Impressions **109**(78) (2011)
8. Manzano, G., Prado, S.A.: Liberalizing trade of environmental goods and services: how to address the free-rider problem. Philippine Inst. Dev. Stud. Policy Notes **11**, 1–8 (2015)
9. Hinnosaar, M, Hinnosaar, T, Kummer, M.E, Slivko, O.: Wikipedia matters. J. Econ. Manage. Strategy 1–13 (2021). https://doi.org/10.1111/jems.12421. Accessed 23 Nov 2022
10. Antin, J., Cheshire, C.: Readers are not free-riders: Reading as a form of participation on Wikipedia. In: Proceedings of the ACM Conf on Computer Supported Cooperative Work, Savannah, Georgia, USA, 127–130 (2010). https://doi.org/10.1145/1718918.1718942. Accessed 23 Nov 2022
11. Olson, F., Cook M. L.: The Complexities of Measuring Free Rider Behavior: Preliminary Musings. ISNIE 2006 (2006). Accessed 23 Nov 2022
12. Kemeny, J.G., Snell, L.J.: Finite Markov Chains. 3rd printing 1983 Edition. Springer-Verlag (1983)
13. Kishor, A. Niyogi, R.: A game-theoretic approach to solve the free-rider problem. In: Tenth International Conference on Contemporary Computing (IC3), Noida, pp. 1–6 (2017)
14. Battaglini, M., Nunnari, S., Palfrey, T.R.: Dynamic Free Riding with Irreversible Investments. Am. Econ. Rev. **104**(9), 2858–2871 (2014)
15. Pyrkina, O., Yudanov, A.: Local resistance to public goods unpaid appropriation (Markov chain approach to "counterfeiter problem"). In: Proceedings of XV International Conference on Mathematics. Computer. Education. Ed: Riznichenko G., Izhevsk: R&C dynamics **1**, 208–218 (In Russ)

16. Yudanov, A., Pyrkina, O., Bekker, E.: On the limits of unsolvability of the "free rider problem". Voprosy Ekonomiki. (11), 57–75 (2016). (in Russ.) https://doi.org/10.32609/0042-8736-2016-11-57-75, last accessed 2022/11/23
17. Ivanenkova, E.D., Ryzhkova, M.V.: Free rider effect and openness: the results of laboratory experiment (2012). http://www.science-education.ru/pdf/2012/5/7046.pdf. Accessed 23 Nov 2022
18. Nordhaus, W.D.: Climate clubs: overcoming free-riding in international climate policy. Am. Econ. Rev. **105**(4), 1339–1370 (2015). https://doi.org/10.1257/aer.150000011339,lastaccessed2022/11/23
19. Nordhaus, W.D.: The Climate Club. How to Fix a Failing Global Effort. Foreign affairs, May/June 2020, pp. 10–17 (2020)
20. Browne, J., Villarreal, D., Lackner, K., Brennan, S.: Incentivizing a carbon-free economy: a method to identify free-riders. Economicheskaya politika **15**(2), 68–85 (2020). https://doi.org/10.18288/1994-5124-2020-2-68-85. (In Russian). Accessed 23 Nov 2022
21. European Commission. Carbon Border Adjustment Mechanism: Questions and Answers. Brussels, 14 July 2021 (2021) https://ec.europa.eu/commission/presscorner/detail/en/qanda_21_3661. Accessed 23 Nov 2022
22. Market intelligence of the housing (mortgage housing credit) loan market in Russia. Statistical digest (Internet version). Moscow, Bank of Russia, 2014–2022, №№ 1–9 http://www.cbr.ru/statistics/bank_sector/bank_sector_review/. Accessed 13 Jan 2023
23. Federal Tax Service. Unified register of small and medium-sized entrepreneur-ships. https://rmsp.nalog.ru/statis-tics2.html?ysclid=lcizj3bi98983087728. Accessed 13 Jan 2023
24. FEDERAL LAW On conducting an experiment to establish a special tax regime Tax on professional income. http://pravo.gov.ru/proxy/ips/?docbody=&nd=102488108. Accessed 13 Jan 2023

Modeling of Sustainability

Econometric Modeling of Adaptation of the Russian Economy to Western Countries' Sanctions

Viktor Byvshev[✉] [ID]

Financial University under the Government of the Russian Federation, GSP-3, Leningradsky Ave., 49, 125993 Moscow, Russia
VByvshev@mail.ru

Abstract. The econometric modeling of the adaptation of the Russian economy to the sanctions of Western countries is being discussed. The exponential adaptation model adopted in this article is an integral part of the production function of the Russian economy constructed here. At the last stage of the production function construction scheme (the post-factum forecasting stage), the production function of the Russian economy with the adaptation model used in it showed high accuracy of forecasting real GDP. This circumstance made it possible to interpret the model of adaptation of the Russian economy to the sanctions of Western countries as adequate. The impact of Western sanctions on the Russian economy is decreasing by about 25% every year.

Keywords: the model of adaptation of the Russian economy to the sanctions of Western countries · the production function of the national economy · the Cobb-Douglas function

1 Introduction

The construction of the production function of the national economy has been discussed by many authors [1-9 et al.], and, as a rule, in the process of constructing the production function, a simple, flexible, easy-to-evaluate and interpret Cobb-Douglas function was used [10]. The construction of the production function of the national economy is invariably carried out according to the observed levels of time series, such as the gross domestic product (GDP) Y_t, fixed capital K_t, number of people L_t employed in the economy *and* hydrocarbon prices p_t [3, etc.]. Time series (Y_t, K_t, L_t, p_t) are nonstationary, and this circumstance gives rise to a serious statistical problem of spurious regression when estimating the parameters of the production function [11]. Indeed, in the case of spurious regression, the least square adjustment method of the parametric production function are untenable, and the statistical tests, used to validate its parameters, are incorrect [12]. This circumstance must be considered when constructing the production function of the national economy.

In this paper the procedure for constructing the production function of the Russian economy begins with a study of the cointagration of time series (Y_t, K_t, L_t, p_t) and

© The Author(s), under exclusive license to Springer Nature Switzerland AG 2023
N. Agarwal et al. (Eds.): MSBC 2022, CCIS 1717, pp. 97–114, 2023.
https://doi.org/10.1007/978-3-031-33728-4_7

including in the specifications of the production function a model of adaptation of the national economy to Western sanctions (the first stage of construction), and ends with post - factum forecasting with the calculation of relative errors in GDP forecasts (the second stage of construction). The statistical information necessary for constructing the production function is borrowed from a recently published article [3]. The Cobb-Douglas function is used as an analytical basis [13], which is invariably used by researchers in modeling macroeconomics objects [14–18].

2   Designations, Prerequisites, and Statistical Information

The symbol Y_t is traditionally used to denote the real GDP, produced in the Russian economy in year t using the level of factors of production $(x_{1t}, x_{2t}, ..., x_{kt})$. The main factors of production are fixed capital K_t, number of people employed in the economy L_t and human capital H_t. ... Note that the mathematical model (1), which explains Y_t by the variables $(x_{1t}, x_{2t}, ..., x_{kt})$ is called the production function of the national economy:

$$Y_t = F(x_{1t}, x_{2t}, ..., x_{kt}). \tag{1}$$

Human capital H_t affects the level of output Y_t in the labor process. In the fundamental work [19], the influence of the variables H_t and L_t on the output level is modeled as $E_t \cdot L_t$. Here E_t is the exogenously (outside the model) specified level of efficiency of live labor. The growth of the variable E_t with the passage of time means exogenous labor-saving scientific and technological progress, or STP in short. It is convenient to model the dynamics of live labor efficiency as an exponential function of time [19]:

$$E_t = E_{t-1} \cdot (1 + g) = E_0 \cdot e^{\gamma \cdot (t - t_0)}. \tag{2}$$

Here, the symbol g indicates the growth rate (in fractions) of the variable E_t per time cycle (usually per year).

Remark 1. In addition to labor-saving STP, economic theory considers capital-saving STP and neutral STP (STP according to Hicks). In the case of a capital-saving STP, its effect on the output level Y_t is modeled as $E_t \cdot K_t$. Here E_t is an exogenously (outside the model) specified level of efficiency of fixed capital. It is also customary to model the growth of the variable E_t with the passage of time as an exponential function of time (2). Finally, in the situation of a neutral STP, the production function of the national economy is given by the equation.

$$Y_t = E_0 \cdot e^{\gamma \cdot (t - t_0)} \cdot F(x_{1t}, x_{2t}, ..., x_{kt}).$$

We emphasize that in the case of the Cobb-Douglas production function, all three approaches are equivalent. Let us add that the exogenous influence of scientific and technological progress on the level of GDP can be equivalently modeled using the index of scientific and technological progress $STP_t = e^{\gamma \cdot t}$ including this variable in Eq. (1) in the set of factors of production that explain Y_t which is done by many researchers [7, 8, etc.].

The level of GDP in modern Russia is significantly influenced by the price of hydrocarbons (and specifically, the price of oil p_t). For this reason, researchers of the production function of Russia reasonably interpret the price of oil as one of the significant factors of production and include the variable p_t in the equation of the production function of the Russian economy [3–7 et al.].

To summarize, let us write Eq. (1) of the production function of Russia first in the general form $Y_t = F(K_t, L_t, STP_t, p_t)$ and then take as a function F the convenient Cobb-Douglas multiplicative function:

$$Y_t = A \cdot e^{\gamma \cdot (t - t_0)} \cdot K_t^{\alpha} \cdot L_t^{\beta} \cdot p_t^{\delta}. \tag{3}$$

Postulating the invariance in time of the coefficients $(A, \alpha, \beta, \gamma, \delta)$ of the function (3), we note their meaning. The constant A is called the coefficient of joint productivity of factors of production, and its value depends on the selected units of measurement of the arguments of function (3). The constants (α, β, δ) are the values of the elasticity of the variable Y_t over, respectively, the variables (K_t, L_t, p_t), so δ is the relative change in Y_t (in %) in response to a relative 1% increase in p_t The coefficient γ has a completely different meaning - it is the relative change in Y_t (in fractions!) for each unit of time (for example, for a year), so γ is the contribution to the rate of gain Y_t of scientific and technological progress. Later (see (11)), specification (3) will be expanded with an indicator of Russia's default in 1998, the global financial crisis in 2009, and Western sanctions, with a model for adapting the Russian economy to them.

After taking the logarithm of Eq. (3) and adding an unobservable random perturbation ξ_t, a statistical model of the production function of Russia appears:

$$lnY_t = lnA + \gamma \cdot (t - t_0) + \alpha \cdot lnK_t + \beta \cdot lnL_t + \delta \cdot lnp_t + \xi_t. \tag{4}$$

The quality of the estimates $\left(\tilde{A}, \tilde{\alpha}, \tilde{\beta}, \tilde{\gamma}, \tilde{\delta} \right)$ of the parameters $(A, \alpha, \beta, \gamma, \delta)$ of the statistical model (4) depends crucially on the properties of the time series $(lnY_t, lnK_t, LnL_t, lnp_t)$ from which these estimates will be calculated. If these time series are stationary (belong to class $I(0)$), then the estimates will be consistent [13]. If these series are non-stationary (specifically, they belong to class $I(1)$), then two situations are possible. In the first situation, the time series $\left(lnY_t, lnK_t, lnL_t, lnp_t \right)$ are completely integrated (they have a general stochastic trend [14]), and then the estimates $\left(\tilde{A}, \tilde{\alpha}, \tilde{\beta}, \tilde{\gamma}, \tilde{\delta} \right)$ will be superconstant. The super constancy of estimates manifests itself in the rapid stabilization of their values as the sample size from which they are calculated increases. In addition, cointegration of time series will smooth out the impact of model specification errors in its trend-stationary part [11]. Thus, cointegration will not smooth out the influence of the possibly incorrect hypothesis H_0 (see (5)) about the constancy of the return of the production function (3) on the scale of production in the non-stationary part of the specification

$$H_0 : \alpha, \beta \in (0, 1); \alpha + \beta = 1, \tag{5}$$

but it will smooth out the impact of the possibly incorrect hypothesis H_0 (see (6)) about the absence of STP in the national economy

$$H_0 : \gamma = 0. \tag{6}$$

In the second situation the series (Y_t, Kt_t, Lt_t, p_t) are not cointegrated, and then the estimates $\left(\tilde{A}, \tilde{\alpha}, \tilde{\beta}, \tilde{\gamma}, \tilde{\delta} \right)$ calculated by the least squares method using the statistical model (4) will be invalid, and all standard tests in the estimated statistical model (4) will be incorrect [12].

Remark 2. In the situation of non-cointegrated time series $(lnY_t, lnK_t, lnL_t, lnp_t)$, after taking the logarithm of the Eq. (3), taking the full differential and adding an unobservable random disturbance ζt, we have to turn to the statistical model (7) with stationary series of relative changes $(\frac{\Delta Y_t}{Y_{t-1}}, \frac{\Delta K_t}{Y_{t-1}}, \frac{\Delta L_t}{L_{t-1}}, \frac{\Delta p_t}{p_{t-1}})$ of the variables of the production function (3):

$$\frac{\Delta Y_t}{Y_{t-1}} = \gamma + \alpha \cdot \frac{\Delta K_t}{Y_{t-1}} + \beta \cdot \frac{\Delta L_t}{L_{t-1}} + \delta \cdot \frac{\Delta p_t}{p_{t-1}} + \zeta_t. \tag{7}$$

Estimating the model (7) will lead to consistent estimates of parameters only in the situation of non - cointegrated non-stationary time series $\left(lnY_t, lnK_t, lnL_t, lnp_t \right)$; if these series are cointegrated, then the estimates of the model parameters (7) will be untenable, and the tests in the estimated model (7) will be incorrect [20]. Note that in this work the model (7) does not need to be evaluated as below will be shown that the time series $\left(lnY_t, lnK_t, lnL_t, lnp_t \right)$ cointegration.

It turns out that testing the hypothesis of cointegrated time series $\left(lnY_t, lnK_t, LnL_t, lnp_t \right)$ is an obligatory part of constructing the production function of the national economy!

The construction of the production function of the Russian economy will be carried out using statistical information in the form of time series (Y_t, K_t, L_t, p_t), borrowed from the work [3] and placed below in the Table 1. Levels Y_t of the real GDP (billion rubles) and fixed capital K_t(billion rubles) are expressed in 1990 prices, oil price levels p_t (dollars per barrel) are expressed in 2010 prices, and the number of people employed in the economy L_t is calculated in millions.

Remark 3. It can be shown that the oil price levels expressed in 1990 prices will differ from the levels p_t accepted in this paper only by a constant multiplier. The expression of p_t levels in 1990 prices will only lead to a change in the free term A in the equation of the production function (3), depending (as noted above) from the accepted units of measurement. The remaining coefficients in Eq. (3) will not change.

Table 1. Levels of time series used to construct the production function of the Russian economy [3]

Year	Y (billion rubles)	K (million rubles)	Z (%)	K (actual) (billion rubles)	L (million rubles)	P (USD/bar)
1990	644	1871649	100	1871,65	75,325	28.65
1991	612	1957288	100	1957,29	73,848	24,5
1992	523	2009054	73	1466,61	72,071	23.14
1993	478	2030396	74	1502,49	70,852	19.72
1994	417	2014984	61	1229,14	68,484	18.91
1995	400	1995229	60	1197,14	66,441	18.57
1996	386	1983823	54	1071,26	65,95	22,9
1997	391	1967098	54	1062,23	64,639	22,22
1998	371	1953216	55	1074,27	63,642	15,48
1999	394	1953747	62	1211,32	63,963	22,1
2000	434	1962932	66	1295,54	64,517	35,54
2001	456	1976006	69	1363,44	64,98	31.89
2002	477	1993845	70	1395,69	65,574	32,99
2003	512	2015564	73	1471,36	65,979	36,24
2004	549	2040209	74	1509,75	66,407	45,05
2005	584	2074736	76	1576,8	66,792	62,07
2006	632	2119496	78	1653,21	67,174	72,72
2007	686	2169707	80	1735,77	68,019	76,18
2008	722	2229842	77	1716,98	68,474	94,95
2009	665	2292706	65	1490,26	67,463	64,13
2010	695	2350079	72	1692,06	67,577	79.64
2011	725	2416816	78	1885,12	67,727	99.97
2012	750	2499424	79	1974,54	67,968	101,61
2013	760	2581327	78	2013,44	67,901	99,21
2014	765	2644159	77	2036	67,813	91,59
2015	744	2673133	75	2004,85	68,389	53,65
2016	742	2696319	77	2076,17	68,43	46.98
2017	753	2730170	79	2156,83	68,127	55,91
2018	771	2762511	78	2154,76	68,016	70,01
2019	781	2853595	79	2254,34	67,388	64,37

3 Methods

The first stage of building the production function is testing the cointegration of time series and clarifying the specification of the production function using the model of adaptation of the Russian economy to Western sanctions.

The first step. The first step in testing the time series cointegration hypothesis

$$\left(x_{1t} = lnY_t, \; x_{2t} = lnK_t, \; x_{3t} = lnL_t, \; x_{4t} = lnp_t\right)$$

it is necessary to test for each of these series the hypotheses of the unit root, that is, the hypothesis

$$H_0 : x_{it} \sim I(1), \tag{8}$$

that the series x_{it} is a non-stationary series from class $I(1)$. Hypothesis (8) opposite alternative

$$H_1 : x_{it} \sim I(0) \tag{9}$$

is investigated by the Dickey-Fuller test [21], which is programmed in the adf.test (x_{it}, k) function of the statistical application R. Below (Table 2) are the results of the Dickey-Fuller test for k = 2 hypotheses (8) for the time series lnY_t, lnK_t, LnL_t, lnp_t. According to the Table 2, we assume hypothesis (8) that the time series (lnY_t, lnK_t, LnL_t, lnp_t) belong to class $I(1)$. The graphs of these series are shown in Fig. 1.

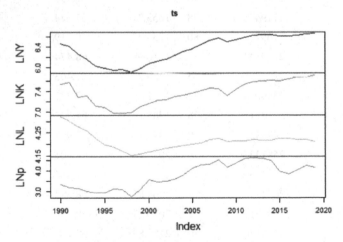

Fig. 1. Time series graphs lnY_t, lnK_t, LnL_t, lnp_t

The second step. Now we can take the second step in investigating their cointegration. Before the second step, we note that the cointegrations of the time series lnY_t, lnK_t, LnL_t, lnp_t visually manifest themselves by a certain similarity in the geometry of the graphs of their implementations (see Fig. 1). The lnY_t graph shows three local minima:

Table 2. Results of the study of hypothesis (8)

Time series	Test Statistics Dickey-Fuller test statistics	Value p – value	Decision rule (significance level $\alpha = 0.05$)
lnY_t	−2.8146	0.2626	Hypothesis (8) accepted
lnK_t	−3.16	0.1313	Hypothesis (8) accepted
lnL_t	−3.18	0.1212	Hypothesis (8) accepted
lnp_t	−1.28	0.8585	Hypothesis (8) accepted

in the year of the Russian default (t = 1998), in the year of the global financial crisis (t = 2009) and in the year when Western sanctions were imposed (t = 2015). This information allows us to clarify the specification of the production function of the Russian economy by appropriately including in its equation the fictitious variable dcs_t (an indicator of default, the Global financial crisis, and Western sanctions with the model (11) of adaptation to sanctions of the Russian economy):

$$dcs_t = \begin{cases} 1 \ when \ t = 1998, 2009, 2015; \\ a_1 \ when \ t = 2016, \\ a_2 \ when \ t = 2017, \\ a_3 \ when \ t = 2018. \\ a_4 \ when \ t = 2019. \\ 0 \ when \ other \ t \ from \ 1990-2019. \end{cases} \tag{10}$$

4 A Model for Adapting the Russian Economy to Western Sanctions

The values $(a_1, a_2, a_3, a_4) \subset [0, 1]$ of the fictitious variable dcs_t taken over the time interval from 2016 to 2019 are intended to reflect the adaptation of the Russian economy to Western sanctions according to the model.

$$dcs_t = \exp(-a \cdot (t - 2015)). \tag{11}$$

Remark 4. The crises of 1998, 2009 and 2015, of course, differ from each other in their effects on the Russian economy. Specifically, the Russian economy overcame the consequences of the crises of 1998 and 2009 in almost one year (this is clearly visible on the lnL_t graph in Fig. 1). The impact of the crisis of 2015 is longer. This circumstance is taken into account in the model (10) – (11).

Consider (10) in specification (3):

$$Y_t = A \cdot e^{\gamma \cdot (t-1990)} \cdot e^{\theta \cdot dcs_t} \cdot K_t^{\alpha} \cdot L_t^{\beta} \cdot p_t^{\delta}.$$

The statistical (regression) model corresponding to this equation has the specification

$$lnY_t = lnA + \gamma \cdot (t - 1990) + \theta \cdot dcs_t + \alpha \cdot lnK_t + \beta \cdot lnL_t + \delta \cdot lnp_t + \varepsilon_t. \quad (12)$$

The value of the coefficient a in the model (11), determined below according to the criterion $R^2 \to$ max where R^2 is the coefficient of determination of the model (12)) in the process of evaluating the parameters of the statistical model (12), turned out to be 0.3.

If the series lnY_t, lnK_t, LNL_t, lnp_t in model (12) are cointegrated, then regression (12) is called cointegrated, but if the series are not cointegrated, then regression (12) turns out to be false. Model (12) is necessary for performing the second step of testing the hypothesis of cointegration of the non-stationary time series included in it. The second step consists of two actions.

Action1. Model parameters (12) are estimated by the least squares method. Below is the protocol (13) for estimating the OLS of model parameters (12), performed according to Table 1 in statistical application R.

Call:

lm(formula = LNY $\sim$ t.1990 + dcs + LNK + LNL + LNp, data = ndata)

Odds :

Evaluation of St.. error t value $\Pr(> |t|)$

(Intercept)	−6.062923	0.782336	−7.750	5.51e − 08 ∗ ∗∗
$t.1990$	0.006514	0.001878	3.469	0.001990 ∗ ∗
dcs	0.071176	0.015866	4.486	0.000153 ∗ ∗ ∗ .
LNK	0.328926	0.063026	5.219	2.39e − 05 ∗ ∗∗
LNL	2.173706	0.282619	7.691	6.29e − 08 ∗ ∗∗
LNp	0.192935	0.013998	13.784	6.75e − 13 ∗ ∗∗

− − −

Residual standard error : 0.01927 on 24 degrees of freedom

Multiple R − squared : 0.9954, Adjusted R − squared : 0.9944

F − statistic : 1038 at 5 and 24 DF, p − value : < 2.2e − 16.   (13)

According to (13), the evaluation (14) of the model (12) by the least squares method turned out to be as follows:

$$lnY_t = − 6, 0629 + 0, 0065 \cdot (t − 1990) + 0, 071 \cdot dcs_t + 0, 33 \cdot lnK_t$$

$$+ 2, 17 \cdot lnL_t + 0, 19 \cdot lnp_t + \varepsilon_t; R^2 = 0, 9954, \tilde{\sigma}_\varepsilon = 0, 01927, \text{t} = 1990, 1991, 2019; \quad (14)$$

Let us discuss the meaning of $\tilde{\sigma}_\varepsilon = 0.019$ in model (14). This is the standard relative error (in fractions) of predictions $\tilde{Y}_t$ according to model (14). In other words, we can expect that the relative mean squared error prediction $\tilde{Y}_t$ according to model (14) will be approximately 2%.

We also note that the value of the coefficient $a = 0.3$ in the model (11) of adaptation of the Russian economy to sanctions is determined according to the criterion $R^2 \rightarrow$ max together with the calculation of parameters in the model (14). Accordingly, the values of the dcs_t over the time interval from 2016 to 2019 ended up as follows:

$$a_1 = 0, 74, \ a_2 = 0, 55, \ a_3 = 0, 41, \ a_4 = 0, 30. \tag{15}$$

Remark 5. Standard tests with trend-stationary explanatory variables can be performed in cointegrating regression [25]. It can be seen from protocols a (13) of model evaluation and (12) that the t-test allows us to confidently accept the hypothesis

$$H_1 : \theta \neq 0 \tag{16}$$

on the significance of the explanatory variable dcs_t. Perhaps, the positive sign of the estimate $\tilde{\theta} = 0.071$ of the coefficient θ for the variable dcs_t causes some confusion (Indeed, from Fig. 1, it seems that the coefficient θ has a negative sign). The following plausible arguments allow us to understand the reason for the positive sign of the estimate $\tilde{\theta}$. According to specification (12), the change $\Delta lnY_{2009} = lnY_{2009} - lnY_{2008} = -0.082$ satisfies the equation:

$$\Delta lnY_{2009} = \gamma + \theta + \alpha \cdot \Delta lnK_{2009} + \beta \cdot \Delta lnL_{2009} + \delta \cdot \Delta lnp_{2009} + \Delta\varepsilon_{2009}.$$

From here.

$$\theta = \Delta lnY_{2009} - (\gamma + \alpha \cdot \Delta lnK_{2009} + \beta \cdot \Delta lnL_{2009} + \delta \cdot \Delta lnp_{2009} + \Delta\varepsilon_{2009}). \tag{17}$$

One might expect a negative value of the coefficient θ in the situation $\Delta lnK_{2009} = \Delta lnL_{2009} = \Delta lnp_{2009} = 0$.
However (see table 1)

$$\Delta lnK_{2009} = -0, 14; \ \Delta lnL_{2009} = -0, 015; \ \Delta lnp_{2009} = -0, 39. \tag{18}$$

The coefficients $(\gamma, \alpha, \beta, \delta)$ and the value $\Delta\varepsilon_{2009} = \varepsilon_{2009} - \varepsilon_{2008}$ are, of course, unknown, but their best estimates are known: $\tilde{\gamma} = 0.0065$; $\tilde{\alpha} = 0.33$; $\tilde{\beta} = 2.17$; $\tilde{\delta} = 0.19$; $\Delta\tilde{\varepsilon}_{2009} = e_{2009} - e_{2008} = 0.0069 - 0.0122 = -0.0053$. We substitute these estimates and values (18) into the Eq. (17), and as a result, we obtain the approximate equality.

$$\theta \approx -0, 082 - (0, 0065 + 0, 33 \cdot (-0, 14),$$
$+2, 17 \cdot (-0, 015) + 0, 19 \cdot (-0, 39) - 0, 0053) = 0, 06965$, which explains the positive sign of the score $\tilde{\theta} = 0.071$. Conclusion: you can see that the values $(lnY_t, lnK_t, lnL_t, lnp_t)$ change in the same direction in the interval from 2008 to 2009, for this reason the sign of the coefficient θ is positive.

Action 2. Calculate the residuals $e_t = \tilde{\varepsilon}_t$ in model (14), and use the residuals e_t to test the hypothesis H_0 (see (19)) that the random perturbation ε_t in model (12) is a non-stationary series $I(1)$:

$$H_0 : \varepsilon_t \sim I(1). \tag{19}$$

If hypothesis (19) is rejected in favor of the alternative

$$H_1 : \varepsilon_t \sim I(0),\tag{20}$$

that the time series is stationary, then the time series lnY_t, lnK_t, $LnlL_t$, lnp_t in model (12) are interpreted as cointegrated and the estimated model (14) is recognized as correct (cointegrating regression). If hypothesis (19) is accepted, then the time series lnY_t, lnK_t, $LnlL_t$, lnp_t are recognized nonintegrated, and the model (12) is interpreted as a false regression.

Note that in the situation of cointegrating regression (14), we can correctly test hypothesis (6) with the t – test about the absence of STP in the national economy for the time interval $t = 1990, 1991, ..., 2019$.

Below, we investigate hypothesis (19) using the Durbin – Watson cointegrating regression test [16]. Тест The Durbin-Watson Cointegrating Regression test examines (attention!) hypothesis (20) versus alternative (19).

We calculate the residuals e_t in the estimated model (14), construct a graph of the time series e_t using the tsdisplay(et) function, as well as (along the way) graphs of estimates of its autocorrelation function ACF and partial autocorrelation function PACF (Fig. 2). Note that the graphs presented in Fig. 2 allow us to interpret the time series e_t as white noise, i.e., as a known stationary series. However, we study the stationarity of the time series ε_t, so we calculate the DW statistics the Durbin-Watson cointegrating regression test:

$$DW = \frac{\sum_{t=1991}^{t=2019}(e_t - e_{t-1})^2}{\sum_{t=1990}^{t=2019}(e_t)^2} = 2,0178.\tag{21}$$

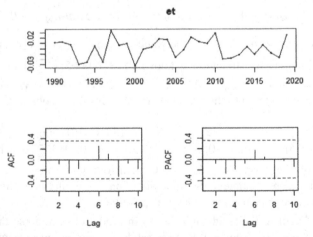

Fig. 2. Graphs of the residuals e_t in model (14) and its functional characteristics ACF and PACF.

Here is the calculation protocol in R statistics (21):

Durbin-Watson test
data: trdcmodel
DW = 2.0178, p-value = 0.2392.
Critical values *of*the DW statistic at the significance level $\alpha = 0.05$ are given in.
[22] and presented in Table 3 below.

Table 3. Critical values *of*DW_{cr} statistics *ofthe*DW hypothesis (16)

Total number of M variables (including y_t) in the model	Number of observations n		
	50	100	200
2	0,72	0,38	0,20
3	0,89	0,48	0,25
4	1,05	0,58	0,30
5	1,19	0,68	0,35

We will not be able to directly use the data in Table 3 for two reasons. First, the number of observations (see Table 1) for which the estimated model (14) is obtained is $n = 30$, and second, the model (14) contains M = 6 variables. We will have to perform a biquadratic extrapolation of the data from Table 3. First, for each fixed value M = 2, 3, 4, 5, we will extrapolate the values of DW_{cr} back (by $n = 30$) using second-order polynomials; we will get the values, respectively, 0.903, 1.11, 1.30, 1.46 (see column n = 30 in Table 4).

Table 4. Biquadratic extrapolation of data from Table 3

M	Number of observations n			
	30	50	100	200
2	**0,90**	0,72	0,38	0,20
3	**1,11**	0,89	0,48	0,25
4	**1,30**	1,05	0,58	0,30
5	**1,46**	1,19	0,68	0,35
6	**1,60**			

Then we extrapolate forward (by M = 6) values of DW_{cr} obtained for n = 30 using a second-order approximating polynomial; the graph of this polynomial is shown in Fig. 3.

As a result, we obtain the desired critical value $DW_{cr} = 1, 60$ *of the DW statistic* of the Durbin-Watson cointegrating regression test. Since the calculated value (21) of the statistic DW of the hypothesis criterion (20) exceeds the value $DW_{cr} = 1, 60$, we accept hypothesis (20), that is, we interpret the estimated model (14) as a cointegrating

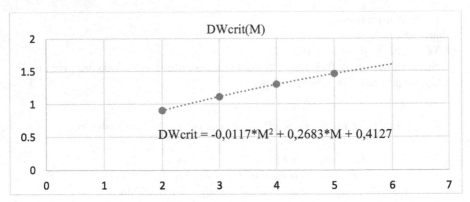

Fig. 3. Biquadratic extrapolation of critical values *oftheDWstatistics* of the cointegrating regression test

regression, and we accept the hypothesis that the time series lnY_t, lnK_t, $LnlL_t$, lnp_t are cointegrated.

The first stage of the methodology for constructing the production function (refinement of its specification using the model of adaptation of the Russian economy to Western sanctions and the procedure for testing the cointegration of the time series lnY_t, lnK_t, $LnlL_t$, lnp_t) has been completed. Evaluation (14) of model (12) passed all the necessary checks which are necessary for confidence in all parameters in the model (14). Specifically,

1) Test the Jarque - Bera test is the normal of the distribution of a random perturbation ε_t in model (12); here is the protocol of this test:

   Jarque Bera Test
   data: et
   X-squared = 0.99478, df = 2, p-value = 0.6081.

2) Test Reset [23] the correctness of the specification, here is the protocol of this test:

   RESET test
   data: trdcmodel
   RESET = 0.15628, df1 = 1, df2 = 23, p-value = 0.6963.

3) The Breusch-Pagan test of conditional homoskedasticity ε_t, here is the protocol of this test:

   Bptest (trdcmodel)
   studentized Breusch-Pagan test
   data: decode
   BP = 6.8948, df = 5, p-value = 0.2286.

   Therefore, any standard tests about the model parameters (12) will be correct. We are interested in the question of the existence of scientific and technological progress (STP) in the Russian economy in the time interval $t = 1990, 1991, ..., 2019$. The answer to this question will be positive if we can reject hypothesis (6) about the absence of STP in this time interval.

5 Results of Testing the Hypothesis of Scientific and Technological Progress in the Russian Economy

Standard tests with trend-stationary explanatory variables can be performed in cointegrating regression [23]. We use the t – test to investigate hypothesis (6), which means that there was no STP in Russia during the time interval t = 1990,…,2019. The statistic $t = 3.47$ of the criterion of this hypothesis is found in protocol (13). Under the fair hypothesis (6), this statistic has the Student distribution with the number of degrees of freedom $df = 24$. Let's set the standard significance level $\alpha = 0.05$. Note that the result of testing hypothesis (6) does not depend on the chosen alternative. Indeed, if you choose an alternative

$$H_1 : \gamma \neq 0, \tag{22}$$

then, at the significance level $\alpha = 0.05$, hypothesis (6) is rejected as contradicting real data (this can be seen from protocol (13), where p – value = 0.00189). If you choose an alternative about the presence of STP in the Russian economy

$$H_1 : \gamma > 0, \tag{23}$$

then hypothesis (6) at the significance level $\alpha = 0.05$ deviates more in favor of (23), since in the situation (23) the critical region of hypothesis (6) is the interval (1.71, + ∞), and with the statistic $t = 3.47$ it confidently falls into this region.

Remark 6. We have an objective reason to say that the Russian economy has STP, and all other things being equal, because of STP, Russia's real GDP increases by about 0.6% per year.

6 The Second Stage of the Methodology for Constructing Variants of the Production Function of the Russian Economy: A Study of the Stability of Coefficient Estimates and an Assessment of the Accuracy of Ex-Post Forecasting

In this section, we investigate the stability of estimates of the coefficients of statistical model (12) on training samples with intervals, respectively [1990, 2000], [1990, 2003], [[1990, 2006], [1990, 2009], [1990, 2012], [1990, 2015], [1990, 2018], and then we will determine the accuracy of ex-post forecasts of Russian GDP for the production function with the coefficient estimates obtained on these samples. Table 5 show the coefficient estimates obtained from the above training samples; standard errors of these estimates are indicated in parentheses. Considering Table 5, we state that with the growth of the training sample size, the estimates of all coefficients in the statistical model (12) quickly stabilize. This is how the cointegrated nature of the time series used to evaluate model data manifests itself! However, we note that in model (12) on the sample [1990,

2000], the estimates of $\tilde{lnA}$, $\tilde{\gamma}$, $\tilde{\beta}$ were determined completely unreliably, and the reasons for this circumstance are most likely the insignificant size of the training sample (11 observations) and the absence of any STP in the Russian economy during this time period (the collapse of the USSR and so on).

Table 5. Values of coefficient estimates in the statistical model (12)

Training sample	$\tilde{lnA}$	$\tilde{\gamma}$	$\tilde{\theta}$	$\tilde{\alpha}$	$\tilde{\beta}$	$\tilde{\delta}$
[1990, 2000]	1,88 (5,0)	−0,025 (0,020)	0,088 (0,035)	0,506 (0,14)	−0,02 (1,38)	0,26 (0,07)
[1990, 2003]	− 6,15 (2,1)	0,0075 (0,0069)	0,075 (0,034)	0,37 (0,11)	2,13 (0,66)	0,18 (0,06)
[1990, 2006]	− 6,27 (1,65)	0,0085 (0,0056)	0,069 (0,028)	0,38 (0,09)	2,16 (0,50)	0,16 (0,046)
[1990, 2009]	− 6,66 (1,20)	0,0095 (0,0046)	0,068 (0,02)	0,36 (0,069)	2,28 (0,38)	0,17 (0,042)
[1990, 2012]	− 6,45 (1,1)	0,0080 (0,0040)	0,073 (0,020)	0,33 (0,071)	2,27 (0,36)	0,18 (0,039)
[1990, 2015]	− 6,00 (0,89)	0,0059 (0,0026)	0,074 (0,018)	0,32 (0,066)	2,17 (0,31)	0,20 (0,023)
[1990, 2018]	− 6,05 (0,78)	0,0061 (0,0019)	0,075 (0,016)	0,32 (0,063)	2,18 (0,28)	0,20 (0,015)
[1990, 2019]	− 6,06 (0,78)	0,0065 (0,0019)	0,071 (0,016)	0,33 (0,063)	2,17 (0,28)	0,19 (0,014)

Let's move on to calculating ex-post forecasts of Y_t values and relative errors of ex-post forecasts Y_t. Table 6 shows the relative errors of ex-post forecasts of Russian GDP for the production function with the equation

$$Y_t = A \cdot e^{\gamma \cdot (t-1990)} \cdot e^{\theta \cdot dcs_t} \cdot K_t^\alpha \cdot L_t^\beta \cdot p_t^\delta \qquad (24)$$

and estimates of coefficients from Table 5. We note the meaning of ex-post forecasts and their relative errors on the example of a training sample over a time interval [1990, 2000]. So, the forecast is based on the rule

$$\begin{cases} ln\ \tilde{Y_t} = +1,883 - 0,0248 \cdot (t-1990) + 0,08765 \cdot dcs_t + 0,506 \cdot lnK_t - \\ \qquad -0,022 \cdot lnL_t + 0,258 \cdot lnp_t, \\ \tilde{Y_t} = EXP(ln\ \tilde{Y_t}) \end{cases} \qquad (25)$$

calculated for each value of the time variable $t = 2001, 2002, ..., 2019$ and, further, the relative forecast error (in %) is determined by the rule:

$$re_t = 100 \cdot \frac{\tilde{Y_t} - Y_t}{\tilde{Y_t}}. \qquad (26)$$

The last line of this table contains the values of absolute values (26).

Table 6. Relative errors $re_t(\%)$ of ex-post forecasts of Russian GDP based on estimates of the production function (24)

Year of forecasting	A temporary period of training samples						
	[1990, 2000]	[1990, 2003]	[1990, 2006]	[1990, 2009]	[1990, 2012]	[1990, 2015]	[1990, 2018]
2001	−6,4						
2002	−11,8						
2003	−16,9						
2004	−19,9	−1,4					
2005	−17,8	1,8					
2006	−22,5	0,43					
2007	−31,4	−1,7	−2,2				
2008	−34,8	−1,1	−1,8				
2009	−38,5	−0,1	−0,8				
2010	−43,6	−2,3	−2,6	−1,4			
2011	−37,2	2,7	2,3	3,4			
2012	−41,5	2,9	2,6	3,7			
2013	−46,4	2,4	2,2	3,5	1,8		
2014	− 53.4	1,2	1,3	2,6	0,6		
2015	−62,1	3,8	4,2	5,5	3,2		
2016	−72,4	2	2,9	4,2	1,4	−1,7	
2017	−71,0	3,4	4,2	5,6	2,7	−0,2	
2018	−71,5	4,4	5	6,5	3,7	1,1	
2019	−79,6	1,3	2,2	3,7	0,3	−2,7	−2,5
	41	**2,1**	**2,6**	**4**	**2**	**1,4**	**2,5**

7 Results

1) The production function of the Russian economy estimated and tested over the entire sample (Table 1) has the following equations:

$$\tilde{Y}_t = 0,002328 \cdot e^{0,0065 \cdot (t-1990)} \cdot e^{0,071 \cdot dcs_t} \cdot K_t^{0,33} \cdot L_t^{2,17} \cdot p_t^{0,19}, \qquad (27)$$

$t = 1990, 1991, \ldots, 2019,$

$$dcs_t = \begin{cases} 1 \ when \ t = 1998, \ 2009, \ 2015. \\ 0{,}74 \ when \ t = 2016. \\ 0{,}55 \ when \ t = 2017. \\ 0{,}41 \ when \ t = 2018. \\ 0{,}30 \ when \ t = 2019. \\ 0 \ when \ other \ t \ from \ 1990-2019. \end{cases} \tag{28}$$

2) The values (28) of the dummy variable dcs_t reflect the impact on Russia's real GDP of the default in 1998, the severe financial crisis in 2009, and, according to model (11), the adaptation of the Russian economy to Western sanctions (see remark 4).

Remark 7. The last conclusion is valid for Western sanctions imposed at the end of 2014. The sanctions imposed in 2022 are much tougher and more diverse. However, there is still no statistical information to assess the approach developed in this paper to adapt the Russian economy to the sanctions of 2022.

3) The accuracy of ex-post forecasts according to model (12), estimated on the training sample [1990, 2000], is unacceptable (average relative error $re \approx 41\%$). This circumstance is due to completely unreliable estimates $\tilde{lnA}, \tilde{\gamma}, \tilde{\beta}$ coefficients (see Table 5), and the reasons for this circumstance, on the one hand, are the small size of the training sample (11 observation equations with 6 determined coefficients) and, probably, the lack of scientific and technological progress (and most likely, the presence of scientific and technological regression) in the economy Russia in the time interval [1990, 2000] - the collapse of the USSR, etc.

4) The accuracy of ex-post forecasts based on the model (12) estimated from training samples [1990, 2003], [1990, 2006], [1990, 2009], [1990, 2012], [1990, 2015] and [1990, 2018], a very high (Table 6) and, equally important, it agrees well with the value of the average quadratic relative error $\tilde{\sigma}_\varepsilon \approx 2\%$ (see (14)), calculated during the evaluation of the model (12) for the full sample [1990, 2019].

5) True forecast errors for model (12) estimated from training samples [1990, 2003], [1990, 2006], [1990, 2009], [1990, 2012], [1990, 2018], have different sign (Table 6), and it looks like that the forecast $\tilde{Y}_t$ for this model is unbiased.

6) In the production function (27), the value $\tilde{\gamma} = 0.0065$ is an estimate of the relative contribution (in shares) of scientific and technological progress to the annual growth rate of Russia's real GDP. Therefore, all other things being equal, scientific and technological progress increases Russia's real GDP by about 0.6% per year.

7) The elasticity values of Russia's real GDP in terms of fixed capital, labor, and oil prices, respectively, are approximately 0.3%, 2% and 0.2%. Consequently, a 1% increase in the levels of the main factors of production Kt and Lt leads to an increase in Russia's real GDP by about 2.3% [25].

8 Conclusions

1) At the last stage of the production function construction scheme (the post-factum forecasting stage), the production function of the Russian economy with the adaptation model used in it showed high accuracy of forecasting real GDP. This circumstance made it possible to interpret the model of adaptation of the Russian economy to the sanctions of Western countries as adequate.

2) We can say that for each year the impact of Western sanctions on the Russian economy decreases by about 25%.

References

1. Douglas, P.H.: The Cobb-Douglas production function once again: its history. Its testing, and some new empirical values. J. Polit. Econ. **84**(5), 903–916 (1976)
2. Fraser, I.: The Cobb-Douglas Production Function: An Antipodean Defence? Econ. Issues **7**(Part 1), 39–58 (2002)
3. Afanasyev, A.A., Ponomareva, O.S.: The spread of the Wuhan coronavirus (SARS-COV-2) in Russia: macroeconomic production function based on the world price of Brent crude oil. Probl. Market Econ. **1**, 24–46 (2021)
4. McCombie, J.S.L.: Are There Laws of Production? An assessment of the early criticisms of the cobb-douglas production function. Rev. Pol. Econ. **10**(2), 141–173 (1998)
5. Shaikh, A.: Laws of production and laws of algebra, the humbug production function. Rev. Econ. Stat. **56**, 115–120 (1974)
6. Weber, C.E.: Pareto and the wicksell-cobb-douglas functional form. J. History Econ. Thought **20**(2), 203–210 (1998)
7. Kirilyuk, I.L.: Models of production functions for the Russian economy. Comput. Res. Modeling **5**(2), 293–31312 (2013)
8. Felipe, J., Adams, F.G.: The estimation of the Cobb-Douglas function: a retrospective review. Eastern Econ. J. **31**, 427–445 (2005)
9. Williams, J.: Professor Douglas' Production Function. Econ. Rec. **25**, 55–64 (1945)
10. Kleiner, G.B.: Production Functions: Theory, Methods, Application, p. 239. Finance and Statistics Publ, Moscow (1986)
11. Granger, C.W.J., Newbold, P.: Spurious regressions in econometrics. J. Econ. **2**, 111–120 (1974)
12. Hamilton,J.D.: Time Series Analysis. Princeton. - Princeton University Press (1994). 786 p.
13. Cobb, Ch.E., Douglas, P.H.: A theory of production. Am. Econ. Rev. **18**(1, Supplement), 139–165 (1928)
14. Akaev, A.A., Sadovnichy, V.A.: Sadovnichy Closed dynamic model for describing and calculating the long wave of economic development of Kondratiev. Bull. Russ. Acad. Sci. **10**, 883–896 (2016)
15. Aghion, P., Howitt, P.: The Economics of Growth, p. 495. The MIT Press Cambridge, Massachusetts London, England (2009)
16. Romer, D.: Advanced Macroeconomics, p. 716. McGraw-Hill, New York (2012)
17. Romanovsky, M.Yu., Romanovsky, Yu.M.: Introduction to econophysics: statistical and dynamic models. Textbook, 2nd Ed., is pr. and additional-Moscow: Izhevsk: Institute of Computer Research (2012). 338 p.
18. Suvorov, N.V., Akhunov, R.R., Gubarev, R.V., Dzyuba, E.I., Fayzullin, F.S.: Application of the Cobb-Douglas production function for the analysis of the region's industrial complex. Econ. Region **16**(1), 187–200 (2020)

19. Solow, R.: A contribution to the theory of economic growth. Quart. J. Econ. 65–94 (1956)
20. Engle, R.F., Granger, C.W.J.: Cointegration and error correction: representation, estimation and testing. Econometrica **55**, 251–276 (1987)
21. Fuller, W.A.: Introduction to Statistical Time Series, 2nd edn., p. 736. Wiley, New York (1996)
22. Banerjee, A., Dolado, J., Gabraith, J.W., Hendry, D.F.: Co-integration, Error-Correction, and the Econometric Analysis of Non-Stationary Data. Oxford University Press (1993). 329 p.
23. Davidson, R., MacKinnon, J.G.: Econometric Theory and Methods. Oxford University Press (2004)
24. Ramsey, J.B.: Tests for specification errors in classical linear least squares regression analysis. J. Roy. Stat. Soc. B **31**, 350–371 (1969)
25. Byvshev, V.A.: Assessment of the level of return on the scale of production in the Russian economy. Soft Measur. Comput. Sci. J. **54**(5), 91–98 (2022)

Improved Free Disposal Hull Methodology for China Provinces Effective Social-Economic Development Modeling

Artem Denisov[1,2] (ID), Wang Qian[3,4(✉)] (ID), and Elizaveta Steblianskaia[5] (ID)

[1] Computer Science Department, Kostroma State University, Kostroma, Russia
[2] Department of Innovation Management, Saint-Petersburg Electrotechnical University (LETI), Saint-Petersburg, Russia
[3] Department of Economics, Organization and Management of Production, Russian University of Transport (RUT MIIT), Moscow, Russia
409563899@qq.com
[4] Jilin Railway Vocational College, Jilin, China
[5] Higher School of Economics, Moscow, Russia

Abstract. One of the key trends in sustainable development is to ensure integrated regions' social development. Strengthening the "social" part of sustainable development leads to new ways of improving people's quality of life. Mathematical modelling is one of the tools needed to transform the region's economy from developing to developed state. A model may help explain a system, study the effects of different components, and make predictions about behaviour. This study critically examines the shortcomings and limitations of the existing VRS model to assess social efficiency in China provinces. The authors analyzed China provinces social effectiveness data to test the Data Envelope Analysis (DEA) obtained models. Social and economic data was used from China Year Statistical Books from 1997 to 2021. The total expenditures on health care and education were taken as input variables, and the Atkinson Index, the number of unemployed people and GDP were taken as output variables. Based on improved DEA models, target indicators of output social parameters were determined. The analysis of the obtained results suggests that using the proposed models would allow determining the directions of China provinces' effective multifactorial development.

Keywords: Social Development Modelling · Data Envelopment Analysis · Free Disposal Hull · Hyperspace of the efficiency parameters · Hyper-triangle · China provinces · Efficiency assessment of social development

1 Introduction

The Covid-19 pandemic has turned social-oriented strategies into the spotlight [1]. Social development is one of the critical elements in complex sustainable development [2, 3]. A social-oriented concept in sustainability appraisal allows for following the new sustainable way of economic development [4]. Strengthening the "social" part of sustainable

N. Agarwal et al. (Eds.): MSBC 2022, CCIS 1717, pp. 115–125, 2023.
https://doi.org/10.1007/978-3-031-33728-4_8

development leads to new ways of people's quality of life [5]. One of the key trends in sustainable development is to ensure integrated regions' development through the social-oriented development concept [6]. Social development stands for social welfare, which are used as factors to judge a company's non-financial performance, and this concept was presented in the UN Global compact as a strategy for sustainable development [7, 8]. The introduction of social development inevitably led to the complication of regional management systems, which, in particular, was reflected in the sustainable-oriented indicators [9–11]. The accent on social development needs to create social welfare across countries and regions [12].

Recent works in social development have emphasised the need for a dynamic and more comprehensive way to develop social development models. This is because of the inconsistency of the concept of the social development framework itself, along with its features, definitions and dimensions. Furthermore, most of the existing social development frameworks are not fully compatible and sufficient to reflect the dynamic of social development [4]. Mathematical modelling is one of the tools needed to transform the regions' economy from a developing to a developed economy [13]. A model may help explain a system, study the effects of different components, and predict behaviour [14].

This study critically examines the shortcomings and limitations of the existing VRS model to assess social efficiency in China provinces. Nowadays, it is significantly complicated to manage the regions, as it makes it difficult to compare the effectiveness of development and, accordingly, the rational choice of areas, that needs to improve. This problem can be solved through the use of Data Envelope Analysis (DEA). DEA models can also be subdivided in terms of returns to scale by adding weight constraints. Charnes, Cooper, and Rhodes (1978) originally proposed the efficiency measurement of the DMUs for constant returns to scale (CRS), where all DMUs operate at their optimal scale. Later Banker, Charnes, and Cooper (1984) introduced the variable returns to scale (VRS) efficiency measurement model, allowing the breakdown of efficiency into technical and scale efficiencies in DEA [15, 16]. These authors developed Constant Returns to Scale model (further- CRS) and Variable Returns to Scale model (further VRS). In this case, all indicators determining the costs of ensuring ESG concept development are defined as inputs, and the effects achieved are defined as inputs.

At the same time, it is advisable to use a VRS model to assess efficiency, which is characterized by the possibility of taking into account the scale of the compared elements, which is vital for the comparative evaluation of the effectiveness of objects (divisions) of different scales. VRS models are input-oriented (focused on optimizing the resources consumed) and output-oriented (focused on achieving maximum effects). Steblyanskaya et al. showed formulas calculations in the paper concerning companies' social-oriented modelling [2].

The primary problem when using VRS models is that they are oriented to assess current efficiency and do not allow setting target values for developing the objects being compared. This disadvantage can be eliminated by transforming the cloud of compared objects of the DEA model. Free Disposal Hull (further- FDH), suggested by Deprins, Simar, Tulkens [17]. Tulkens further developed models for measuring regions' social and economic development [18]. The main idea of this approach is to present data on all the objects under analysis in the form of a multidimensional body limited by a convex hull. To describe the convex hull, it was suggested to use the rectangle mesh the vertices of which are the objects with the maximum efficiency (drivers). The primary problem of the FDH's traditional representation is the orthogonal representation of its surface. This significantly worsens the quality of determining the optimal parameters, since the values are selected from the list of parameter values of the objects being compared.

The rest of the paper is organized the following way: Sect. 2 outlines the methodology; the data analysis case are presented in Sect. 4. Finally, in the concluding remarks the authors indicate research limitations and future research directions and give a few concluding recommendations.

2 Methodology

The authors suggest improving the quality simulation results by transforming of an orthogonal grid into a finite element system (hyper-triangles), as shown in Fig. 1. This approach will allow not only to determine the efficiency using traditional VRS models (Fig. 1.a), but also to find the nearest point on the FDH, which will allow finding the coordinates of the closest point on the shell for an object with low relative efficiency (Fig. 1.b). Such a point makes it possible to determine for such an object the development targets closest to it, transferring it from relatively inefficient to practical efficiency.

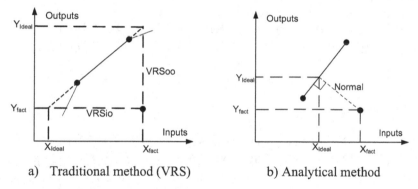

a) Traditional method (VRS)   b) Analytical method

Fig. 1. (a. b). Defining the object efficiency line crossing with the hyper-triangle's plane

This approach also makes it possible to determine development targets for objects located on the FDH surface (which are relatively efficient). This problem can be solved by perceiving the formed hyper-triangles as efficiency trends are set in hyperspace. Then, in order to determine the target values of indicators for such an object, it is necessary to exclude all trends associated with it (hyper-triangles) from the FDH surface, extend the remaining hyper-triangles by closing the FDH, and find the nearest point by lowering the normal to the resulting surface.

Matrix calculations can be used to build the proposed models. The suggested system of definitions is as follows:

Hyper-space of dimension N, where $N = q + m$ (1) is a space of factors where the analyzed objects are described.

Hyper-plane of dimension N is the main element of the hyper-space which can be presented as a hyper-space of dimension N-1.

Hyper-triangle of dimension N is the simplest figure in the hyper-space consisting of N points through which a hyper-space can be set (in a two-dimension space – a segment; in a tri-dimension space – a triangle; in a four-dimension space – a tetrahedron). On the analogy of a tri-dimension space the hyper-plane is set with the help of a hyper-triangle as follows:

$$
\begin{vmatrix}
x_1 - x_{11} & \cdots & x_m - x_{m1} & y_1 - y_{11} & \cdots & y_q - y_{q1} \\
x_{12} - x_{11} & \cdots & x_{m2} - x_{m1} & y_{12} - y_{11} & \cdots & y_{q2} - y_{q1} \\
\cdots & \cdots & \cdots & \cdots & \cdots & \cdots \\
x_{1N} - x_{11} & \cdots & x_{mN} - x_{m1} & y_{1N} - y_{11} & \cdots & y_{qN} - y_{q1}
\end{vmatrix} = 0 \qquad (1)
$$

where $\{x_1, \ldots, x_m, y_1, \ldots, y_q\}$ are coordinates of a point belonging to the hyper-plane; $\{x_{1N}, \ldots, x_{mN}, y_{1N}, \ldots, y_{q1}\}$| are coordinates of N vertices of the hyper-triangle.

This representation allows to evaluate the VRS-efficiency of the compared objects relative to the hyper-triangles formed by use of VRSio and VRSoo modelы. VRSio (input-oriented model) focused on optimizing resources (reducing costs) while maintaining current performance indicators. VRSoo model focused on increasing effects while maintaining current resource levels.

For VRSio model:

$$
\begin{vmatrix}
\alpha_k \cdot x_{1k} - x_{11} & \cdots & \alpha_k \cdot x_{mk} - x_{m1} & y_{1k} - y_{11} & \cdots & y_{qk} - y_{q1} \\
x_{12} - x_{11} & \cdots & x_{mk} - x_{m1} & y_{12} - y_{11} & \cdots & y_{q2} - y_{q1} \\
\cdots & \cdots & \cdots & \cdots & \cdots & \cdots \\
x_{1N} - x_{11} & \cdots & x_{mN} - x_{m1} & y_{1N} - y_{11} & \cdots & y_{qN} - y_{q1}
\end{vmatrix} = 0 \qquad (2)
$$

For VRSoo model:

$$
\begin{vmatrix}
x_{1k} - x_{11} & \cdots & x_{mk} - x_{m1} & \alpha_k \cdot y_{1k} - y_{11} & \cdots & \alpha_k \cdot y_{qk} - y_{q1} \\
x_{12} - x_{11} & \cdots & x_{m2} - x_{m1} & y_{12} - y_{11} & \cdots & y_{q2} - x_{q1} \\
\cdots & \cdots & \cdots & \cdots & \cdots & \cdots \\
x_{1N} - x_{11} & \cdots & x_{mN} - x_{m1} & y_{1N} - y_{11} & \cdots & y_{qN} - y_{q1}
\end{vmatrix} = 0 \qquad (3)
$$

where $\{x_{1k}, \ldots, x_{mk}, y_{1k}, \ldots, y_{qk}\}$ – coordinates of the object under analysis; α_k – its efficiency concerning drivers; $\{x_{1N}, \ldots, x_{mN}, y_{1N}, \ldots, y_{q1}\}$| – coordinates of N vertices of the hyper-triangle of the convex hull.

The formula of the square matrix determinant is as follows:

$$
|M| = \sum_{i=1}^{N} (-1)^{i-1} \cdot m_{i1} \cdot |M_{i1}|
$$

where M is a square matrix of N dimension; mi1 is an element of the matrix; M_{i1} is a minor corresponding to the element. Thus, it is possible to determine the coefficient of efficiency a:

For VRSio model:

$$\alpha_k = \frac{\sum_{i=1}^{m}\left((-1)^{i-1}x_{i1} \cdot |M_{i1}|\right) - \sum_{r=1}^{q}\left((-1)^{r+m-1}\left(y_{rk} - y_{r1}\right) \cdot |M_{r+m-1}|\right)}{\sum_{i=1}^{m}\left((-1)^{i-1}x_{ik} \cdot |M_{i1}|\right)} \qquad (4)$$

$\alpha_k = \{\alpha \cdot x_{1k}, \ldots, \alpha \cdot x_{mk}, y_{1k}, \ldots, y_{qk}\}$

For VRSoo model:

$$\alpha_k = \frac{\sum_{r=1}^{q}\left((-1)^{r+m-1}y_{r1} \cdot |M_{r+m-1}|\right) - \sum_{i=1}^{m}\left((-1)^{i-1}(x_{ik} - x_{i1}) \cdot |M_{i1}|\right)}{\sum_{r=1}^{q}\left((-1)^{r+m-1}y_{rk} \cdot |M_{r+m-1}|\right)} \qquad (5)$$

$\alpha_k = \{x_{1k}, \ldots, x_{mk}, \alpha \cdot x_{mk} \ldots, \alpha \cdot y_{qk}\}$

where C*k are coordinates of the point of crossing of the efficiency line of the object under analysis with a hyper-plane of the hyper-triangle.

The resulting expressions allow, in particular, to find those hyper-triangles that form the FDH surface and thereby find objects with maximum relative efficiency. This can be done using the convexity property FDH. This property determines that any hyper triangle FDH is characterized by the property:

- If the hyper-triangle belongs to FDH, then all the objects being compared will either lie below the hyper-plane formed by this hyper-triangle, or belong to it.

Based on this, according to the VRSoo model, all efficiency coefficients ak for hyper-triangles forming FDH should be greater than or equal to 1. If this condition is not met, then triangle is not included in FDH and should be excluded from the analysis.

After finding the hyper-triangles lying on the FDH, can determine the current efficiency of all the analyzed objects, as well as find for each of their objects the point closest to it on the FDH and thereby set performance targets for it. When using analytical geometry methods, the nearest hyper triangle FDH is determined through the length of the normal from the DMU to its projection onto the corresponding hyper plane:

$$r = \frac{||M||}{\sqrt{\sum_{i=1}^{m}\left(|M_{i1}|^2\right) + \sum_{r=1}^{q}\left(|M_{r+m-1}|^2\right)}} \rightarrow \min \qquad (6)$$

In this case, the coordinates of the closest point with high efficiency C*k = {x1*,..., xm*, y1 C*,..., yqC*} can be determined using the formulas: the coordinates of the projection onto the plane of the hyper-triangle are determined by the formulas:

$$\forall j = 1..m : x_{jC^*} = x_{jk} - \frac{(-1)^{j-1} \cdot M_{j1} \cdot |M|}{\sum_{i=1}^{m}\left(|M_{i1}|^2\right) + \sum_{r=1}^{q}\left(|M_{r+m-1}|^2\right)} \qquad (7)$$

$$\forall j = 1..q : y_{jC^*} = y_{jk} - \frac{(-1)^{j+m-1} \cdot M_{(j+m)1} \cdot |M|}{\sum_{i=1}^{m}\left(|M_{i1}|^2\right) + \sum_{r=1}^{q}\left(|M_{r+m-1}|^2\right)} \qquad (8)$$

When constructing a normal, the values of part of the projection coordinates may be worse than those of the analyzed object. In this case, it will be necessary to adjust the position of the projection point: the values for all degraded indicators are determined by the coordinates of the starting point, and the values of the remaining indicators are recalculated by following formulas:

$$x_{jC^{**}} = x_{jC^*} - \frac{\left(\sum_i\left((x_{ik} - x_{iC^*}) \cdot (-1)^{i-1} \cdot |M_{i1}|\right) + \sum_r\left((y_{rk} - y_{rC^*}) \cdot (-1)^{r+m-1} \cdot |M_{r+m-1}|\right)\right) \cdot |M_{j1}|}{\sum_i\left(|M_{i1}|^2\right) + \sum_r\left(|M_{r+m-1}|^2\right)} \quad (9)$$

$$y_{jC^{**}} = y_{jC^*} - \frac{\left(\sum_i\left((x_{ik} - x_{iC^*}) \cdot (-1)^{i-1} \cdot |M_{i1}|\right) + \sum_r\left((y_{rk} - y_{rC^*}) \cdot (-1)^{r+m-1} \cdot |M_{r+m-1}|\right)\right) \cdot |M_{j+m-1}|}{\sum_i\left(|M_{i1}|^2\right) + \sum_r\left(|M_{r+m-1}|^2\right)}$$

$$(10)$$

where
$\left(\sum_i\left((x_{ik} - x_{iC^*}) \cdot (-1)^{i-1} \cdot |M_{i1}|\right) + \sum_r\left((y_{rk} - y_{rC^*}) \cdot (-1)^{r+m-1} \cdot |M_{r+m-1}|\right)\right)$ – the sum of pairwise products of deviations in the degradable indicators and their corresponding minor; $\sum_i\left(|M_{i1}|^2\right) + \sum_r\left(|M_{r+m-1}|^2\right)$ – the sum of the squares of minor recalculated indicators.

3   Application of the New Models in Assessing China' Socio-economic Development

The authors analyzed the China provinces' social development data to test the obtained models. Chinese provinces' social and economic imbalances have seen the adoption of a succession of policies designed initially to promote a more equilibrated model of coordinated national development and more recently a more sustainable and more equitable development path consistent with the recent emphasis on the goal of harmonious development [19]. Social and economic data was used from China Year Statistical Books from 1997 to 2021. The authors use the Atkinson index an inequality measure [20].

The results of the analysis concerning social development effectiveness according to the VRSio model from 1997 to 2021 are shown in Fig. 2. The total expenditures on health care and education were taken as input variables. The Atkinson Index, the number of unemployed people and GDP were taken as output variables. The last two indicators

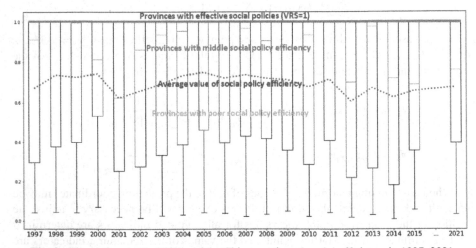

Fig. 2. The change in the VRSio of the China provinces' social efficiency in 1997–2021

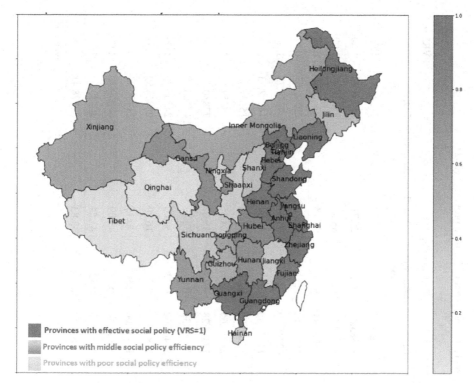

Fig. 3. VR Sio efficiency of social development of Chinese provinces in 2021

in the calculations were given per capita. The effectiveness of the social development of Chinese provinces in 2021 is shown in Fig. 3.

#Based on models (10)–(14), target indicators of output social parameters were determined (while maintaining the current levels of input parameters) (Table 1). The analysis of the obtained results suggests that using the proposed models will allow for determining the directions of effective multifactorial development.

Table. 1. Actual and target (model) indicators of social development of Chinese provinces (2021)

Provinces	Input		Output (Fact)			Output (Target)			VRSio
	Wealth	Education	Atkinson Index	Unemployment level	GDP	Atkinson Index	Unemployment level	GDP	
Beijing	935,62	400,73	0,25	8,00	25669,13	0,23	7,38	27273,77	1,00
Tianjin	529,81	204,65	0,23	25,80	17885,39	0,23	25,71	18268,83	1,00
Hebei	1196,61	551,68	0,32	39,70	32070,45	0,31	38,33	33351,15	1,00
Shanxi	639,97	302,96	0,34	26,10	13050,41	0,31	24,78	17570,70	0,38
Inner Mongolia	585,15	286,62	0,33	26,70	18128,10	0,32	26,20	20302,69	0,57
Liaoning	668,43	309,45	0,30	47,30	22246,90	0,30	46,51	22244,73	1,00
Jilin	526,87	275,53	0,30	25,70	14776,80	0,30	25,69	14812,73	0,41
Heilongjiang	589,26	282,52	0,29	39,60	15386,09	0,29	39,53	15631,07	1,00
Shanghai	886,70	385,77	0,24	24,30	28178,65	0,24	24,21	28459,13	1,00
Jiangsu	1943,15	717,74	0,29	35,20	77388,28	0,28	35,07	77830,18	1,00
Zhejiang	1370,72	546,22	0,27	33,90	47251,36	0,27	32,79	47368,98	1,00
Anhui	960,40	483,47	0,33	30,40	24407,62	0,33	30,00	24367,29	1,00
Fujian	832,02	380,21	0,30	16,30	28810,58	0,30	16,29	28844,59	0,92
Jiangxi	895,04	441,78	0,32	31,30	18499,00	0,30	30,15	21496,22	0,21
Shandong	1925,28	795,70	0,31	45,80	68024,49	0,31	45,09	68099,10	1,00
Henan	1416,83	783,44	0,32	43,60	40471,79	0,32	43,54	40733,66	1,00
Hubei	1104,32	593,01	0,31	32,90	32665,38	0,31	32,83	32728,41	0,76

(continued)

Table. 1. (*continued*)

Provinces	Input		Output (Fact)			Output (Target)			VRSio
	Wealth	Education	Atkinson Index	Unemployment level	GDP	Atkinson Index	Unemployment level	GDP	
Hunan	1088,50	550,08	0,34	44,90	31551,37	0,33	43,89	35979,03	0,66
Guangdong	2444,54	1129,66	0,30	38,00	80854,91	0,30	37,91	81080,92	1,00
Guangxi	901,02	471,45	0,36	18,10	18317,64	0,36	17,95	18296,22	1,00
Hainan	225,89	114,97	0,32	5,10	4053,20	0,29	4,80	4838,56	0,16
Chongqing	606,46	333,49	0,31	15,70	17740,59	0,31	15,65	17885,98	0,56
Sichuan	1372,64	777,63	0,34	56,30	32934,54	0,33	55,00	37405,24	0,32
Guizhou	889,41	395,25	0,40	14,80	11776,73	0,40	13,72	11623,31	0,47
Yunnan	918,51	470,24	0,39	20,10	14788,42	0,39	19,06	14641,61	0,65
Tibet	178,86	70,46	0,40	1,80	1151,41	0,42	1,31	1081,59	0,04
Shaanxi	819,81	384,32	0,36	22,70	19399,59	0,32	21,08	26526,50	0,27
Gansu	578,80	275,16	0,41	9,80	7200,37	0,41	9,34	7135,81	0,77
Qinghai	180,68	103,78	0,37	4,60	2572,49	0,31	4,19	3968,04	0,05
Ningxia	160,87	82,60	0,34	5,10	3168,59	0,30	4,81	4171,36	0,11
Xinjiang	700,65	258,22	0,36	9,70	9649,70	0,36	9,65	9642,69	0,57

4 Conclusion

In the paper, the authors give attention to the new evaluation methods of Chinese provinces' sustainable development. The authors suggest improving the quality of simulation results by transforming of an orthogonal grid into a finite element system (hyper-triangles). Such an approach allows to comprehensively manage the regions' effectiveness.

The authors analyzed China provinces' social development data to test the obtained models. The analysis results concern the social development effectiveness according to the VRSio and VRSoo model from 1997 to 2021. VRSio model focused on optimizing resources while maintaining current performance indicators. VRSoo model focused on increasing revenue while maintaining current resource levels. This representation allows evaluating of the VRS-efficiency of the compared objects relative to the hyper-triangles formed by them.

The total expenditures on health care and education were taken as input variables, and the Atkinson Index, the Number of Unemployed people and GDP were taken as output variables.

In the research the authors proved the idea of some authors, like Niu Weinan and co-authors [21], Yi and Liu [22], Steblyanskaya and co-authors [7], Vasiev and co-authors[1] that the social development of some provinces is more efficiency than another one. Thus, Beijing, Guandong, Shandong has the highest level of social efficiency, while western provinces have the middle level of social development.

References

1. Vasiev, M., Bi, K., Denisov, A., Bocharnikov, V.: How coronavirus pandemics (COVID-19) influences Chinese economic sustainability. Foresight STI Govern. 14(2), 7–22 (2020). https://doi.org/10.17323/2500-2597.2020.2.7.22
2. Steblyanskaya, A.N., Wang, Z., Denisov, A.R., Bragina, Z.V.: Company sustainable growth as the result of interaction between finance, energy, environmental and social factors (in case of JSC "Gazprom"). St Petersburg Univ. J. Econ. Stud. 36(1), 134–160 (2020). https://doi.org/10.21638/spbu05.2020.107
3. Potapova, A., Wang, Z., Steblyanskaya, A.: The impact of corporate social responsibility on the company's financial performance. Korporativnye finansy = J. Corporate Fin. Res. 15(4),18–35 (2021). https://doi.org/10.17323/j.jcfr.2073-0438.15.4.2021.18-35
4. Baines, J., Morgan, B.: Sustainability appraisal: a social perspective' in sustainability appraisal. A review of international experience and practice. In: Dalal-Clayton, B., Sadler, B. (eds.), First Draft of Work in Progress. International Institute for Environment and Development, London (2004)
5. Cuthill, M.: Strengthening the 'Social' in sustainable development: developing a conceptual framework for social sustainability in a Rapid Urban Growth Region in Australia. Sustain. Dev. 18(6), 362–373 (2010)
6. Tsang, A., Frost, T., Cao, H.: Environmental, Social, and Governance (ESG) disclosure: a literature review. Br. Account. Rev. 55(1), 101149 (2023). https://doi.org/10.1016/j.bar.2022.101149

7. Steblianskaia, E., Vasiev, M., Denisov, A., Bocharnikov, V., Steblyanskaya, A., Wang, Q.: Environmental-social-governance concept bibliometric analysis and systematic literature review: do investors becoming more environmentally conscious? Environ. Sustain. Indicators **17**, 100218 (2023). https://doi.org/10.1016/j.indic.2022.100218

8. Lee, E.; Kim, G.: Analysis of domestic and international green infrastructure research trends from the ESGP perspective in South Korea. Int. J. Environ. Res. Public Health, **19**, 7099 (2022). https://doi.org/10.3390/ijerph19127099

9. Amel-Zadeh, A., Serafeim, G.: Why and how investors use ESG information: evidence from a global survey. Financ. Anal. J. **74**(3), 87–103 (2018). https://doi.org/10.2469/faj.v74.n3.2

10. Satsuk, T., Botasheva, F., Rachek, S., Pak, M.: Social economic development control and management in the context of integration transformations. In: Manakov, A., Edigarian, A. (eds.) TransSiberia. LNNS, vol. 402, pp. 37–45. Springer, Cham (2022). https://doi.org/10.1007/978-3-030-96380-4_5

11. Bernardi, C., Stark, A.W.: Environmental, social and governance disclosure, integrated reporting, and the accuracy of analyst forecasts. Br. Account. Rev. **50**(1), 16–31 (2018). https://doi.org/10.1016/j.bar.2016.10.001

12. Midgley, J.: Social Development: The Developmental Perspective in Social Welfare. SAGE Publications Ltd, London (1995)

13. Daniel, U.O.: Mathematical modelling: An introductory Guide to Practical Applied Mathematical, Modelling Techniques. Analysis and Methods. Mindex Publishing Co., Ltd Benin City (2011)

14. Dangelmayr, G., Kirbi, M.: Mathematical Modelling: A Comprehensive Introduction Prentice Hall, New Jersey 07458 (2005)

15. Charnes, A., Cooper, W.W. and Rhodes, E.: Measuring the efficiency of decision making units. Eur. J. Oper. Res. **2**, 429–444 (1978)

16. Banker, R.D., Charnes, A., Cooper, W.W.: Some models for estimating technical and scale inefficiencies in data envelopment analysis. Manage. Sci. **30**, 1078–1092 (1984)

17. Deprins, D., Simar, L., Tulkens, H.: Measuring labor-efficiency in post offices. In: M. Marchand, et al. (eds.) The Performance of Public Enterprises: Concepts and Measurement, 243-267. Elsevier, Amsterdam (1984)

18. Tulkens, H.: The performance approach in public sector economics: An introduction and an example. Annales de l'économiepublique, sociale et cooperative **57**(4), 429–443 (1986)

19. Dunford, M., Li, L.: Chinese spatial inequalities and spatial policies. Geogr. Compass **4**(8), 1039–1054 (2010)

20. Cowell, F.A.: Measurement of Inequality in Atkinson. A. B. / Bourguignon, F. (Eds): Handbook of Income Distribution. Amsterdam (2000)

21. Niu, W.: The Quality Index of China's Gross Domestic Product (GDP). China Acad. Sci. J. **1**(1), 516–525 (2011). (in Chinese)

22. Yi, H., Liu, Y.: Green economy in China: Regional variations and policy drivers. Glob. Environ. Chang. **31**, 11–19 (2015)

Dynamics of the Long-Term Orientation in Russian Society Over the Past 100 years: Results of the Analysis of the Russian Subcorpus of Google Books Ngram

Timofei Nestik[1]([✉]) [iD], Vladimir Bochkarev[2] [iD], and Vera Levina[3] [iD]

[1] Institute of Psychology of the Russian Academy of Sciences, 13 Yaroslavskaya Str., Moscow 129366, Russian Federation
nestikta@ipran.ru

[2] Kazan Federal University, Republic of Tatarstan, 18 Kremlevskaya Str., Building 1, Kazan 420008, Russian Federation
vladimir.Bochkarev@kpfu.ru

[3] Peoples Friendship University of Russia (RUDN University), 6 Miklukho-Maklaya Str., Moscow 117198, Russian Federation

Abstract. Methods of computational linguistics were used to study orientation towards long-term future as one of the characteristics of psychological state of society. Analysis of the dynamics of the use of nouns and verbs, which are semantic markers of long-term orientation, in Russian-language texts of the 20th-21st centuries was carried out. The analysis was performed employing the third version of the Russian subcorpus of Google Books Ngram presented in 2020. To identify the main trends in frequency of use of the corresponding phrases, methods of cluster analysis were employed. Our analysis shows that since the mid-1970s, the frequency of the nouns "planning", "plan", "forecasting" and "forecast" in combination with the adjective "long-term" has decreased. The frequency of use of verbs with the semantics of long-term planning had decreased from the mid-1970s to the mid-1990s, and then grew until 2018. Apparently, the revealed dynamics reflects the crisis of the planned economy, which led to the abandonment of long-term indicative planning. In addition, we have shown that since the 1960s, the frequency of use of verbs with the semantics of forecasting has been increasing, and the frequency of those with the semantics of hope, goal-setting and achievements has been decreasing. Positive correlation of linguistic markers of forecasting with the growth of the urban population, growth of per capita gross national income and overall life expectancy has been revealed. Prospects for further research in this area are outlined.

Keywords: The long-term orientation · The Russian society · Google Books Ngram

N. Agarwal et al. (Eds.): MSBC 2022, CCIS 1717, pp. 126–136, 2023.
https://doi.org/10.1007/978-3-031-33728-4_9

1 Introduction

Long-term orientation is a multidimensional phenomenon that includes value-motivational, cognitive, affective and behavioral components [22, 23]. Long-term orientation can be considered not only as a characteristic of individual, but also as a characteristic of large social groups and even society as a whole, closely related to culture and macroeconomic processes. Like social optimism, it is one of the important indicators of the psychological state of society, since it indicates the degree of the citizens faith in their own strength and the ability to their personal and collective future [24]. In this case, of particular interest is the study of the dynamics of the long-term orientation of society and its connection with economic, social and demographic processes. Case study provides opportunity for such analysis.

Analysis of linguistic markers of cultural and macropsychological changes in the 1800s - 2000s is a growing stem of research [4, 12–14, 16, 18, 28, 31, 34–36], however, in the field of corpus studies the long-term orientation as a cultural trait and its relationship with economic and demographic indicators hasn't been addressed.

In our study methods of computational linguistics were used to shed light on the orientation towards long-term future as one of the characteristics of psychological state of society. We analyzed the dynamics of the use of nouns and verbs as semantic markers of long-term orientation in Russian-language texts of the 20th-21st centuries. The analysis was performed employing the Russian subcorpus of Google Books Ngram, which is the largest diachronic corpus of the Russian language. To identify the main trends in frequency of use of the corresponding phrases, methods of cluster analysis were employed. These trends were further correlated with a number of socio-economic indicators, including the level of GDP, the number of urban population, fertility and mortality.

2 Objectives and Methods

The purpose of the study was to prove the relationship between markers of long-term orientation in Russian-language texts and socio-demographic dynamics in 1920 – 2019. The hypothesis was that the usage of long-term orientation linguistic markers correlates positively with urbanization and economic development.

In order to determine the list of the analyzed words, a lexical-semantic field was constructed and lexical markers of long-term orientation in Russian-language tests of the 20th-21st centuries were identified. The collocations with the word *dolgosrochnyj* 'long-term' (with case inflexions *-aya*, *-ye*, *-oe*) were established on the basis of the data of the National Corpus of the Russian language, which can be used in determining the semantic markers of the phenomenon of long-term orientation in the content analysis: *osnova* 'basis', *mery* 'measures', *celi* 'objectives', *tendencii* 'trends', *sledstviya* 'consequence', *vlozheniya* 'investment', *prisutstvie* 'presence', *proekty* 'projects', *programma* 'program', *plany* 'plans', *kontakty* 'contacts', *sohranenie* 'conservation', *delo* 'case', *strategiya* 'strategy', *bumagi* 'papers', *investicii* 'investment', *arenda* 'lease', *reshenie* 'decision', *preimushchestvo* 'advantage', *manevr* 'maneuver', *pozitivnye effekty* 'positive effects', *prioritet* 'priority', *finansirovanie* 'funding', *krizis* 'crisis', *razvitie* 'development', *fondirovanie* 'funding', *zaimstvovanie* 'borrowing', *den'gi* 'money', *elementy* 'elements', *ustojchivost'* 'sustainability', *instrument* 'tool', etc. [29]. In lexicographic sources the lexeme long-term is in the synonymic row: *dolgovremennyj* 'long-term', *dlitel'nyj* 'continuous', *dolgij* 'long', *fondirovannyj* 'funded' [8]. The lexeme "orientation" forms a synonymic series of 24 synonyms, of which such lexemes as *kurs* 'course', *napravlenie* 'direction', *napravlennost'* 'orientation', *nastroennost'* 'disposition', *nacelivanie* 'targeting', *ustremlennost'* 'aspiration', *tendenciya* 'tendency', etc. may be related to the semantics of "future tense" [8]. The concept of long-term orientation in economic discourse can also be semantically marked by such single lexemes and collocative constructions as: *nastojchivost'* 'persistence', *budushchee* 'future', *nepreryvnost'* 'continuity', *dolgosrochnaya perspektiva* 'long-term perspective', *vremennoj gorizont* 'time horizon', *dolgosrochnyj gorizont* 'long-term horizon', *dolgosrochnaya zhiznesposobnost'* 'long-term resilience', *planirovanie* 'planning', *prognozirovanie* 'forecasting'. Different morphological forms of words have been taken into account.

Based on the data from the National Corpus of the Russian language, 42 verbs forming word combinations with the semantics of long-term orientation were identified: *dostignut' postavlennyh zadach* 'to reach the set goals', *planirovat' na dolgij srok* 'plan over a long period of time', *prognozirovat' posledstviya* 'predict the consequences', *zhdat' v otdalennom budushchem* 'look forward to the distant future', *verit' v budushchee* 'believe in the future', *videt' budushchee* 'see the future', *vystroit' dolgosrochnye otnosheniya* 'build long-term relationships', *mechtat' o budushchem* 'dream of the future', *stavit' cel'* 'set a goal', etc. [29].

The data on frequencies of words and word combinations were obtained from Google Books Ngram corpus [20]. The third version of the Russian Google Books Ngram corpus, presented in 2020, is based on the texts of over a million books published between 1486 and 2019, with a total size of 89.4 billion words. Thus, it is the largest diachronic corpus of the Russian language. For comparison, the other largest diachronic corpus, The Russian National Corpus [29] is based on texts with a total size of 1.5 billion words. The analysis was conducted for the time interval 1920–2019. First, the texts from this period are best represented in the Google Books Ngram corpus. Second, this choice avoids the difficulties associated with the 1918 spelling reform. Since the size of the corpus varies from year to year, we used relative (i.e., normalized to the size of the corpus) frequencies everywhere.

The time series of frequencies extracted from the corpus were analyzed by cluster analysis methods to identify major trends. Since the number of classes is not known in advance, hierarchical clustering was used. We used Weighted Pair Group Method with Arithmetic Mean (WPGMA) algorithm. Cosine similarity, as well as Pearson and Spearman correlation coefficients, were used as a measure of similarity between series. The best results were obtained using the latter measure.

For the selected clusters, we plotted the total frequencies of the words assigned to these clusters, which were then compared with the series of socio-economic and demographic indicators. Statistical sociological data only covers last 100 years, since the first All-Russia population census was conducted only in 1897. Data of a rural population is taken from [32, 33,], gross domestic product (GDP) data - from [9, 19], life expectancy – from [2, 19], total fertility rate – from [30].

3 Results

An hierarchical cluster analysis of the frequency of use of nouns combined with the adjective "long-term" in 1920–2019 identified six groups of nouns (see Fig. 1): 1) "future" (*budushchee* 'future', *vremya* 'time', *plan* 'plan', *srok* 'term'); 2) "planning" (*planirovanie* 'planning', *prognoz* 'forecasting', *prognozirovanie* 'foresight'); 3) "development" (*razvitie* 'development', *cel'* 'goal'); 4) "vision" (*perspektiva* 'perspective', *strategiya* 'strategy'); 5) "relationships" (*otnosheniya* 'relations'); 6) "orientation" (*orientaciya* 'orientation, direction').

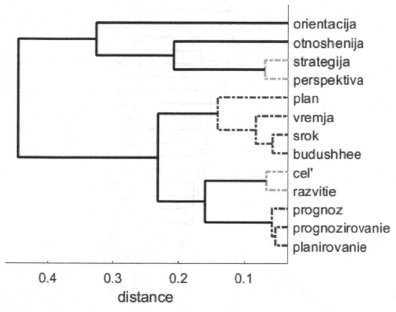

Fig. 1. Results of a hierarchical cluster analysis of the frequency of use of nouns combined with the adjective "long-term" in 1920 - 2019 (based on the Russian subcorpus of Google Books Ngram).

The results of a hierarchical cluster analysis of the frequency of use of verbs with the semantics of long-term orientation in 1920–2019 show that several groups of verbs can be identified (see Fig. 2): 1) "forecasting" (*prognozirovat'* 'to forcast', *sprognozirovat'* 'to prognose, *videt'* 'to see', *zaglyanut'* 'to look inside', *povliyat'* 'to affect', *popast'* 'to get to', *predugadat'* 'to anticipate', *smotret'* 'to watch', *formirovat'* 'to shape'); 2) "planning" (*planirovat'* 'to plan', *splanirovat'* 'to schedule'); 3) "prediction" (*predskazyvat'* 'to prophesy', *predskazat'* 'to predict'); 4) "achieving" (*dostignut'* 'to achieve', *stavit'* 'to put'); 5) "dreaming" (*mechtat'* 'to dream', *postavit'* 'to set').

The results of the cluster analysis of pronouns and nouns are in good agreement with studies of long-term orientation as a complex socio-psychological phenomenon, including future orientation, optimism and hope for rewarding efforts, long-term goal setting and planning, the value of continuous development, as well as orientation towards building long-term relationships and accumulation of social capital [3, 5, 17, 22].

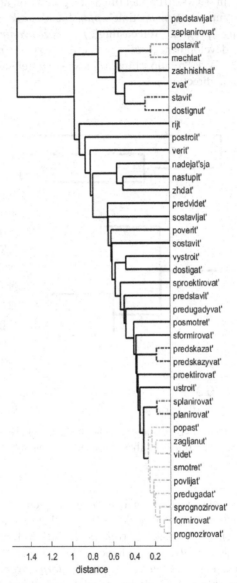

Fig. 2. Results of a hierarchical cluster analysis of the frequency of use of verbs with the semantics of long-term orientation in 1920–2019

Due to the fact that "forecasting" is located in the same cluster of nouns as "planning", it can be assumed that, unlike the use of verbs with similar meaning, the use of these nouns reflected the indicative function of forecasting in a planned economy: in official documents, forecasts were declared as the basis for plans.

For selected clusters, graphs of the total frequencies of verbs assigned to these clusters were found, which were then analyzed visually (see Fig. 3). Our analysis shows that since the mid-1970s, the frequency of the nouns of the cluster "planning", in combination with the adjective "long-term" has decreased.

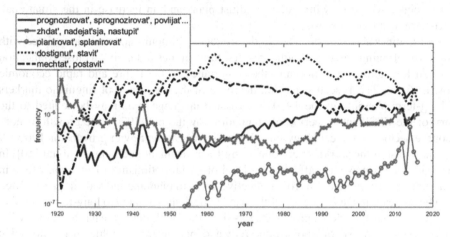

Fig. 3. Trends in the frequency of use of verbs with the semantics of long-term orientation in 1920 - 2019

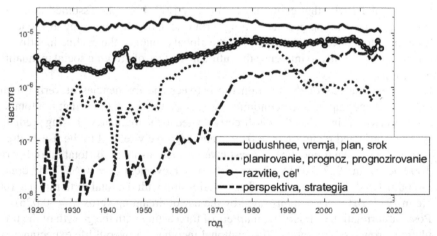

Fig. 4. Trends in the frequency of use of nouns with the semantics of long-term orientation in 1920 - 2019

The dynamics of the use of verbs of the group "planning" (*planirovat'* 'to plan', *splanirovat'* 'to schedule')" is similar to the use of nouns of the group "planning" (see Fig. 4). The frequency of use of verbs with the semantics of long-term planning had decreased from the mid-1970s to the mid-1990s (from 1976 to 1994 the decrease was 48.6%), and then grew until 2018 (from 1994 to 2018 the increase was 107%). For example, the share of the verb "to plan" in the size of the corpus for the corresponding year decreased from 0.000026% in 1976 to 0.000015% in 1984 and 0.000013% in 1996. Apparently, this reflected the decline of the planned economy. The increase in the use of the verbs *prognozirovat'* 'to forecast, to predict' and *sprognozirovat'* 'to prognose' (from 1976 to 2018 the increase in the use of the verb *prognozirovat* was 169%) can be associated with a growing need to adjust plans and an increase in the situational, short-term nature of forecasts.

Our findings about the decrease in the frequency of nouns and verbs associated with long-term planning agree well with cross-cultural studies indicating a close connection between long-term orientation and the importance of the future and rapid economic growth [6, 15, 21]. It seems that the decrease in the frequency of linguistic markers of long-term planning in the 1970s in Russian-language texts may be related to the entry of the USSR into a period of stagnation: by the mid-1970s, the growth of non-resource sectors of the economy had slowed significantly. Soviet growth for 1960–89 was the worst in the world, after controlling for investment and human capital [10]. In our opinion, this may have affected the level of social optimism of Russians, which in turn led to a shift of attention from collective goals to planning individual, private life.

The decrease in the frequency of the use of vocabulary related to long-term planning may also be related to global processes: it is since the 1970s that there has been a growing gap between the growth of labor productivity and income growth, which was reflected in the growth of depression markers in English- and Spanish-speaking texts [4]. A number of economists view the period since the 1970s as the great stagnation [7, 26]. Finally, there are indications of a decline in the rate of breakthrough discovery and innovation in the 1960s and 1970s that continues to this day [27]. It can be assumed that a key psychological factor in the decline of long-term orientation has been the awareness of the limitations to the continuous growth of the global economy, the decline in individual confidence in their ability to influence the future in the face of growing social inequalities and global risks.

Correlation analysis of the relationship between the frequencies of verb use and indicators of demographic and economic changes showed ($p < 0,05$) that the total life expectancy in Russia in 1946–2014 is directly related to the frequency of using predictive verbs ($r = 0.569$) and planning ($r = 0.574$) and negatively related to the use of dream verbs ($r = -0.378$). We found the strongest inverse relationship of the total mortality rate per 1000 people in 1927–2014 with the verbs of achievement ($r = -0.627$) and dreams ($r = -0.600$). On the contrary, the weakest relationship with the total birth rate per 1000 people in 1927–2014 was demonstrated by the use of dreaming verbs ($r = -0.026$).

Positive correlation of linguistic markers of forecasting with the growth of the urban population, growth of per capita gross national income and overall life expectancy has been revealed (see the Table 1).

At the same time, the frequency of use of the verbs with the semantics of hope is negatively related to fertility and life expectancy. It was found a negative correlation between total life expectancy and the frequency of use of the dreaming verbs.

Table 1. Relationship between the use of verbs that have the semantics of long-term orienta-tion and economic and demographic indicators.

Demographic and economic indicators	Period	Group 1 "Forecasting"	Group 2 "Planning"	Group 3 "Prediction"	Group 4 "Achieving"	Group 5 "Dreaming"
Total fertility rate (per 1000)	1927–2014	-0,861	-0,714	-0,636	-0,446	-0,026
Crude death rate (per 1000)	1927–2014	-0,385	-0,435	-0,089	-0,627	-0,6
Total rate of natural increase	1927–2014	-0,76	-0,507	-0,731	-0,023	0,49
Total fertility rate	1927–2014	-0,828	-0,683	-0,591	-0,469	-0,139
Total fertility rate of the urban population	1946–2014	0,289	0,473	0,082	0,522	-0,087
Total fertility rate of the rural population	1946–2014	0,268	0,456	0,063	0,519	-0,074
Life expectancy (male)	1927–2014	0,678	0,69	0,389	0,592	0,324
Life expectancy (women)	1927–2014	0,746	0,71	0,464	0,562	0,263
Total life expectancy	1946–2014	0,569	0,574	0,378	0,305	-0,378
Share of urban residents in total population	1926–2014	0,794	0,407	0,5	0,271	-0,079
Per capita gross national income (1990$)	1920–2012	0,823	0,918	0,538	0,595	0,254

(continued)

Table 1. (*continued*)

Demographic and economic indicators	Period	Group 1 "Forecasting"	Group 2 "Planning"	Group 3 "Prediction"	Group 4 "Achieving"	Group 5 "Dreaming"
Per capita gross national income (1990$)	1960–2012	0,442	0,78	0,362	-0,256	-0,283

Based on the results of the correlational analysis we can suggest that urbanization and the growth of orientation towards individualistic values increase the need for forecasting and planning of the individual future. On the contrary, the experience of collective threats and orientation towards collectivist values increase hope and orientation towards collective goals, that is, the construction of a positive collective future that performs the functions of protecting a positive group identity.

4   Conclusion

The features of the dynamics of the use of dreaming verbs that we have discovered allow us to put forward a hypothesis about the compensatory nature of dreams in a crisis and their direct connection with the level of collectivism and generalized trust in society. The data obtained are consistent with other results of the analysis of linguistic markers of cultural changes in the 1800s–2000s: for example, an increase in socioeconomic status and an increase in tolerance for violations of the social order are associated with an increase in the level of individualism [12, 31, 34], focus on individual achievement [13], creativity and scientific and technological development [16].

Apparently, the urbanization and atomization of society strengthens the orientation towards forecasting and planning the individual future. It can be assumed that the experience of a collective threat and an orientation towards collectivistic values enhance the construction of a positive collective future that performs the functions of protecting a positive group identity.

Recognizing the limitations of this study, we should take into account not only the different size of texts representing certain years, but also the wide time interval we have chosen from 1920 to 2014. The first half of this period is less represented in the corpus, but the years of intensive industrialization fell on it, which could affect the results of the correlation analysis.

Further research is needed to clarify the relationship between the various components of long-term orientation and the expression of individualistic and collectivistic values in culture.

Also promising is the analysis of the relationship between long-term orientation and the dynamics of anxiety and depression in Russian, English, German and Spanish texts. Such studies of the dynamics of the psychological state of society can help to take another step towards the development of mathematical models of social processes and the creation of digital twins that allow predicting the impact of economic changes on the psychological well-being of large social groups.

Acknowledgements. This research was financially supported by the Russian Foundation for Basic Research, grant №19–29-07463.

References

1. Aggarwal, C.C., Reddy, C.K. (Eds.): Data Clustering: Algorithms and Applications. 1st edn. Chapman and Hall/CRC (2014)
2. Andreev, E.M., Darsky, L.E., Harkova, T.L.: Demographic history of Russia: 1927–1959. Moscow (1998)
3. Bearden, W.O., Money, R.B., Nevins, J.L.: A measure of long-term orientation: development and validation. J. Acad. Mark. Sci. **34**, 456–467 (2006)
4. Bollen, J., et al.: Historical language records reveal a surge of cognitive distortions in recent decades. PNAS **118**(30), e2102061118 (2021)
5. Brigham, K.H., Lumpkin, G.T., Payne, G.T., Zachary, M.A.: Researching long-term orientation: a validation study and recommendations for future research. Fam. Bus. Rev. **27**(1), 72–88 (2014)
6. Bukowski, A., Rudnicki, S.: Not only individualism: the effects of long-term orientation and other cultural variables on national innovation success. Cross-Cult. Res. **53**(2), 119–162 (2019)
7. Cowen, T.: The Great Stagnation: How America Ate All The Low-Hanging Fruit of Modern History, Got Sick, and Will (Eventually) Feel Better. Dutton, New York (2011)
8. Dictionary of Russian Synonyms. http://web-corpora.net/synonyms. Accessed 21 Nov 2022
9. Dzis-Voynarovskiy, N.: The graph of the century: Russia's economy for 1913–2012 years. Moscow (2012)
10. Easterly, W., Fischer, S., DEC: The Soviet economic decline: historical and republican data. Policy Research Working Paper Series 1284, The World Bank (1994)
11. Everitt, B.: Cluster analysis. Wiley, UK (2011)
12. Greenfield, P.: The changing psychology of culture from 1800 through 2000. Psychol. Sci. **24**(9), 1722–1731 (2013)
13. Grossmann, I., Varnum, M.: Social structure, infectious diseases, disasters, secularism, and cultural change in America. Psychol. Sci. **26**(3), 311–324 (2015)
14. Hills, T., Proto, E., Sgroi, D., Seresinhe, C.: Historical analysis of national subjective wellbeing using millions of digitized books. Nat. Hum. Behav. **3**, 1271–1275 (2019)
15. Hofstede, G., Minkov, M.: Long- versus short-term orientation: new perspectives. Asia Pac. Bus. Rev. **16**(4), 493–504 (2010)
16. Jackson, J., Gelfand, M., De, S., Fox, A.: The loosening of American culture over 200 years is associated with a creativity–order trade-off. Nat. Hum. Behav. **3**(3), 244–250 (2019)
17. Joireman, J., King, S.: Individual differences in the consideration of future and (more) immediate consequences: a review and directions for future research. Soc. Pers. Psychol. Compass **10**(5), 313–326 (2016)
18. Lorenz-Spreen, P., Mønsted, B., Hövel, P., Lehmann, S.: Accelerating dynamics of collective attention. Nat. Commun. **10**, 1759 (2019)
19. Markevich, A., Harrison, M.: Great war, civil war, and recovery: Russia's national income, 1913 to 1928. J. Econ. Hist. **71**(3), 672–703 (2011)

20. Michel, J.-B., et al.: Quantitative analysis of culture using millions of digitized books. Science 331(6014), 176–182 (2011)
21. Milfont, T. L., Gapski, E.: Cross-cultural differences in time orientations: integrating culture-level data. In: Paper presented at the 20th Congress of the International Association for Cross-Cultural Psychology, Melbourne, Australia (2010)
22. Nestik, T.: Long-term orientation of the person: the state and prospects of research. Institut psihologii Rossiĭskoĭ akademii nauk. Social'naya i ekonomicheskaya psihologiya 5(3), 110–140 (2020). http://soc-econom-psychology.ru/engine/documents/document830.pdf
23. Nestik, T.: Socio-psychological predictors and types of personal long-term orientation. Psihologicheskij Zhurnal 42(4), 28 (2021)
24. Nestik, T., Selezneva, A., Shestopal, E., Yurevich, A.: Problema psikhologicheskogo sostoyaniya obshchestva i politicheskikh protsessov v sovremennoi Rossii. Voprosy Psikhologii 67(5), 3–14 (2021)
25. Nestik, T.: Obraz budushchego, sotsial'nyi optimizm i dolgosrochnaya orientatsiya rossiyan: sotsial'no-psikhologicheskii analiz. SotsioDigger 9(14), 6–48 (2021)
26. Pagano, P., and Sbracia, M.: The secular stagnation hypothesis: a review of the debate and some insights. Bank of Italy Occasional Paper No. 231 (2014)
27. Park, M., Leahey, E., Funk, R.J.: Papers and patents are becoming less disruptive over time. Nature 613, 138–144 (2023)
28. Rautionaho, P., Nurmi, A., Klemola, J. (eds.): Corpora and the changing society: studies in the evolution of English. John Benjamins, Amsterdam and Philadelphia (2020)
29. RNC, The Russian National Corpus, 2003—2022, http://ruscorpora.ru. Accessed 21 Nov 2022
30. Russia, Total fertility rate, 1960–2019, Demoscope Weekly (03.09.2020), http://www.demoscope.ru/weekly/ssp/rus_tfre.php. Accessed 21 Nov 2022
31. Solovyev, V., Bochkarev, V., Kaveeva, A.: Variations of social psychology of Russian society in last 100 Years. In: 2015 IEEE International Conference on Smart City/SocialCom/SustainCom (SmartCity), pp. 519–523. IEEE, Chengdu, China (2015)
32. Statistical year-book of Russia, 2014: statistical compilation/Goskomstat of Russia. Moscow (2014)
33. The population of Russia for 100 years (1897–1997): statistical compilation. Goskomstat of Russia, Moscow (1998)
34. Velichkovsky, B., Solovyev, V., Bochkarev, V., Ishkineeva, F.: Transition to market economy promotes individualistic values: analysing changes in frequencies of Russian words from 1980 to 2008. Int. J. Psychol. 54(1), 23–32 (2019)
35. Younes, N., Reips, U.-D.: The changing psychology of culture in German-speaking countries: a Google Ngram study. Int. J. Psychol. 53(S1), 53–62 (2018)
36. Yu, F., et al.: Cultural value shifting in pronoun use. J. Cross Cult. Psychol. 47(2), 310–316 (2016)

Sustainable Development Issues of the Belt and Road Initiative in Educational Modeling Cases

Alina Steblyanskaya ⓘ and Zhinan Wang⁽✉⁾ ⓘ

School of Economics and Management, Harbin Engineering University, Harbin, China
alina_steblyanskaya@hrbeu.edu.cn, wzn6768@163.com

Abstract. China's Belt and Road Initiative (BRI) is a massive development plan in scale and scope. It aims at facilitating China's connectivity with the rest of the world through trade, investment, and infrastructure projects. Therefore, understanding the human and social dynamics and socio-behavioral tendencies through Belt and Road development, and quantifying, and mapping the spatial-temporal distribution of environmental vulnerability caused by natural and human-made impacts are needed for understanding environmental protection and Road restoration issues. Understanding the trends in ecological, cultural and behavioral evolution and their driving factors is critical to revealing changes in ecosystem's structure and function. However, less is known about the nonlinear relationship between greening trends and statistical instrumentation. Thus, we want to share HEU experience concerning new Business Statistics cause implementation. In the example of a practical case concerning Belt and Road initiative development, the authors show for students sampling distribution and sampling modeling processes, and understand their implementations. On the example of Belt and Road case, the students learn sampling to collect data and the theorems of sampling distribution.

Keywords: China University · Education for Sustainable Development (ESD) · Sustainable Development Goals · Business Statistics course · "Belt and Road" modelling · Ecological Civilization

1 Introduction

Sustainability is an umbrella concept encompassing modern solutions for an improved society and environment [1]. The eminent quest to construct sustainable resolutions for environmental degradation requires many attractive pillars, including an environmentally responsible economy development [2]. But even if weighing cost against benefits does not entirely answer what should be done about implementing environmentally-oriented behaviour or responsible production and consumption, it is an essential part of the answer [3, 4]. The sustainability or green economy framework needs a better understanding of the ethical concepts for supporting responsible decisions for Nature protection [5, 6]. The crucial moral problem is to focus on environmental protection issues, and how to encourage people to make environmentally-oriented decisions. Environmentally-oriented ethics is the treasure part of knowledge that people will investigate in the nearest future [7, 8].

In the paper the authors give attention to the Education for Sustainable Development (ESD) as education that promotes changes in knowledge, skills, values and attitudes to create a more sustainable and equitable society for all [9, 10]. ESD is a dimension component in the indicator for Sustainable Development Goal 12 (SDG) for "responsible consumption and production". SDG 12 has 11 goals, and target 12.8 is "By 2030, ensure that people around the world have relevant information and awareness about sustainable development and lifestyles in harmony with nature" [11]. According to the research by Clark, William K. and Alicia G. Harley, from the article "The Science of Sustainability: Towards a Synthesis", the capacity linking knowledge to action is one of the primary forms of implementing sustainable development [12].

The authors consider the Business Statistics course as a base for achieving SDG 12 and SDG 13. The authors built the practical cases for Ecological Civilization sustainable development under Belt and Road initiative. The introduction of HEU statistical cases regarding the Belt and Road' sustainable development has enriched the statistical course. Using survey methodology, students can build understandable models and learn how to use various programs to build models. We show the students the unity and interconnection of society, culture and natural factors in achieving ecologically oriented life through Belt and Road construction.

The rest of the paper is organized the following way: Sect. 2 outlines the preliminary literature review concerning sustainable education. Section 3 describes 4 cases methodology; the results of data analysis are presented in Sect. 4. Finally, in the conclusion remarks the authors indicate research limitations and future research directions and give a few concluding recommendations.

2 Literature Review

2.1 Belt and Road Initiative Towards Sustainability in Education

BRI is a transcontinental long-term policy and investment program which aims at infrastructure development and acceleration of the economic integration of countries along the route of the historic Silk Road. The Initiative was unveiled in 2013 by China's president Xi Jinping and until 2016, was known as Belt and Road Initiative. On March 28, 2015, the official outline for the Belt and Road Initiative was issued by the National Development and Reform Commission (NDRC), the Ministry of Foreign Affairs (MOFA) and the Ministry of Commerce (MOFCOM) of the People's Republic of China (PRC), with authorization of the State Council [13]. According to the official outline, BRI aims to "promote the interrelation between Asian, European and African continents an establish all-dimensional, multi-tiered and composite connectivity networks, and realize diversified, independent, balanced and sustainable development in these countries."[1]

Increased cooperation and joint action by the Belt and Road countries in education are an important part of what the Belt and Road Initiative aims to achieve, and in turn, can provide the talent needed to make the Initiative a success. Thus, in July 2016, Ministry of Education of the People's Republic of China issued "Education Action Plan for

---

[1] *The Belt and Road Big Data Service Platform on Ecological and Environ-mental Protection.* www.greenbr.org.cn, *last accessed 2022/11/13.*

the Belt and Road Initiative"[2]. The plan has 6 sections, like mission of education, principles and priorities for cooperation, chinese education in action and working together to create bright future for education. This official government publication demonstrates the importance that China places on education within the BRI. Some recipient countries face difficulties providing basic higher education, while others have problems related to the quality, efficiency and cost of higher education. This, in turn, has an effect on the availability of skilled labour. Workers and students in the recipient countries need to be trained with the appropriate skills to be employed as part of the BRI [14, 15].

2.2 Education Towards SDG Implementation

Promoting sustainability is essential to resolving the world's environmental and social challenges, including climate change, environmental degradation, conflict and injustice, and poverty and inequality [16]. In articulating the Sustainable Development Goals (SDGs) in 2015, the United Nations (UN) positioned sustainability as the critical issue shaping our future. The subsequent COVID-19 pandemic has been hailed a catalyst for management educators to reconsider, and perhaps recalibrate, how best to serve the people and planet by fostering greater compassion and collaboration, to overcome longstanding neglect of ecosystems and social wellbeing.

Over the past few decades, future sustainability has been framed as requiring equilibrium or a balance between societal, environmental and economic interests [17]. Sometimes cast as 'people, planet and profit', these interconnected dimensions have served as the classic three-pillar framework guiding sustainability, including sustainable management education and triple bottom line corporate reporting [18, 19, 20]. The economic pillar of sustainable development encompasses the global economy, as well as corresponding business activities responsible for many negative environmental and social impacts, such as industrial pollution and unsustainable consumption. It has therefore been recognised that future sustainability requires the education of governments, businesses and consumers to more consciously create positive environmental and societal outcomes, rather than only focusing on financial outcomes [21]. Financial targets have often been realised via production cost-cutting, fuelled by an excessive consumption culture that demands low prices. Since environmentally-friendly manufacturing practices and corresponding sustainable products are generally more costly and less convenient, these options are often overlooked by governments, businesses and consumers [22]. Educators therefore need to consider how they can facilitate a shift away from these unsustainable attitudes and behaviours, which could include a global citizenship pathway and improved sustainability curricula [23, 24]

3 Methodology

Nowadays, when the environmental agenda has become the most relevant, more and more attention is paid to education with elements of sustainable development (see **Fig. 1**).

---

[2] *Education Action Plan for the Belt and Road Initiative - Xinhua Silk Road (imsilkroad.com), last accessed 2022/11/13.*

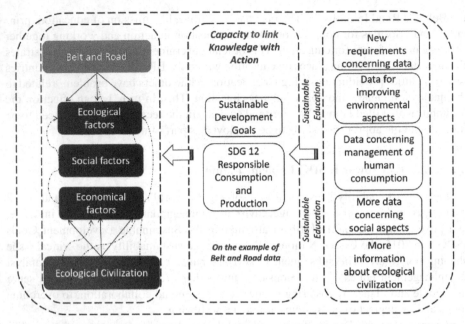

Fig. 1. Authors vision of the BRI ecologically-oriented sustainable education case-studies background.

The scheme shows the concept of implementing the sustainable development goals in a Business statistics course. The authors built the course based on the SDG 12 "responsible consumption and production" as the primary goal for achieving sustainable education. A vital condition for our cases was the importance of the connection between knowledge and action. Thus, by mean of practical cases, we hoped to enrich HEU students sustainable education. First, we have introduced new requirements for the use of environmentally-oriented Belt and Road data, as well as data described the social and economic development. We gave student more data concerning ecological civilization, any social aspects and data concerning management of human consumption as a new requirements to the data set [25]. Then, we asked students to build the cases oriented on the SDG 12 and develop interactions between economy, environmental, and social data under the Belt and Road initiative.

For the Business Statistics course environmental-oriented case-study, we use data from the Belt and Road Initiative official web-site http://eng.greenbr.org.cn/ or making the research questionnaire in two languages – in Chinese and English. In this case we use survey methodology. Thus, the research questionnaires with answers could be found on the website Wenjianxing, https://www.wjx.cn/vj/h46hUOc.aspx and in supplementary materials.

The green economy has a correlative role with the implementation of SDGs, which could revive human well-being, social equity, and substantially decrease environmental risks and ecological scarcities. But how the green activities correlate with the students' expectations and evaluation of the green future? Are people ready to do something necessary to support Nature?

On this case example, the authors show to the students the unity and interconnection of society, culture and nature factors in the way to achieving ecological oriented life through Belt and Road construction.

This case is about Sampling and sampling distribution; thus students need to compile survey and manage it. On the example of this practical case concerning Sampling and Sampling Distributions, the students should learn how to compile surveys and how to ask questions. New economic practices and policies need to be developed towards sustainable development goals (SDGs). In this case we do Survey and evaluate the survey results.

First, for our Survey we have developed scenarios with six hypotheses inside:

1. Plastic Bag (PB) with a hypothesis: "Better to buy a plastic bag that is cheaper".
2. Violated contract (VC): "My lawyer says there is a loophole through which contracts with long-term partner can be terminated and contract with new partner could be signed. Everyone must choose better decision for his profit".
3. Eco-meeting (EM): "It is necessary to go to the eco-meeting while they didn't send me an invitation. It is necessary to find information about the meeting".
4. GDP control (GDP): "The correlation between economic growth and the environmental protection is overstated".
5. Eco-civilization (EC):" The ego-cantered humanism with the dominant of freedom must be replaced by the eco-centric humanism with the dominant of responsibility".
6. My responsibility (MR): "The environmental movement can facilitate the solution to the problem as a social influence of the population on the management of the climate-determining business".

The research survey process can reveal students' valid opinions, enable them to share ideas in a safe and comfortable environment [26]. The authors used the following steps to manage the survey process: (1) To determine who will participate in the survey (in our case students); (2) To decide the type of survey (in our case online and in-person), (3) To design the survey questions and layout (we need to ask about six situations); (4) To distribute the survey (in our case through the University information system); (5) To aanalyse the responses (through the online system and offline calculations); (6) To analyse the result; (7) To give feedback to students concerning research results. The full survey process description the authors show in Fig. 2.

The research is based on the School of Economics and Management, Harbin Engineering University (SEM HEU), China (2875 students). Selection units: course, person. We have formed a sample in three stages. At the first step, we were looking for respondents from the School of Economics and Management' faculties. Then we selected students based on the grade, thus, we chose, bachelors, masters and doctors. Finally, at the last step, we got the final sample and proceeded to the survey.

To calculate the sample size, we used the Rukavishnikov formula [27]:

$$n = [30; 50] \times k_1 \times k_2$$

where:

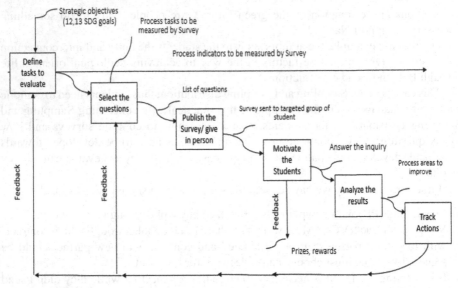

Fig. 2. Survey processes

n – sample size

k_1 – the number of gradations of the first attribute

k_2 – the number of gradations of the second attribute

In our case:

k_1 – the number of degrees of the level of education (bachelor's, master's, doctoral studies)

k_2 – number of faculties-departments (statistics, enterprise economics, green and energy economics, international economics)

Thus, we determined the boundaries of our sample size: 360 – the minimum number of respondents, 600 – the maximum. Therefore, our study involved 517 people of different ages, 240 men and 277 women, less than 25 years old – 291 people, 25–35-year-old - 169 people, 35–45-year-old – 42 people and more than 45 years old – 15 people, totally 276 people with education no less than bachelor degree and 241- with master and doctoral degree.

$$\Delta = Z\sqrt{\frac{pq}{n}}, \text{ where}$$

n- sample size

Z- is a coefficient that depends on the confidence interval chosen by the researcher

p- p is the proportion of respondents with the presence of the studied trait

q = 1-p is the proportion of respondents who do not have the studied futured. Δ-the maximum sampling error

We calculate the error of a sample of 2875 people at a 95% confidence level, if the general population is significantly larger than the sample size:

$$\Delta = 1,95\sqrt{\frac{0,5*0,5}{2875}} = \pm1,82\%$$

If a sample of 2,875 people is used for the study, then for conclusions on the sample as a whole, the error is 1.82%, which is quite acceptable for evaluating the decisions made.

The analysis addresses only ethical acceptability, not optimality. Therefore, in our study we focused on the ethical reasons for achieving environmentally-oriented decisions.

Confirmatory factor analysis and tests of predictive reliability on six one-dimensional ethical indicators showed that this revised measure exceeded the predictive one and corresponded to the realities. The results showed that 51% of respondents had chosen the environmental – oriented behaviour, 31% of the respondents have the neutral position and 18% do not care about ecological questions at all (see Table 1).

Table 1. Evaluation results

SDG	Abbr	1	2	3	4	5	6
12 Responsible production and consumption	Plastic bag (PG)	53%	11%	10%	9%	9%	8%
	Violated contract (VC)	37%	17%	16%	11%	9%	9%
	Eco-meeting (EM)	13%	11%	13%	15%	14%	33%
13 Climate Action	GDP changes (GDP)	42%	13%	14%	13%	9%	9%
	Eco-civilization (EC)	11%	7%	20%	19%	21%	23%
	My responsibility (R)	9%	3%	19%	20%	24%	25%

Table 1 shows that many people do not care about the SDG at all, are frustrated with the ecological questions and don't want to take action for Nature conservation. Thus, concerning SDG 12 41% involves environmental questions, 14% almost discuss ecological conservation issues. However, 20% of interviewees do not care about ecological matters (see Figs. 3 and 4).

The most "heart-touching" situation in environmental protection was the situation with plastic bags: 64% preferred to use nature-oriented bags from another material. 54% of the respondents are also against violated contracts if it would be helpful for the environment. However, only 24% of the respondent in "Eco-meeting" situation ready to act, to move for the purpose of environmental protection. Concerning SDG 13 situation is even worse. 55% of people involve with ecological questions and have understandings concerning GDP growth and industrial postilions. However, only 18% involves with the "Ecological civilization" points of view. And only 11% ready to take responsibility about environmental issues.

First PG scenario action "Better to buy a plastic bag that is cheaper" shows that totally 53% of respondents chose the environmental – oriented behaviour with only 8%

of respondents replied that it is "Just" and "Fair" behaviour. For 42% of respondents to buy plastic bag if Nature is damage is culturally unacceptable and morally wrong. However, from 6% till 11% of the respondents will buy it nevertheless circumstances. The 67% of respondents sure that buying plastic bags is action violated the unspoken duty before society, however almost 6% have their own position without any reference to the standard commitment. Indeed, the ethics problem with plastic bags in oceans is enormous and many researchers and students try to start investigations concerning this theme. Plastics that were initially created to help humans are now destroying the environment and hurting human and animal health. First, we need efforts to lessen our consumption and reduce wastes to prevent pollution. Second, we need efforts to clean up the plastic in the ocean. Third, we need efforts to develop our communities more sustainably.

Second VC scenario action "My lawyer says there is a loophole through which contracts can be terminated. The research results show that the respondents chose better decision for their profit. Results showed that only 37% chose the environmental – oriented behaviour. 37–40% of respondents answered that terminated contract behaviour was "Just", and only 10% emphasized their negative position. Other respondents have a neutral position or "not decided for themselves" positions. It is a matter of concern that for 30% of respondents terminated contract is "culturally acceptable" and "morally right" or "violated the unspoken duty before society" and only 6% of respondents were disagree with this position. Thus, we can see that profit -oriented behaviour are dominant among people.

Third EM scenario action "It is necessary to go to the environmental protection meeting, even though they didn't send me an invitation" shows that only 33% chose the environmental – oriented behaviour. Thus, 34% of respondents replied that they would go to seek information about the meeting nevertheless they have no invitation. However, only 12% of the respondents answered that going to seek the meeting without invitation is "culturally acceptable" or "morally right" for them. And 38% of the respondent decided that this action violated the unspoken duty before society and only 14% negatively replied that not violated at all.

Fourth GDP scenario action "The relationship between economic growth and the state of the environment is overstated" shows that totally 42% chose the environmental – oriented behaviour ("Just", "Fair", "Culturally acceptable"). Thus, in general, respondents understand that progress leads to the killing of Nature, unless people change the types of consumption. However, we found some narrow understandings concerning morality. Thus, people don't understand that economic growth can immoral or could violate society's unspoken duty.

Fifth EC scenario action "The ego-cantered humanism with the dominant of freedom should be replaced by the eco-centric humanism with the dominant of responsibility." shows that totally 53% agree with trends to sustainable and environmental – oriented behaviour. However, the majority of respondents do not have a clear answer to the question. That is why the majority adheres to a neutral position. Only about 20% of respondents answer with a clear agreement that the transition to Eco-civilization is morally correct. The rest part of respondents adheres to a neutral position.

Sixth MR scenario action "The environmental movement can facilitate the solution to the problem as a social influence of the population on the management of the climate-determining business" shows that totally 49% chose the environmental – oriented behaviour. However, only a quarter of respondents have an explicit idea that it is necessary to take green technologies and environmentally-oriented behaviour. The remaining three-quarters of the respondents do not understand what steps they should take.

4 Conclusion

In the paper, the authors gave attention to the sustainable development, green finance and environmental-oriented education questions [28]. In the research the authors proved the idea of Yan Jun and co-authors that ESD promotes changes in knowledge, skills, values and attitudes to create a more sustainable and equitable society for all [29].

The authors considered the Business Statistics course as a base for explaining necessety to achieve sustainable development goals. The authors shared the Business Statistics case-study as an example to explain how students can involve environmentally-oriented problems in the educational process. The case aimed to improve learning skills under the Belt and Road framework. As a result, the authors formed among students a global vision of environmentally-oriented ethical behaviour using the Belt and Road as an example.

In these case-study, results showed that many students do not care about the SDG, are frustrated with the ecological questions and don't want to take action for Nature conservation. Thus, concerning SDG 12 41% involves environmental questions, 14% almost discuss ecological conservation issues. However, 20% of interviewees do not care about environmental matters.

References

1. Ivlev, V.Y., Ivleva, M.I., Ivleva, M.L.: Ethical aspects of the theory of green economy. In: Proceedings of the 2nd International Conference on Contemporary Education, Social Sciences and Ecological Studies (CESSES 2019), vol. 356, (2019). https://doi.org/10.2991/cesses-19.2019.245
2. Abid, N., Ceci, F., Ceci, F., Aftab, J.: Financial development and green innovation, the ultimate solutions to an environmentally sustainable society: evidence from leading economies. J. Clean. Prod. 369 (2022). https://doi.org/10.1016/j.jclepro.2022.133223
3. Peña-Vinces, J., Solakis, K., Guillen, J.: Environmental knowledge, the collaborative economy and responsible consumption in the context of second-hand perinatal and infant clothes in Spain, Resources, Conservation and Recycling, vol. 159, 104840 (2020). ISSN 0921-3449.https://doi.org/10.1016/j.resconrec.2020.104840
4. Broome, J.: The ethics of climate change. Inaugural Roseman Lecture in Practical Ethics. University of Toronto, 23 October (2009)
5. Akhtar, R., Sultana, S., Masud, M.M., Jafrin, N., Al-Mamun, A.: Consumers' environmental ethics, willingness, and green consumerism between lower and higher income groups. Resour. Conserv. Recycl. **168**(105274), 591–600 (2021). https://doi.org/10.1016/j.resconrec.2020.105274

6. Steblyanskaya, A., Bobylev, S., Yan, J.: Green economy for nature conservation: new paradigm for the future. BRICS J. Econ. **3**(4), 203–207 (2022). https://doi.org/10.3897/brics-econ.3.98753

7. Pla-Julián, I., Guevara, S.: Is circular economy the key to transitioning towards sustainable development? Challenges Perspect. Care Ethics, Futures **105**, 67–77 (2019). https://doi.org/10.1016/j.futures.2018.09.001

8. Vasiev, M., Bi, K., Denisov, A., Bocharnikov, V.: How coronavirus pandemics (COVID-19) influences Chinese economic sustainability. Foresight STI Gov. **14**(2), 7–22 (2020). https://doi.org/10.17323/2500-2597.2020.2.7.22

9. Kalsoom, Q., et al.: Inquiry into sustainability issues by preservice teachers: a pedagogy to enhance sustainability consciousness. J. Clean. Prod. (2017)

10. Vargas, C.M.A.: Sustainable development education: averting or mitigating cultural collision. Int. J. Educ. Dev. (2000)

11. Sterling, S.: sustainable education: re-visioning learning and change, schumacher briefing № 6. Green Books for the Schumacher Society, Dartington, p. 94 (2001). https://www.greenbooks.co.uk/sustainable-education

12. Clark, W.C., Harley, A.G.: Sustainability science: towards a synthesis. Sustainability Science Program Working Paper 2019–01, John F. Kennedy School of Government, Harvard University, Cambridge (2019)

13. Yii, K.J., Bee, K.Y., Cheam, W.L., Chong, Y.M., Lee, C.: Is Transportation Infrastructure Important to the One Belt One Road (OBOR) Initiative? Empirical Evidence from the Selected Asian Countries. Sustainability, 10(11) (2018)

14. United Nation environment programme, Emissions gas report 2019, https://www.unep.org/resources/emissions-gap-report-2019. Accessed 10 Nov 2022

15. Liu, B., Efimova, O., Vasiev, M., Quan, W.: Belt and road initiative for environmental economic development: a case study of cooperation between China and Russia in transport sector. BRICS J. Econ. **3**(4), 299–316 (2022). https://doi.org/10.3897/brics-econ.3.91318

16. Hansmann, R., Mieg, H.A., Frischknecht, P.M.: Principal sustainability components: empirical analysis of synergies between the three pillars of sustainability. Int. J. Sustain. Dev. World **19**, 451–459 (2012)

17. Elkington, J.: Towards the sustainable corporation: win-win-win business strategies for sustainable development. Calif. Manage. Rev. **36**(2), 90–100 (1994). https://doi.org/10.2307/41165746

18. Elkington, J.: Cannibals with Forks: The Triple Bottom Line of 21st Century Business. New Society Publishers, Gabriola Island, Stony Creek (1998)

19. Savelyeva, T., Douglas, W.: Global consciousness and pillars of sustainable development: a study on self-perceptions of the first-year university students. Int. J. Sustain. High. Educ. **18**(2), 218–241 (2017). https://doi.org/10.1108/IJSHE-04

20. Hunter, M.C., Smith, R.G., Schipanski, M.E., Atwood, L.W., Mortensen, D.A.: Agriculture in 2050: recalibrating targets for sustainable intensification. Bioscience **67**(4), 386–391 (2017). https://doi.org/10.1093/biosci/bix010

21. Greenland, S., Levin, E., Dalrymple, J.F., O'Mahony, B.: Sustainable innovation adoption barriers: water sustainability, food production and drip irrigation in Australia. Soc. Responsib. J. **15**(6), 727–741 (2019)

22. Estelles, M., Fischman, G.E.: Who needs global citizenship education? A review of the literature on teacher education. J. Teach. Educ. **72**(2), 223–236 (2021). https://doi.org/10.1177/0022487120920254

23. Khoo, S.M., Jørgensen, N.J.: Intersections and collaborative potentials between global citizenship education and education for sustainable development. Glob. Soc. Educ. **19**(4), 470–481 (2021). https://doi.org/10.1080/14767724.2021.1889361

24. Aoyama, R.: "One Belt, One Road": China's new global strategy. J. Contemp. East Asia Stud. **5**(2), 3–22 (2016). https://doi.org/10.1080/24761028.2016.11869094

25. Nikulchev, E., Gusev, A., Ilin, D., Gazanova, N., Malykh, S.: Evaluation of user reactions and verification of the authenticity of the user's identity during a long web survey. Appl. Sci. **11**(22), 11034 (2021). https://doi.org/10.3390/app112211034

26. Rukavishnikov, V.: Public opinion structures and environmental concerns in modern Russia. The "Current Developments in Environmental Sociology" Symposium, Woudshoth (1992)

27. Bacchetti, P., Wolf, L.E., Segal, M.R., McCulloch, C.E.: Ethics and sample size. Am. J. Epidemiol. **161**(2), 105–110 (2005)

28. Steblyanskaya, A., Wang, Z., Gabdrahmanova, N.: Mathematical dynamic model for "green finance" sustainable growth. Int. J. Q. Res. (Serbian' journal), 15(1) 259–27 (2021). https://doi.org/10.24874/IJQR15.01-15

29. Yan, J., Feng, L., Steblyanskaya, A., Kleiner, G., Rybachuk, M.: Biophysical economics as a new economic paradigm. Int. J. Public Adm. **2**(7), 2019 (2019)

Carbon Dioxide Emissions Modelling Along the Route Using Various Transportation Modes

Maksim Vasiev[1]($\boxtimes$) (iD), Olga Efimova[2] (iD), Evgeniy Baboshin[2] (iD), Irina Matveeva[3] (iD), and Olga Malysheva[2] (iD)

[1] School of Economics and Management, Harbin Engineering University, Harbin, China
vasievmp@hrbeu.edu.cn

[2] Department of Economics, Organization and Management of Production, Russian University of Transport (RUT MIIT), Moscow, Russia

[3] Department of International Finance and Accounting, Russian University of Transport (RUT MIIT), Moscow, Russia

Abstract. Growth trends in global demand for passenger and freight transportation will lead to the growth of the transport sector of the economy by 2050 more than double. Such growth is a sign of social and economic progress, the inevitable concomitant of which is increased energy consumption, carbon dioxide emissions and air pollution. In this regard, the economic assessment of the environmental component of the transportation industry becomes relevant. In the paper the authors consider a transport route as an example of the green route formation. The primary criterion is to minimize the carbon footprint when delivering goods from the starting point of Krasnoyarsk to the station Hani. To select a transportation option based on the volume of emissions, the authors calculated options for all route sections, which can be structured according to the "data cube" methodology. The calculations show that a complete railway route is preferable to transportation by road, because the volume of emissions of 1.87 tons is almost 500 times less than by road transport. Nevertheless, it is necessary to consider a more significant number of parameters for a more accurate comparison of the efficiency of transportation routes.

Keywords: carbon dioxide emissions from cargo transportation · the carbon footprint of railway transportation · modelling

1 Introduction

In the context of the 2030 Agenda for Sustainable Development, the transition to sustainable transport systems plays a central role in the changes needed for economic equality, and the creation of social-oriented infrastructure [1–3]. Railway transportation is well suited to urban needs in an increasingly urbanized world. High-speed rail can be an alternative to short-haul air travel, and conventional and freight rail can complement other modes of transport for efficient mobility.

N. Agarwal et al. (Eds.): MSBC 2022, CCIS 1717, pp. 148–157, 2023.
https://doi.org/10.1007/978-3-031-33728-4_11

In 2015, the Paris Agreement was signed, under which countries committed to reducing their greenhouse gas emissions. Since then, the development of a low-carbon economy began: taxes and duties began to be introduced on products with a high carbon footprint, goods and raw materials acquired a new characteristic. The companies are forced to reduce their carbon footprint in whatever way they can to support competitiveness [4, 5].

Since 2016 much attention has been paid to the issues of long-term scenarios for reducing greenhouse gas emissions in Russia, and the accompanying effects from the implementation of these scenarios, including environmental consequences, impact on the environment and public health, aspects of low-carbon development have been considered. In Russia new goals were established: keeping the net greenhouse gas emissions below 70–75% of the 1990 level, with a likely shift in targets to 60–65% by 2030–2035. Russia has developed a strategy to reduce greenhouse gas emissions until 2050.

Transport infrastructure is key in achieving sustainable development and directly impacts over 80% of the United Nation sustainable development goals (further- UN SDG). Through the creation and use of sustainable infrastructure, countries achieve economic, social and environmental results under the sustainable development goals framework. The target state of railway transport can be defined as an environmentally efficient and all-season transport with traditional technologies for integrating with other modes of transportation. To achieve above-mentioned goals, it is necessary to implement the following development directions, presented in Fig. 1.

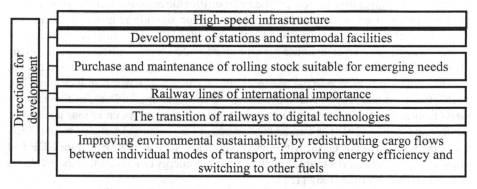

Fig. 1. Directions for the railway transport development

The activities of the largest railway company - Russian Railways JSC in the field of climate impact reduction are based on the provisions of the following regulatory documents:

• Environmental strategy of Russian Railways for the period up to 2020 and the future up to 2030;
• Energy strategy of Russian Railways for the period up to 2020 and for the future up to 2030;
• Climate Doctrine of the Russian Federation.

It is necessary to consider the energy-optimal train traffic control parameters to build a route using railway transport.

The research has some unique contributions: (1) The authors propose a new methodology for determining the amount of greenhouse gas emissions in Russian Railways. The "data-cube matrix" presents a new approach to calculating the railway carbon footprint matrix; (2) There are few studies concerning railway carbon footprint calculations in Russia. Thus, the research data set is valuable; (3) Research contributes to the literature review concerning railway footprint evaluation method development.

The rest of the paper is organized as follows. The following section contains a literature review. Section 3 contains a description of the materials and methodology, followed by presenting the Krasnoyarsk-Hani case results in Sect. 4. Then follow the conclusions, including the research limitations explanation and discussions of the directions for future research.

2 Literature Review

Studies of academic publications on the sustainable development of transport systems [6–9] have shown great attention to the ideas of environmentally friendly logistics and supply chain control, the energy efficiency of transportation. The publications analyze the balance between different aspects, such as economic, environmental and social stability, and consider the performance of transportation systems, and seek the various ways of sustainable systems development.

Many researchers emphasized that to control carbon dioxide emissions in transport effectively, it is imperative to measure their carbon dioxide emission factors. Thus, Zhang with co-authors measured models concerning carbon dioxide reduction on transport using the double exponential function for the variables [10, 11]. Ran et al. showed how to reduce transportation greenhouse gas emissions by developing policies targeting goals [12]. Steblianskaia et al. showed that nowadays ESG-concept development and carbon dioxide emission reduction in the transport industry increase in words in literature [13]. Vallés-Giménez and Zárate-Marco evaluated the dynamic Spatial Panel of Subnational GHG Emissions and measured the environmental effectiveness of emissions taxes [14]. Andrés and Padilla (2018) examined the sources of carbon dioxide emissions in the EU transport sector by considering vital macro variables, such as real per capita GDP and population, and transport variables, such as transport energy efficiency, transport volume and modal share in their study [15].

Transport is a source of emissions of greenhouse gases and other environmentally harmful issues. Some research indicates that the balance between the various sustainable development goals is skewed towards the economy at the expense of environmental and social equity issues. As an example, we can cite the works of Porfiriev and Safonov [16, 17], which show the existence of a conflict between classical and green logistics. Thus, decarbonized transportation sector is one of the primary goals for all countries. For example, You B. with co-authors suggested a way to decarbonise road transport using meta-analysis models and proved a new emission reduction model [18].

In Russia, few scientists concern with carbon footprint methodology development. Professor Postol developed the carbon emissions evaluation model [8]. George Kleiner and Maksim Rybachuk evaluated carbon dioxide emission assessment using system methodology [19]. Ilsheva and Baldesku classified harmful emissions for railways [20].

Aleksandr Tkachenko developed some ideas for the railway sector' carbon dioxide reduction assessment, however, his ideas didn't have opportunities for implementation [21]. Olga Efimova from the Russian University of Transport developed the carbon footprint evaluation for Russian Railways using energy consumption and ecological data. As a result, a model for carbon footprint evaluation for route was built without empirical data [22]. Tatiana S. Nokelaynen from the World data center for Geography Moscow State University mapped the environmental impacts of railway transport in Russia. His research was based on the Karlson' design and evaluation of railway corridors based on spatial ecological and geological criteria [23] The map represents linear pollution connected with railway transportation systems, which is accessed according to the traffic intensity and types of freight transported on the routes [24].

3 Methodology

3.1 Data

Many research data is collected from fieldwork. The transportation parameters, like traffic intensity and freight volumes, the presence of polluting cargos and passenger train frequency were used from the Russian Railway website https://eng.rzd.ru/. Russian Railway financial data was used from financial department information[1].

3.2 Research Methodology

With an increase in the speed of the locomotive, energy costs inevitably increase. Hense, the correct choice of the train's speed is a complex technical and economic problem that must solved by the Russian Railways' automated traffic control systems. The greenhouse gas emissions economic assessment algorithm see in Fig. 2.

When transporting by road, the driver also considers the need to save fuel, but his actions are often intuitive. In addition, when the movement of cars becomes difficult, the number of harmful emissions increases disproportionately to the length of the route. A particularly significant impact on the amount of fuel and energy resources used can accompany road transport in winter and conditions of unforeseen traffic jams, when crossing checkpoints at the border, and other cases that are not amenable to rationing. The energy consumption for traction of trains depends not only on the type of locomotive and profile characteristics, but also on the train' mass and the train'length.

Transportation task desition can be structured according to the "data cube" principle (Fig. 3). In the "data cube" on the axis (x) are the transport types, on the axis (y) cargo types, on the axis (z) route sections (from departure to destination), t- time.

The "data cube" contains information in cells that display the route traveled by a particular mode of transport, considering time, carbon dioxide emissions, carbon footprint, energy consumption, cargo weight and volume.

The authors selected the optimal route for cargo, which displays a combination of transport' various modes that helps to reduce carbon dioxide emissions.

---

[1] https://www.ceicdata.com/en/russia/company-financial-data-railway-russian-railways.

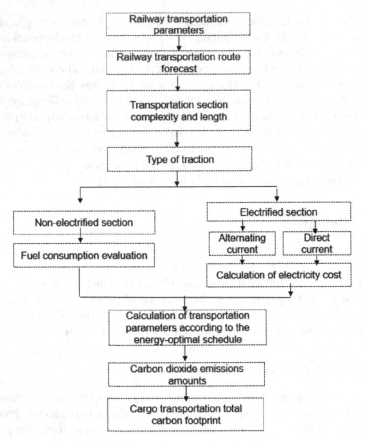

Fig. 2. Greenhouse gas emissions' economic assessment algorithm

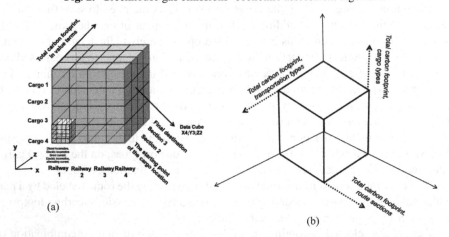

Fig. 3. (a, b) The structure of information about the transportation'carbon footprint.

Since 2017, the methodology for determining the amount of GHG emissions in Russian Railways has been in force, approved by Order No. 1602/r of Russian Railways, approved by order of the Ministry of Natural Resources dated June 30, 2015 No. 300. The approved Methodology provides measures to save fuel and energy resources, and, accordingly, reduce greenhouse gas emissions.

Calculate the consumption of fuel and energy resources for the implementation of transportation along the route using various modes of transport.

Implementing the overland transportation route from the consignor to the consignee has several options, which are characterized by economic parameters (profitability and costs) and environmental parameters, primarily the amount of emissions and environmental damage. To assess the magnitude of this damage, the most critical parameter is the volume of consumption of fuel and energy resources.

The carbon footprint calculation is based on the methodology for determining the amount of greenhouse gas emissions of Russian Railways.

As the leading indicators characterizing the train' energy consumption, it is customary to consider its specific values depending on whether the route section is electrified or diesel traction is used. We can evaluate the fuel consumption for train traction - in tons of equivalent fuel per 1 km (cf/km) or the electricity consumption (kWh/tkm gross).

Thus, the fuel or electric energy consumption spent by the locomotive related to the transport production unit (specific consumption) can be calculated by use of the folowing formula:

– for heating capacity in kg/104t km gross

$$n = \frac{3{,}35}{\eta} \frac{(m_{\text{л}} + m_c)}{m_c} \times (w_o + i_{\text{э}}) \tag{1}$$

– for electric traction in kWh /104t·km gross

$$e = \frac{27{,}25}{\eta} \frac{(m_{\text{л}} + m_c)}{m_c} \times (w_o + i_{\text{э}}) \tag{2}$$

To calculate the emitted gases volume, the authors consider the characteristics of the fuel burned (the coefficients used in the formulas will depend on this factor). Energy consumed parameters and the corresponding emissions depend on whether electricity or diesel is used for traction.

In most cases, due to the lack of the possibility of delivering goods by railways only, it becomes necessary to combine railways with other modes of transport. Aa result, the carbon footprint will be calculated considering the entire route length.

For onboard cargo vehicles, the expected value of fuel consumption is calculated by the next formula:

$$Q_H = 0,001 \times (H_{san} \times S + H_W \times W) = (1 + 0,001 \times D) \tag{3}$$

where Q_H is the standard fuel consumption, l;
S - car or road train mileage, km;
H- fuel consumption rate per vehicle mileage in running order without load, l/100 km;

$$H_{san} = H_s + H_g \times G_{np} \tag{4}$$

where H_{san} is the base rate of fuel consumption per vehicle (tractor) mileage in running order, l/100 km (=, l/100 km, for a single vehicle);

H_s- fuel consumption rate for the additional mass of a trailer or semi-trailer, l/100 t km;

H_g- the unladen weight of the trailer or semi-trailer, t;

G_{np}- the rate of fuel consumption for transport work, l/100 t km;

W – the volume of transportation work, t km:

$$W = G_{gr} \times S_{gr} \qquad (5)$$

G_{gr} - a mass of cargo, t;

S_{gr} - mileage with cargo, km;

D - correction factor (total relative allowance or reduction) to the norm, %.

4   Krasnoyarsk-Hani Case Calculation Results

The authors consider an example of the minimum carbon footprint route formation when delivering goods from Krasnoyarsk city to Khani station with the combination in the transportation route of construction materials and coal. Calculations are presented in Table 1. In this example, CO_2 emissions are calculated using the methodological part formulas. According to normative documents, a specific cost per ton of emissions could be set for the Russian Railways and not exceed 2,500–3,000 Rub per ton. Thus, the value of the cost expression could be calculated as the amount of CO_2 emissions multiplied by the tariff equal to 2,500 Rub. Per ton.

Table 1. The carbon footprint of cargo transportation using road and railway.

Name of goods, cargo	Route	Kind of transport	Energy consumption,t	CO2 Emissions	Carbon footprint
Building materials (100 tons)	Krasnoyarsk-Taishet (423 km) 7 h 26 min	Automobile (Ford F-Max)	11.2 l/100 t km	4.15 tons	RUB 10,375
Coal + Building Materials (5496 tons)	Taishet-Taksimo (1469 km) 37 h 26 min	J.D electric locomotive (alternating current)	102.6 kWh /104t km gross	0.566 tons	RUB 1,415
Coal + Building Materials (5496 tons)	Taksimo Honey (393 km) 13 h 23 min	J.D Locomotive	56.2 kg / 104t km gross	1.304 tons	RUB 3,260
The CO2 emissions, total					6.02 tons
The total cost of carbon footprint					RUB 15,050

Source: Data from Russian Railways https://eng.rzd.ru/ *(date of access: 17.01.2023)*

Table 1 shows the transportation route of two types of cargo, from Krasnoyarsk to Khani by sections: the transportation of the first cargo, weighing 100 tons, was carried out by road from Krasnoyarsk to Taishet with a section distance of 423 km. In this section, 19 kg/104 t·km of gross energy was spent, accompanied by 4.15 tons of CO2 emissions. Subsequently, the transportation of two types of cargo with a total weight of 5,496 tons on the Taishet-Taksimo section with a distance of 1,469 km was carried out on electric traction with alternating current, 102.6 kWh / 104t km gross was spent, CO2 emissions amounted to 0.566 tons. On the last, third section of Taksimo-Khani with a distance of 392 km, the cargo was transported by rail using diesel traction, energy consumption was 56.2 kg/104t km gross, and CO2 emissions amounted to 1.304 tons.

The total amount of CO2 emissions during the transportation of cargo amounted to 6.02 tons, the cost of the carbon footprint for the entire route was 15,050 rubles. To select the optimal transportation option, the authors compile a table with data concerning various options for implementing the transportation route for a given volume of goods (see Table 2).

Table 2. Transportation carbon footprint matrix.

Name of goods, cargo	Route	Railway route		Automobile route	
		FER consumption	CO2 emissions, t	FER consumption, l/100t km	CO2 emissions, t
building materials (100 tons)	Krasnoyarsk-Taishet (423 km)	0.538 kWh /104t km gross	0,003	11,2	4,15
Coal + Building Materials (5496 tons)	Taishet-Taksimo (1469 km)	102.6 kWh /104t km gross	0,566	2134,78	791,0147
Coal + Building Materials (5496 tons)	Taksimo Honey (393 km)	56.2 kg / 104t km gross	1,304	571,8958	211,9078

Source: Data from Russian Railways https://eng.rzd.ru/ *(date of access: 17.01.2023)*

The performed calculations show that a complete railway route is preferable to transportation by road, because the volume of emissions of 1.87 tons is almost 500 times less than by road transport. Hovever, it is necessary to consider a more significant number of parameters for a more accurate comparison of the transportation routes'efficiency.

The comparison of routes (Fig. 3) begins with allocating sections using road and rail transportation. The first section of the route from the consignor depends on the cargo dispatch point remoteness from the railway station and the junction of the railway track to the enterprise - the consignor. At the same time, it should be taken into account that, delivery to the station can be carried out by the road, and in this case, there is a need for loading and unloading operations, during which equipment that generates CO2 emissions can also be used. When transporting by rail to the destination, there is also a need for loading and unloading operations, including using loading and unloading equipment.

5 Conclusion

The penetration of the environmental agenda, primarily in terms of carbon regulation, is changing the existing competitive landscape in international freight transportation. The green trend brings competitive advantages to rail transport. However, this effect is discrete and depends on several other factors, such as how successful other modes of transport will be in responding to the environmental agenda. Additional opportunities for railways include technological innovations that highlight the objective environmental benefits of this mode of transport. International and Russian investors confirm the environmental focus of Russian Railways: in 2019 and 2020, the company was one of the first to place two issues of "green" Eurobonds for EUR 500 million and CHF 250 million, respectively, at 0.84% per annum. In 2020, the company also placed perpetual "green" bonds for 100 billion rubles.

Currently, data and tools to support carbon dioxide emission impact analysis in the transport sector are inadequate to address emerging public policy analysis needs. As a result, this study develops a new impact analysis tool for evaluating different transport modes. The study has some research limitations. First, analysis was done on the example of some routes in one country with a limited dataset. Thus, the authors plan to enhance research on evaluating "Belt and Road" countries' transportation routes. The authors see directions for future research in the carbon footprint methodology development emphasizing the more comprehensive set of indicators used for calculation. Authors plan to develop suitable methods and decision-making tools to encourage planning to reduce energy consumption and carbon dioxide emissions. The authors would like to compare the ways of reducing carbon dioxide emissions on railways in different countries. Using the cube methodology, the authors plan to determine whether the number of passengers in the railway carriage affects the environmental friendliness of the route. The exciting question is whether different materials railway carriage was built from also influence emissions.

References

1. Zhao, H.: Problems of carbon neutrality in China: strategies and countermeasures/H. Zhao, H.M.A, B. Chen, K. Zhang, M. Song. Resources, conservation and recycling, T. 176 (2022). https://doi.org/10.1016/j.rcsconrec.2021.105959
2. Li, M. Thoughts on public transport management in a low-carbon economy/M. Li Modern Economic Information, No. 15, p. 375 (2015)
3. Malo, S.: The practice and study of transport in large cities during the construction of Land and spatial planning - On the example of the Third round of strategic planning of transport development in Guangzhou, Ma, S., Zhang, H., Urban Planning, № 44(9), pp. 100–105 (2020)
4. Jian Shen, H.: Institute of Climate Change and Sustainable Development, Tsinghua University, Report, Research on China's Low-carbon Development Strategy and Transformation Path (中国低碳发展战略与转型路径研究) (2021)
5. Guan, D., Hubacek, K., Weber, C.L., Peters, G.P., Reiner, D.M.: The drivers of Chinese CO2 emissions from 1980 to 2030. Glob. Environ. Chang. 18, 626–634 (2008). https://doi.org/10.1016/j.gloenvcha.2008.08.001
6. Vasiev, M., Bi, K., Denisov, A., Bocharnikov, V.: How coronavirus pandemics (COVID-19) influences Chinese economic sustainability. Foresight and STI Governance 14(2), 7–22 (2020). https://doi.org/10.17323/2500-2597.2020.2.7.22
7. Decree of Russian railways dated 08.08.2017 No. 1602r "On approval of the methodology for determining the amount of greenhouse gas emissions in Russian railways"
8. Postol, B.G.: Rationing of fuel and electric energy consumption for train traction per trip: methodological guide for diploma design. Khabarovsk: Publishing House of the Far East State University of Transportation, p. 36 (2001)

9. Decree of the Ministry of Transport of Russia dated March 14, 2008 No. AM-23-r (as amended on September 20, 2018) "On the implementation of the guidelines "Norms for the consumption of fuels and lubricants in road transport"

10. Zhang, G., Wu, L., Chen, J.: Measurement models for carbon dioxide emission factors of passenger cars considering characteristics of roads and traffic. Int. J. Environ. Res. Public Health. **18**(4), 1594 (2021). https://doi.org/10.3390/ijerph18041594.PMID:33567571;PMCID:PMC 7914933

11. Zhang, G., Wu, L.; Factors impacting carbon dioxide emissions of automobiles on the streets of Chinese counties. In: Proceedings of the CICTP 2020 Proceedings: Transportation Evolution Impacting Future Mobility; Xi'an, China. 14–16 August 2020

12. Ran, T., Islam, K., Baher, A., Hatzopoulou, M.: Reducing transportation greenhouse gas emissions through the development of policies targeting high-emitting trips. Transp. Res. Rec. **2672**, 11–20 (2018)

13. Steblianskaia, E., Vasiev, M., Denisov, A., Bocharnikov, V., Steblyanskaya, A., Wang, Q.: Environmental-social-governance concept bibliometric analysis and systematic literature review: do investors becoming more environmentally conscious? Environmental and Sustainability Indicators **17**, 100218 (2023). https://doi.org/10.1016/j.indic.2022.100218

14. Vallés-Giménez, J., Zárate-Marco, A.: A dynamic spatial panel of subnational GHG Emissions: environmental effectiveness of emissions taxes in Spanish regions. Sustainability **12**, 2872 (2020)

15. Andrés, L., Padilla, E.: Driving factors of GHG emissions in the EU transport activity. Transp. Policy **61**, 60–74 (2018). https://doi.org/10.1016/j.tranpol.2017.10.008

16. Safonov, G.V., et al.: Strategy for low-carbon development of Russia, opportunities and benefits of replacing fossil fuels with "green" energy sources. ANO Center for Ecological Innovations, p. 74 (2016)

17. Porfirev, B.N., Shirov, A.A., Kolpakov, A.Y.: Low-Carbon development strategy: prospects for the Russian economy. Mirovaya ekonomika i mezhdunarodnye otnosheniya, vol. 64, no. 9 (2020)

18. You, B., Qiao, F., Yu, L.: An exploration of CO2 emission models for horizontal curves on freeways. J. Civ. Environ. Eng. **6**, 219 (2016). https://doi.org/10.4172/2165-784X.1000219

19. Kleiner, G.B., Rybachuk, M.A.: System structure of the economy: qualitative time-space analysis. Fronteiras. **2**, 61–81 (2016)

20. Ilysheva, N.N., Baldescu, E.V.: Improving methodological tools for quantifying greenhouse gas emissions taking into account international experience/N.N. Ilysheva, E.V. Baldescu (in Russian)

21. Tkachenko, A.A.: National and planetary interests in preserving the balance of nature and economic growth. Economy. Taxes. Right. **12**(5), 6–17 (2019). (in Russian)

22. O.V. Efimova Methods of justifying management decisions when introducing new information technologies. Scientific Monograph/E.B. Baboshin, Efimova O.V., M. MIIT, p. 56 (2009)

23. Karlson, M., Karlsson, C.S.J., Mörtberg, U., Olofsson, B., Balfors, B.: Design and evaluation of railway corridors based on spatial ecological and geological criteria. Transp. Res. Part D: Transp. Environ. **46**, 207–228 (2016)

24. Nokelaynen, T.S.: GIS-Mapping of the environmental impacts of road transport in Russia. In: Proceedings of the International Conference InterCarto/InterGis 21 «Sustainable Development of Territories: GIS Theory and Practice»-Krasnodar, Sochi, pp. 97–100 (2015)

Data Science and Modeling

Research on the Prediction of Highly Cited Papers Based on PCA-BPNN

Tian Yu$^{(\boxtimes)}$ and Changxu Duan

School of Economics and Management, Harbin Engineering University, Harbin 150001,
People's Republic of China
yutian@hrbeu.edu.cn

Abstract. With the increase in scientific research investment, the number of papers has increased significantly, and the evaluation of the impact of papers has received extensive attention from scholars. The citation frequency is the most convenient and widely used index to measure the academic influence of papers. Still, the citation frequency can only measure the real impact of papers some period of time after those have been published. Therefore, to be able to identify highly cited papers at the early stage of publication, this paper collects data on 1025 academic papers published under the library and information discipline of the Web of Science library in 2007 and then extracts 24 predictive characteristics from three aspects: papers, authors, and journals. On this basis, 7 principal component vectors are constructed by feature screening based on PCA. Also, combined with the BP neural network model, the PCA-BPNN highly-cited paper classification prediction model is constructed and finally compared with the other 5 models. The results show that the PCA-BPNN model built in this paper has better prediction performance and provides an effective model for the prediction of paper influence.

Keywords: Paper Influence Prediction · Highly Cited Paper Prediction · PCA-BPNN · Classification Model

1 Introduction

Scientific papers are the basic unit of scientometric research. As a carrier of knowledge, published papers affect the communication and progress of science [1]. Currently, the evaluation methods for the influence of academic papers mainly include peer review and scientometric index quantification. Although the peer review method can evaluate the value of papers more comprehensively, it is time-consuming and of high cost. In this way, citation frequency has been used as an index to measure the influence of papers. However, while the citation frequency index is widely used, it can only measure a paper's current and past scientific impact. In many cases, people want to go beyond this to predict future scientific impact; therefore, we need to go beyond the current citation date of papers and forecast its future citations to reflect its future scientific implications as well [2].

Bai [3] and Hou [4] have given an overview of the methods for evaluating and forecasting the impact of papers, and summarized the forecasting process as data collection, data preprocessing, data analysis, feature selection, model design, model optimization, and model evaluation, where the construction of prediction features and prediction models is the primary factor that affects prediction accuracy. Existing literature has conducted a series of studies based on databases such as Web of Science and Scopus or large datasets such as AMiner and the American Physical Society (APS). Scholars have tried to use the influencing factors related to the citation frequency of papers as prediction features. However, only using a single category or fewer prediction features cannot achieve ideal prediction results. For example, Wang [5] constructed four features attempting to predict ESI highly cited papers. Still, the prediction results were only superior to random selection, indicating that four factors may partially but not sufficiently explain the pattern of highly cited papers in ESI. However, even using prediction features with higher dimensions will still face the problems of feature redundancy and irrelevance, which may lead to long model training time, dimensional disaster, model overfitting, and generalization decline. Therefore, it is an urgent issue to construct a multi-dimensional feature space and select prediction features with higher dimensions to build a higher-accuracy prediction model for paper influence.

In view of these problems and limitations, this paper uses real paper data and focuses on solving the problem of citation number modeling and prediction based on time series papers. Our first contribution is constructing an efficient prediction feature space from several aspects. Secondly, based on principal component analysis (PCA), feature selection and dimensionality reduction are performed on prediction features. Also, combined with BP neural network (BPNN), a highly cited paper recognition model (PCA-BPNN) is proposed based on the characteristics in the early publication stage. PCA-BPNN can eliminate the redundancy between features, reduce the input dimension of the BP neural network, and has good generalization performance. Compared with other common linear or nonlinear classification models, the results show that PCA-BPNN has better accuracy.

2 Review of Related Studies

Existing studies on the impact prediction of papers can be roughly divided into two categories: predicting the citation frequency of papers and identifying highly cited papers. Predicting the citation frequency of papers, i.e., defining the prediction of paper influence as a regression problem [1, 6, 7], sing related features in papers to predict the citation frequency of papers sometime in the future. For example, Kosteas [8] took 60 economics journals in SSCI in 1994 as the research object and built a regression model based on three characteristics of papers, initial citations, and journals, exploring the contribution of three types of attributes to predicting the long-term impact of papers; Abramo [9] took 123,128 papers published by Italian authors on WOS as the research object and predicted the citation rate of papers nine years after the publication based on the regression model constructed from the journal impact factor and the citation data of papers since the first eight years of publication. Amjad [10] used AMiner's dataset to build a regression model with 14 features in four aspects: author, society, journal, and papers and compared the impact of different features in the prediction of journal papers and conference papers; Ma [11] took 20 journals in the field of artificial intelligence as the research object, used the Doc2Vec algorithm to encode the metadata text, and then applied the BiLSTM with attention mechanism to further extract high-level semantic features. On this basis, a prediction model is built combined with initial citation features to predict the citation frequency of papers 8 years after publication; Wang [12] improved the AVG model and proposed a nonlinear citation prediction combination model (NCFCM) based on neural network to predict the potential growth of citation count; Zhao [13] based on deep learning and from the perspective of information cascade prediction, built the cited count prediction model (DeepCCP), which takes the citation network in the early stage (3–5 years) after the publication of the paper as the input to predict the cited frequency in the years after the publication of the paper.

Regarding the relationship between the citation frequency and the academic value of papers, the generally accepted view in the academic circle is: that higher citation of papers indicates higher academic value. Therefore, many studies define the research on paper impact prediction as a classification issue to identify and predict valuable papers. For example, Dong [14] pointed out that because the citation of papers is of an apparent long-tail effect, the influence prediction of papers is not suitable for regression, so they define the influence prediction of papers as a classification issue, namely only predicting whether the citation frequency of an article of a particular author at a specific time in the future can exceed the H index. If yes, it means that this article is conducive to improving the author's influence; if no, it means that this article is not conducive to improving the author's influence. Wang [5] took 617 papers published in seven journals in the field of the public library of science as the research object and explored the prediction performance of metrological indicator and surrogate metrological indicator features on the influence of papers. They used three feature selection techniques, namely Relief-F, principal component analysis, and entropy weight, to rank the contribution of features and constructed three classifiers, namely Naive Bayes, KNN and random forest to verify the classification performance of features; Hassan [15] used the Twitter data collected by Altmetric to construct papers and surrogate metrology features and built classifiers based on random forest and SVM. They then ranked features by importance and revealed the relationship between influential tweets and highly cited papers in the field of information science. After the citation frequency prediction is transformed from regression to classification issue, data can be more in line with the real distribution since the prediction granularity becomes coarser. In this way, the trained model also has better generalization ability, making the research more practical; Wang [16] took the American Physical Society (APS) data set as the research object, extracted four characteristics related to the author and content, and predicted whether the paper would become an ESI high-impact paper 3 and 10 years after its publication based on the multi-layer perceptron model; Hua [17] took 746 papers in the fields of marketing and management information system as the research object, extracted five key word popularity (KP) indicators based on LDA model, and combined with the bibliometric characteristics, used C4.5, logistic regression, support vector machine and other models to classify and predict highly cited articles; Chowdhury [18] proposed the general function form of the generalized linear model (GLM), and used a new hierarchical Bayesian estimation method to carry out logical regression analysis on the highly cited papers in the field of management information system (MIS). The convergence time and fitting effect of the model are good. Through simulation research, it is proved that its prediction accuracy is equal to or even exceeds some prediction models based on machine learning and artificial neural network.

3   Data and Methods

3.1   Problem Definition

This paper defines the prediction of paper influence as a classification prediction problem. A classification model is then constructed by analyzing and collecting characteristic factors related to the citation frequency of papers to identify high-level papers in the early stage of publication. Since the citation frequency of a paper five years after publication is a crucial reflection to indicate the quality of papers [19, 20], existing studies on paper influence the prediction mostly choose to use a five-year citation window to measure and predict the quality and impact of papers [1, 10, 21–23]. Meanwhile, this paper defines highly cited papers based on the "Pareto principle," e.g., papers with a cumulative citation frequency of 80% (in this paper, papers with a citation frequency of more than 5) are defined as highly cited papers.

3.2   Feature Analysis

The selection of characteristic factors that affect the citation frequency is the basis for prediction, which directly determines the effect. This paper believes that the distinguishing elements of paper citation frequency can be considered from the following three aspects: author, paper, and journal characteristics. All relevant features are shown in Table 1.

Author Characteristics.   Papers represent the thought of authors and the crystallization of their wisdom and knowledge. Authors with strong academic ability, the so-called "academic bulls," represent the development level of a discipline, receiving more attention from people. Existing studies have found that the number of authors, authors' institutions [24], as well as the number of authors' publications, citations, and h-index [1, 25] will have an impact on the citation frequency of papers. Therefore, this paper extracts 9 author characteristics, namely the number of authors, the h-index of the first author before publishing this paper, the total number of papers published by the first author before publishing this paper, the total citation frequency of the first author before publishing this paper, the average citation frequency of the first author before publishing this paper, the highest h-index of all authors before publishing this paper, the highest number of papers published by all authors before publishing this paper, the highest total citation frequency of all authors before publishing this paper, and highest average citation frequency of all authors before publishing this paper.

Paper Characteristics.   After being published, the literature type, title form and length, and length may all affect readers' judgment, which in turn will have a certain impact on citation frequency. This part can be called external influencing factors of papers. In addition, the quality of papers directly determines the value, which can be measured by the initial characteristics of papers, categorized into internal influencing factors of

Table 1. List of relevant characteristics.

Feature Category	List of influencing factors	Tag
Author Characteristics	Number of authors	X_1
	H index of the first author before publishing this paper	X_2
	Total number of papers published by the first author before publishing this paper	X_3
	Total citation frequency of the first author before publishing this paper	X_4
	Average citation frequency of the first author before publishing this paper	X_5
	Highest h-index of all authors before publishing this paper	X_6
	The highest number of papers published by all authors before publishing this paper	X_7
	Highest total citation frequency of all authors before publishing this paper	X_8
	Highest average citation frequency of all authors before publishing this paper	X_9
Paper characteristics	Number of literature	X_{10}
	Year of first citation	X_{11}
	Citation frequency in the first two years of publication	X_{12}
	Number of citing countries in the first two years of publication	X_{13}
	Type of citing literature in the first two years of publication	X_{14}
	Number of cited journals in the first two years of publication	X_{15}
	Number of citing disciplines in the first two years of publication	X_{16}
Journal characteristics	Total citation frequency of journals	X_{17}
	Journal impact factors	X_{18}
	5-year impact factors of journals	X_{19}
	Immediacy index of journals	X_{20}
	Published article volume of journals	X_{21}
	Cited half-life of journals	X_{22}
	Value of characteristic factors	X_{23}
	Value of paper impact	X_{24}

papers. Therefore, this paper selects 7 paper characteristics, namely number of literature, year of first citation, citation frequency in the first two years of publication, number of citing countries in the first two years of publication, type of citing literature in the first two years of publication, number of citing journals in first two years of publication, and number of citing discipline in first two years of publication.

Journal Characteristics. Journals are the carrier of papers, and it is easier to attract people's attention if papers are published in high-quality journals. Referencing journal indicators used in existing studies, the cumulative publication volume of journals before the paper was published, cumulative citation volume of journals, composite impact factor, and composite impact factor [1], this paper selects all indicators for evaluating journals in the Journal Citation Report (JCR) to describe the characteristics of journals, including8 journal characteristics, namely total citation frequency of journals, influencing factors of journals, 5-year influencing factors of journals, immediacy index of journals, published article volume of journals, citation half-life period of journals, the value of characterization factors and value of paper influence.

3.3 Data Sources and Analysis

The basic data used in this paper are 1025 articles published in 20 journals under Information Science and Library Science in JCR in 2007. The relevant characteristics of journals are obtained through the journal indicators published by JCR, and relevant characteristics of authors and papers are obtained through the Web of Science discovery tool. Before determining the threshold for low citations, it is necessary to know the distribution of citations five years after publication. This paper makes statistics on the citation frequency of papers in the dataset five years after publication and uses the citation frequency and count as the Y-axis and X-axis, as shown in Fig. 1.

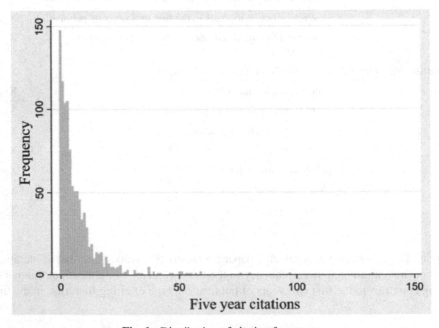

Fig. 1. Distribution of citation frequency.

It can be seen from Fig. 1 that the citation frequency of papers five years after publication is a discrete integer greater than or equal to 0, showing prominent long-tail characteristics. A large number of articles are cited in a frequency ranging from 0 to 5. This study further compares papers with citations less than or equal to 5 and those greater than 5, as shown in Fig. 2. Although the number of papers with a citation frequency less than or equal to 5 accounts for about 60%, their cumulative citation frequency only accounts for 16.7%, which is a considerable gap. More than 80% of cumulative citation frequency is completed by 40% of the literature. It can be considered that the remaining 60% of literature has a minimal contribution to cumulative citation frequency in a low-cited state. This indicates that the distribution of citation frequency of papers is basically in line with the "Pareto principle" and it is appropriate to define highly cited papers on this basis.

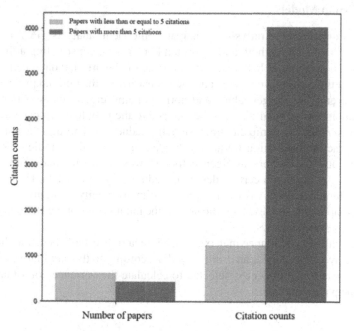

Fig. 2. Comparison of papers with citations less than or equal to 5 and those greater than 5.

3.4 Data Labeling and Standardization

Data Labeling. Based on the problem definition of this paper and the above analysis, if the citation frequency of papers five years after publication is greater than 5, it is defined as highly cited papers, marked as positive type, and the classification value Y_c is represented by 1; if the citation frequency is less than or equal to 5, it is considered as non-highly cited papers, marked as negative type, and the classification value Y_c is represented by 0.

Normalization of Original Samples. Since the data size of 24 indicators is different, and the data unit is also different, it is necessary to normalize the original data to eliminate the influence of dimension and absolute value. The normalization formula is:

$$X = \frac{X^* - X^*{}_{min}}{X^*{}_{max} - X^*{}_{min}} \tag{1}$$

In the formula: X^* is the original data of an indicator; $X^*{}_{min}$ and $X^*{}_{max}$ are the maximum and minimum values of an indicator; X is the normalized data of an indicator, $X \in [0,1]$.

3.5   Prediction Models

Principal Component Analysis. Principal component analysis (PCA) is a linear descending dimension method, and its principle is: firstly, constructing a linearly independent covariance matrix between features based on the original data, then solving the eigenvalue of the covariance matrix, and then constructing the optimal projection matrix based on several large eigenvalues and corresponding eigenvectors. After the above transformation, the original data can be mapped to the new feature space according to the projection matrix to complete dimensionality reduction. Through the analysis of the influencing factors of citation frequency, this paper selects three indicators, including papers, journals, and authors, as eigenvectors. However, the dimension of selected data features is 24, indicating a certain degree of redundancy in the data. Hence, to reduce the feature dimension, PCA is used to process dimensionality reduction, extracting the principal components of these 24 indicators as the input vector of the BP neural network. Specific steps are as follows:

The normalized covariance matrix of each indicator is established, and the eigenvalues and eigenvectors of the matrix are solved. According to the cumulative contribution rate, the principal component is selected to calculate the variance contribution rate of the ith principal component:

$$\rho_i = \lambda_i / \sum_{j=1}^{k} \lambda_j \tag{2}$$

where, ρ_i is the variance contribution rate of the ith principal component, k is the number of principal components, λ_i and λ_j are the eigenvalues of main components i and j respectively. In order to ensure that the extracted principal component can represent most of the information reflected by the original data, this paper selects the principal component vector required for greater than 90% of the cumulative variance contribution rate.

The principal component formula is established to solve the value of each principal component: the formula of each principal component value is $c_i = \sum\limits_{j=1}^{m} a_j x_j$, where m is the number of the principal component vector required for greater than 90% of the cumulative variance contribution rate, a_j is the component of eigenvectors and x_j is the normalized value of each variable.

According to formula (2), the variance contribution rate of each principal component is calculated, and the principal component structure with a cumulative variance contribution rate greater than 90% is selected, as shown in Table 2. It can be seen from Table 2 that the cumulative contribution rate of the variance of the first seven factors reaches 90%, recorded as F1, F2, F3, F4, F5, F6, and F7. Seven eigenvectors composed of 24 eigenvectors are used as the new eigenvariables, and the composition coefficient of each factor is shown in Table 3.

Table 2. Using principal components to explain the total variance of original variables.

Component	Principal component 1	Principal component 2	Principal component 3	Principal component 4	Principal component 5	Principal component 6	Principal component 7
Eigenvalue	2.9339	1.7882	1.2227	1.2024	1.1543	1.0951	1.0904
Contribution rate %	45.6	14.3	11.1	7.2	5.5	3.5	2.9
Cumulative contribution rate %	45.6	59.9	71.0	78.2	83.7	87.2	90.1

Table 3. Factor component coefficient.

Component factor	F1	F2	F3	F4	F5	F6	F7
X1	−0.0289	−0.0921	0.3514	0.1067	−0.1677	0.0757	−0.1215
X2	−0.4563	0.6826	0.0102	0.0938	−0.0416	0.0005	−0.1520
X3	0.0076	0.0138	0.4277	0.0042	0.4757	−0.2216	−0.2411
X4	0.0191	0.0279	−0.0656	−0.4025	−0.3567	−0.1482	−0.1243
X5	1.1543	−0.0787	0.2262	0.6326	−0.1003	−0.2234	0.0460
X12	−0.0556	0.0578	−0.0693	−0.1305	0.5532	−0.0604	0.1441
X13	1.0904	−0.0577	−0.4474	0.1955	0.1337	−0.4921	−0.2905
...	...	...	...	...	...	...	...
X23	−0.0172	0.0491	0.0261	0.2217	0.0393	0.2089	0.1625
X24	−0.5661	−0.0718	−0.0268	−0.0461	0.0134	0.0230	−0.0091

PCA-BPNN Prediction Model. The full name of the BP neural network is Back-Propagation Network, which Rumelhart and McClelland proposed in 1985. It is a multi-layer forward network with one-way propagation, which uses the error back-propagation method for training [26]. It has a simple structure, strong plasticity, and high tolerance to noisy data, so it has been widely used in the fields of information classification, pattern recognition, and prediction. The structural design of the BP neural network model includes the number of layers of the network, the number of neurons in each layer, as well as learning and training methods.

The number of network layers is determined according to the comparison of the final prediction effect for the influence of the number of hidden layers, and this paper adopts a double-hidden network structure, including an input layer, two hidden layers, and an output layer. Generally, the best scenario is that the selection of the number of nodes in the input layer and output layer is with irrelevant input data. According to the calculation, there are 7 feature vectors obtained after the principal component analysis of 24 related factors, and they are not correlated with each other. Therefore, the number of neurons in the input layer is determined as 7. In this paper, both low-cited and highly cited papers need to be predicted, that is, a binary classification problem. The highly cited papers are represented by 1, while low cited papers are represented by 0. In this way, the output variable ranges from 0 to 1, so the number of neurons in the output layer is 1.

There is currently no accurate calculation method for the selection of the number of neurons in the hidden layer. In this paper, the optimal range of the number of neurons in the hidden layer is roughly determined according to formula (3) based on the empirical formula:

$$\begin{cases} l < n - 1 \\ l < \sqrt{n + m} + a \\ l = \log_2 n \end{cases} \tag{3}$$

In this formula: l is the number of hidden neurons; m is the number of neurons in the output layer; n is the number of neurons in the input layer; a is a constant between 1 and 10. The basic structure of the BP neural network model is shown in Fig. 3.

In the binary classification problem, the activation function usually adopts the nonlinear Sigmoid activation function and the linear ReLU activation function. In developing neural networks, especially in the BP neural network covered with sigmoid functions, a concept has been gradually formed: the nonlinear activation function is more advanced than the linear activation function. However, this stereotype is broken as the sparsity of neurons is steadily confirmed. In back-propagation, the gradient of the Sigmoid function is easy to disappear, and the use of the ReLU function can significantly accelerate the gradient descending process and reduce the training time.

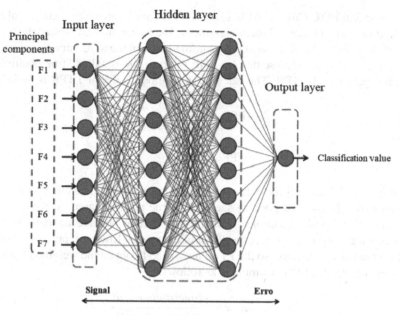

Fig. 3. PCA-BPNN structure.

3.6 Evaluation Indicators

This paper adopts the commonly used indicators of classifier performance evaluation ROC (Receiver Operating Characteristic Curve), Area Under Curve (AUC), and F1 value for evaluation. These two values have also been commonly used in the field of citation classification prediction to evaluate the prediction effect. Some indicators need to be defined to calculate the AUC and F1 values. TP (True Positive) represents the number of samples in which the forecast is true and the actual value is also true; FP (False Positive) represents the number of samples in which the forecast is true but the actual value is false; FN (False Negative) represents the number of samples in which the forecast is false but the actual value is true, TN (True Negative) represents the number of samples in which the forecast is false and the actual value is also false, shown in Table 4.

Table 4. Confusion matrix of classification results.

Predicted True	Negative	Positive
Positive	FN	TP
Negative	TN	FP

AUC Value and ROC Curve. AUC value and ROC curve are often used to evaluate the classification performance of binary classifiers. The larger the AUC value, the better the effect of classifiers. The abscissa of the coordinate axis of the ROC curve is called: "false positive rate", which is represented by FPR; the ordinate is called "true positive rate", which is represented by TPR. The calculation method of FPR and TPR is as follows:

$$\text{FPR} = \frac{FP}{FP + TN} \tag{4}$$

$$\text{TPR} = \frac{TP}{TP + FN} \tag{5}$$

F1 Value. The F1 value is the harmonic mean of precision and recall. The precision is the proportion of predicted positive samples in true positive samples; the recall is the proportion of real positive samples correctly predicted as positive samples. The higher the precision and recall, the better the effect of the model. However, precision and recall are often mutually restrictive, so the F1 value is used to obtain the weighted harmony of precision and recall, and the formula is as follows:

$$F1value = \frac{2 \cdot precision \cdot recall}{precision + recall} \tag{6}$$

4 Experiment and Result Analysis

This paper uses the Python3.7 version for programming and completes data processing, drawing, and modeling in the Anaconda environment. In addition to the PCA-BPNN model, other models are also added for comparison, including the K-nearest neighbor model (KNN), logistic regression model (LR), support vector machine model (SVM), random forest model (RFC), and AdaBoost model. Among them, KNN, logistic regression, and support vector machine are three classic classification models, and their effectiveness has been verified in different data sets. AdaBoost and random forest are both excellent integrated learning models, especially for the AdaBoost integrated learning model, which has been widely used in academic research and practical work in recent years due to its excellent generalization ability. The BP neural network model is constructed using the Keras deep learning framework, and the PCA and other five models for comparison are constructed using the Scikit-learn library. According to the above, the experimental process includes data preprocessing, feature extraction, modeling, parameter determination, model evaluation, etc. The specific process is shown in Fig. 4.

The original data is classified, including 604 positive classes and 421 negative classes. The classification value Yc is represented by 1 and 0, and the data is basically symmetrical. The data normalization is performed according to formula (1), and scholars can also call the MinMaxScaler function already in the scikit-learn library. The PCA-based feature selection is performed according to formula (2), and the PCA model that has been packaged in the scikit-learn library can also be called. Based on the discussion above, a four-layer neural network model is constructed, in which the number of neurons in the

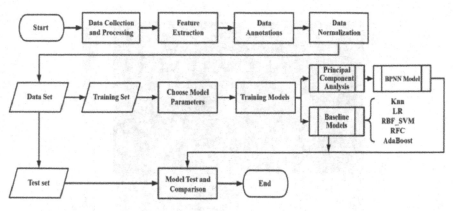

Fig. 4. Experimental flow chart.

input layer is 7 and that in the output layer is 1. The number of neurons in the hidden layer is calculated according to formula (3), and the range is roughly between 3 and 13, which is finally determined as 10 according to the principle of minimum experimental average error after repeated experiments. The topology structure of the model 7–10-10–1 is finally obtained, and there are 201 output parameters of the model. The activation function in the hidden layer adopts the ReLU function, and in order to ensure that the range of output values is between (0,1), the Sigmoid function is used in the output layer. The optimizer adopts the Adam optimizer, and the loss function uses the cross-entropy function. Also, the learning rate is selected as 0.001, and the maximum number of iterations is 2000. The specific parameter settings are shown in Table 5.

Table 5. Model parameter settings.

N	Training parameter	Parameter value
1	Activation function in the hidden layer	ReLU
2	Activation function in the output layer	Sigmoid
3	Optimizer	Adam
4	Loss function	Binary_crossentropy
5	Evaluation function	Binary_accuracy
6	Learning rate	Lr = 0.001
7	Maximum number of training	Epochs = 2000

Due to the limited size of the data set in this paper, in order to make more comprehensive use of the data, we randomly divide the training set and the test set according to 9:1 to obtain the confusion matrix of the prediction results, as shown in Fig. 5.

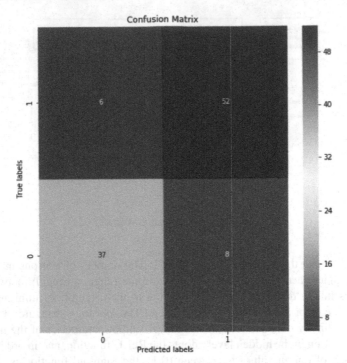

Fig. 5. Confusion matrix in the test set.

It can be seen from the Figure that among the 103 test samples, the number that both the actual value and predicted value belong to the positive class (TP) is 52; the number that the actual value belongs to the positive class while the predicted value belongs to the negative class (FN) is 6; the number that both the actual value and predicted value belong to the negative class (TN) is 37; the number that the actual value belongs to the negative class while the predicted value belongs to the positive class (FP) is 8. According to formula (4) and formula (5), the false positive rate (FPR) is calculated to be 0.178, and the true positive rate (TPR) is 0.897. Then, the ROC curve of each model is drawn, taking TPR as the vertical axis and FPR as the horizontal axis, as shown in Fig. 6. The larger the area under the ROC curve (AUC), the better the performance of the classification model. The classification model with an AUC value above 0.8 indicates good performance, and the classification model with an AUC value above 0.9 indicates excellent performance. It can be seen from Fig. 6 that the AUC value of the neural network model constructed in this paper is significantly higher than that of other classification models, close to 0.9, indicating that the model proposed in this paper has an excellent performance in classification prediction.

In order to further compare the prediction performance of different models, we calculate the average value of AUC value and F1 Score of each prediction model via a fivefold cross-validation method.It can be seen from Fig. 7 that the AUC of the PCA-BPNN model constructed in this paper is significantly higher than that of other classification models, more than 0.8, showing that the prediction ability is stronger than other models.The F1 value of each model is then compared, as shown in Fig. 8. It can be seen from Fig. 8 that

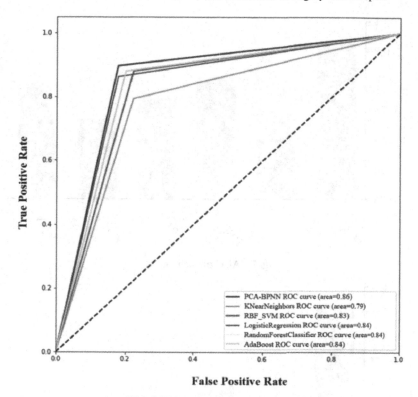

Fig. 6. ROC curve of each model.

the F1 score of the neural network model constructed in this paper is significantly higher than that of other classification models, close to 0.8, indicating excellent performance.

Meanwhile, misclassification items are observed, most of which are concentrated in the citation frequency between 4 and 7, showing that the classification model has low accuracy in terms of the classification category with the citation frequency between 4 and 9. After analysis, the reason for this phenomenon is that papers with a citation frequency between 4 and 9 are near the classification threshold. For example, papers with a citation frequency of 5 may not be significantly different from those with a citation frequency of 6. Such papers have similar characteristics in all aspects but are manually divided into two completely separate categories. In this way, the classification model based on feature learning cannot effectively learn category features during the training. Also, performing effective classification when predicting cases close to the classification boundary is complex.

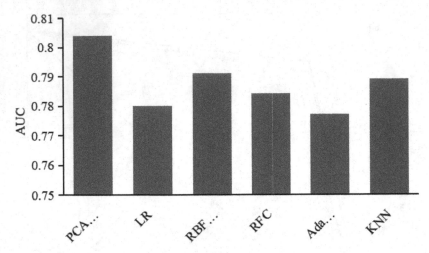

Fig. 7. AUC of each model.

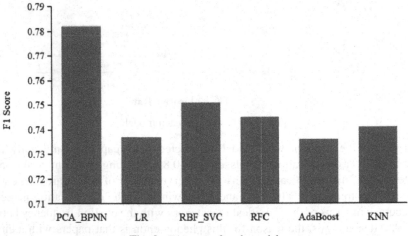

Fig. 8. F1 score of each model.

5   Conclusion and Future Work

The prediction of the influence of scientific literature has always attracted the attention of many scholars, and most existing studies focus on the prediction of highly cited papers. However, the number of low citation papers is significant; thus, it is of great practical significance to predict and identify such papers.

The contributions of this paper are as follows: (1) the problem of predicting the influence of scientific literature is defined as a binary classification problem to realize the prediction and identification of highly cited papers in the early stage of publication; (2) the influencing factors are summarized and classified, obtaining three types of influencing factors: authors, journals and papers. Also, according to the collected data distribution, the threshold of highly cited papers is determined combined with the "Pareto principle"; (3) the PCA is used for feature extraction, and the PCA-BNNN highly cited paper prediction model is constructed combined with BP neural network, achieving good results. This paper can help researchers predict high-impact papers in the early stage of publication, thus providing a basis for evaluating and screening the massive scientific literature in their own research fields.

However, this paper also has the following limitations: (1) due to limited time, the dataset collected in this paper is small and only contains one field of discipline, which may lead to limited applicability and persuasiveness of the constructed model; (2) the determination of the threshold of high and low citation frequency is still vague, and more effective methods are needed for the classification of papers near the threshold; (3) in addition to the three influencing factors proposed in this paper, there are many other factors affecting the citation frequency of papers, such as webometrics, number of users of literature management software, social bookmarking, reprint/comment, etc. In future studies, data sets covering more disciplines will be used so as to obtain more accurate classification standards. Also, studies will be conducted on more discipline data, extracting more factors that may affect the citation of papers to develop a relatively complete framework for predicting paper citations.

References

1. Yu, T., Yu, G., Li, P.-Y., Wang, L.: Citation impact prediction for scientific papers using stepwise regression analysis. Scientometrics **101**(2), 1233–1252 (2014). https://doi.org/10.1007/s11192-014-1279-6
2. Cao, X., Chen, Y., Liu, K.R.: A data analytic approach to quantifying scientific impact. J. Informet. **10**, 471–484 (2016)
3. Bai, X., et al.: An overview on evaluating and predicting scholarly article impact. Information **8**(3), 73 (2017)
4. Hou, J., Pan, H., Guo, T., Lee, I., Kong, X., Xia, F.: Prediction methods and applications in the science of science: a survey. Comput. Sci. Rev. **34**, 100197 (2019)
5. Wang, M., Wang, Z., Chen, G.: Which can better predict the future success of articles? Bibliometric indices or alternative metrics. Scientometrics **119**, 1575–1595 (2019)
6. Lokker, C., McKibbon, K.A., McKinlay, R.J., Wilczynski, N.L., Haynes, R.B.: Prediction of citation counts for clinical articles at two years using data available within three weeks of publication: retrospective cohort study. BMJ **336**, 655–657 (2008)
7. Pobiedina, N., Ichise, R.: Citation count prediction as a link prediction problem. Appl. Intell. **44**(2), 252–268 (2015). https://doi.org/10.1007/s10489-015-0657-y
8. Kosteas, V.D.: Predicting long-run citation counts for articles in top economics journals. Scientometrics **115**(3), 1395–1412 (2018). https://doi.org/10.1007/s11192-018-2703-0
9. Abramo, G., D'Angelo, C.A., Reale, E.: Peer review versus bibliometrics: which method better predicts the scholarly impact of publications? Scientometrics **121**(1), 537–554 (2019). https://doi.org/10.1007/s11192-019-03184-y
10. Amjad, T., Shahid, N., Daud, A., Khatoon, A.: Citation burst prediction in a bibliometric network. Scientometrics **127**(5), 2773–2790 (2022)
11. Ma, A., Liu, Y., Xu, X., Dong, T.: A deep-learning based citation count prediction model with paper metadata semantic features. Scientometrics **126**(8), 6803–6823 (2021). https://doi.org/10.1007/s11192-021-04033-7
12. Wang, K., Shi, W., Bai, J., Zhao, X., Zhang, L.: Prediction and application of article potential citations based on nonlinear citation-forecasting combined model. Scientometrics **126**(8), 6533–6550 (2021). https://doi.org/10.1007/s11192-021-04026-6

13. Zhao, Q., Feng, X.: Utilizing citation network structure to predict paper citation counts: A Deep learning approach. J. Informet. **16**(1), 101235 (2022)
14. Dong, Y., Johnson, R.A., Chawla, N.V.: Will this paper increase your h-index? In: Bifet, A., May, M., Zadrozny, B., Gavalda, R., Pedreschi, D., Bonchi, F., Cardoso, J., Spiliopoulou, M. (eds.) ECML PKDD 2015. LNCS (LNAI), vol. 9286, pp. 259–263. Springer, Cham (2015). https://doi.org/10.1007/978-3-319-23461-8_26
15. Hassan, S.-U., Bowman, T.D., Shabbir, M., Akhtar, A., Imran, M., Aljohani, N.R.: Influential tweeters in relation to highly cited articles in altmetric big data. Scientometrics **119**(1), 481–493 (2019). https://doi.org/10.1007/s11192-019-03044-9
16. Wang, F., Fan, Y., Zeng, A., Di, Z.: Can we predict ESI highly cited publications? Scientometrics **118**(1), 109–125 (2018). https://doi.org/10.1007/s11192-018-2965-6
17. Hu, Y.H., Tai, C.T., Liu, K.E., Cai, C.F.: Identification of highly-cited papers using topic-model-based and bibliometric features: the consideration of keyword popularity. J. Informet. 14, (2020)
18. Chowdhury, K.P.: Functional analysis of generalized linear models under non-linear constraints with applications to identifying highly-cited papers. J. Informet. 15(1), (2021)
19. Wang, M., Yu, G., Yu, D.: Mining typical features for highly cited papers. Scientometrics **87**(3), 695–706 (2011)
20. Wang, M., Yu, G., An, S., Yu, D.: Discovery of factors influencing citation impact based on a soft fuzzy rough set model. Scientometrics **93**(3), 635–644 (2012)
21. Bai, X., Zhang, F., Lee, I.: Predicting the citations of scholarly paper. J. Informet. **13**(1), 407–418 (2019)
22. Ruan, X., Zhu, Y., Li, J., Cheng, Y.: Predicting the citation counts of individual papers via a BP neural network. J. Informet. **14**(3), 101039 (2020)
23. Yan, R., Tang, J., Liu, X., Shan, D., Li, X.: Citation count prediction: learning to estimate future citations for literature. In: Proceedings of the 20th ACM international conference on Information and knowledge management, pp. 1247–1252 (2011)
24. So, M., Kim, J., Choi, S., Park, H.W.: Factors affecting citation networks in science and technology: focused on non-quality factors. Qual. Quant. **49**(4), 1513–1530 (2014). https://doi.org/10.1007/s11135-014-0110-z
25. Xie, J., Gong, K., Li, J., Ke, Q., Kang, H., Cheng, Y.: A probe into 66 factors which are possibly associated with the number of citations an article received. Scientometrics **119**(3), 1429–1454 (2019). https://doi.org/10.1007/s11192-019-03094-z
26. McClelland, D.C.: How motives, skills, and values determine what people do. Am. Psychol. **40**(7), 812–825 (1985)

Logical Dimension in Modeling

Gisin Vladimir[✉] [iD]

Financial University under the Government of the Russian Federation,
Leningradsky Prospect 49/2, Moscow 125167, Russia
vgisin@fa.ru

Abstract. The paper analyzes the proof of equivalence of the efficient market hypothesis and the hypothesis P = NP. The basis of this proof is enabling behavioral characteristics of the decision-making agent into the financial market model and, accordingly, characteristics of the observer into the computing model. Economic models, in which the market is efficient, are based on the same simplifying assumptions about the agent as the assumptions that make it possible to justify the hypothesis P = NP. A similar methodological approach makes it possible to show the incompatibility of Minsky's hypothesis of financial instability with the hypothesis of an efficient market. A key element in the analysis of all three hypotheses is the ability of a person to generate solutions that go beyond the framework of the system in which he is initially immersed. In the context of our analysis, an important aspect is applying non-classical logic. An additional justification for this statement provides the analysis of Arrow's impossibility theorem and FLP's impossibility theorem.

Keywords: Efficient Market · Computability · Impossibility Theorems · Formal Contexts · Non-classical Logics

1 Introduction

Hypotheses are at the heart of the construction of any model. The relationship between hypotheses and facts can be quite complex. Facts can be consistent with a hypothesis, serving as evidence in favor of its plausibility or contradict the hypothesis by refuting it. Another correlation of facts and phenomena with the hypothesis is also possible: the ability or inability of a hypothesis to explain the observed phenomena. In any case, the correlation of facts and phenomena with a hypothesis is investigated within the framework of some formalized model in which both facts and hypothesis are interpreted as some statements.

In this investigation, the meta-theory that provides the tools for such research is also important. It is generally accepted to use the tools of classical logic. There has been a growing interest in softer logical methods in recent decades. In some cases, this allows to increase the dimension of the model space, and by looking at the problem from a new dimension, it is possible more deeply understand the relationship between facts and hypotheses. A striking example here is Arrow's theorem. Its paradoxical statement

N. Agarwal et al. (Eds.): MSBC 2022, CCIS 1717, pp. 179–190, 2023.
https://doi.org/10.1007/978-3-031-33728-4_13

can be proved rather strictly within the framework of classical logic. If we assume that the logic of the group may differ from the classical one, the inconsistency of the statement of Arrow's theorem disappears. For example, if a complete distributive lattice with multiplication is taken as the logical scale of the group, the paradoxical conclusion of Arrow's theorem remains true only if there are no zero divisors in the logical scale.

Impossibility theorems, such as Arrow's theorem, play a fundamental role in economics. The role of some results about impossibility in mathematics is equally fundamental. The general scheme of proving impossibility theorems in economics and mathematics looks quite similar. In both cases, within the framework of some formalized system modeling a real system, the impossibility of the existence of some object with specified properties is established. If such an object can be observed in "reality," the question arises as to what conditions in the model can be adjusted to bring the model in line with the prototype. In economics, we are talking, as a rule, about an adequate modeling of the behavior of economic agents, in mathematics—about an adequate reflection of thought processes, i.e., about the adjustment of metatheory.

The appearance of the additional dimension mentioned earlier makes it possible to reveal the similarity of concepts that seem far apart. "Illuminated" from an external point, they begin to cast shadows that reveal unexpected similarities. An example is [1], where it is shown that under certain assumptions, the efficient market hypothesis (EMH) is equivalent to the hypothesis $P = NP$. A new "projection center" allows us to establish a connection between the efficient market hypothesis and the Minsky's financial instability hypothesis (FIH). As a result, the latter becomes an unexpected argument in favor of the validity of the hypothesis $P \neq NP$.

A deep reconsidering of the basic principles (postulates) of the construction of mathematical models was carried out by Sergeyev, see [2]. One of the main ideas put forward in [2] is that in mathematics and science, it is essential what instruments a researcher uses. The observation results and, accordingly, the model constructed by the researcher depend on the tools. Manipulations with infinity lead to "paradoxical" statements when using the instruments of classical theories. Paradoxes can get an explanation and lose their paradoxicality when the research instruments are replaced. In particular, Sergeyev introduces the concept of a gross unit $\boxed{1}$, which reflects the observer's idea of infinity (a key example is the number of grains in a bag when counting grains). This allows us to include the so-called infinity in the numerical system and consider, for example, a number $\boxed{1} + 1$ that differs from $\boxed{1}$ (a bag of grains plus another grain). Using the gross unit helps us take a fresh look at many fundamental concepts of modern mathematics, particularly the limiting behavior of dynamical systems. Changing the point of view on the number makes strange attractors less "strange" [3]. In this regard, it seems no coincidence that similar objects appear in the theory of numerical systems with a gross unit and in V.V.Tarasenko's fractal logics [4, 5].

The general idea of the dependence of the result on the instruments may well be extended to economic models. The logic of the researcher can play the role of the instrument. Modeling of researcher's logics forms the basis of metatheory.

Replacing classical vision with non-classical versions, in particular, the use of an updated numerical system or non-classical logic, leads to the appearance of a new additional dimension in the theory being developed. The most significant to the author is the connection between the three hypotheses: the efficient market hypothesis, the effective computability hypothesis, and Minsky's financial instability hypothesis.

The general context of "highlighting" classical hypotheses and impossibility theorems with the help of non-classical logic helps fully reveal these hypotheses' relation. For this purpose, the paper includes a summary of results related to these.

The paper is organized as follows. Section 1 illustrates the general ideas outlined in the introduction. It describes the emergence of non-standard concepts in the theory of formal contexts with the instrumental use of a non-classical logical scale. Section 2 explores Arrow's paradox in a situation where the logic of group decision-making is not classical. Here we analyze the connection between the Arrow impossibility theorem and the Fisher-Lynch-Paterson impossibility theorem. Finally, in Sect. 3, the result from [1] is analyzed, establishing the equivalence of the efficient market hypothesis and the efficient computability hypothesis and its relation to the financial instability hypothesis. Section 4 summarizes and outlines the directions for further research.

2   Tolerance Relations and Substructural Logics

Recall that a formal context is a triple (G, M, I) such that G is a set of objects, M is a set of attributes and

$$I \subseteq G \times M$$

is a binary relation relating objects and attributes. The formal context generates a Galois correspondence between the subsets of G and the subsets of M. Given a set of objects $A \subseteq G$, we denote by A' the set of their common attributes. Dually, if $B \subseteq M$ then B' denotes the set consisting of those objects in G that have all attributes from B.

A pair (A, B) is called a formal concept if $A \subseteq G$, $B \subseteq M$, $A' = B$, and $B' = A$.

If (A, B) is a formal concept then A is called the extent, and B is called the intent.

A formal context (G, M, I) generates a similarity (tolerance) relation T on the set of objects G: two objects are connected by this relation if they have a common attribute. In turn, given a tolerance relation (reflexive and symmetric relation) T on G, tolerance classes form an attribute space. The membership relation serves as an object-attribute relation.

In the classical approach, it is assumed that the truth degrees of statements are evaluated in a binary scale $\{0, 1\}$. This requirement can be waived, and a more flexible 1 scale of truth degrees L can be used to evaluate the relationship between objects and attributes (see [6]). In particular, let L be a complete lattice with zero and unit. In addition we suppose that L is endowed with associative operation $*$ such that L turns to be an ordered monoid with zero and unit. Tolerance relation T can be presented as a mapping

$$T : G \times G \to L$$

such that $T(x, x) = 1$ and $T(x, y) = T(y, x)$ for all $x, y \in G$.

The problem of building an attribute space can be reformulated as follows: we have to build M and correspondence

$$S : G \times M \to L$$

such that $T = SS^{-1}$, i.e.,

$$T(x, y) = \sup\{S(x, m) * S(y, m) | m \in M\} \text{forall} x, y \in G.$$

This problem admits a general solution [7].

By definition, an L-subset K of G is defined by a mapping.

$$K : G \rightarrow L.$$

If x is an object then $K(x)$ may be treated as the truth value of the statement "x is an element of K."

It can be shown [7] that an L-subset K is a tolerance class if and only if K satisfies the following equation.

$$K(x) = \bigwedge_{w}(K(w) \rightarrow T(x, y)).$$

where $\rightarrow$ and $*$ are adjoint.

A tolerance class K can be considered as a feature. The relation of K and an object x being defined by.

$$S(x, K) = K(x)$$

.

An interesting situation arises when the tolerance relation is understood in the usual classical sense, i.e., the similarity of objects is evaluated in binary logic, and the relationship of objects with attributes is evaluated on L. In this case (assuming that the set of objects is finite) if K is a tolerance class then $K(x)$ is a Boolean element of L for any object x.

Using non-binary L leads to the emergence of new concepts that do not arise if we limit ourselves to classical logic [8].

Consider the following example.

Let $G = \{x, y, z\}$ be a set of objects. We define a tolerance relation T in G as follows:

$$T(x, x) = T(y, y) = T(z, z) = 1, T(x, z) = T(z, x) = 0,$$

$$T(x, y) = T(y, x) = 1; T(z, y) = T(y, z) = 1.$$

Then a tolerance class K is defined by the equations

$$K(y) = 1, K(x) = \neg K(y).$$

Using binary logic we get two tolerance classes:

$$K_1(y) = K_1(x) = 1, K_1(z) = 0 \text{ and } K_2(y) = K_2(z) = 1, K_1(x) = 0.$$

So, there are three formal concepts:

$$(\{y\}, \{K_1, K_2\}), (\{x, y\}, \{K_1\}), (\{y, z\}, \{K_2\}).$$

Now, let $L = \{0, 1, u, v\}$ be a Boolean algebra such that $u \wedge v = 0$ and $u \vee v = 1$. We can present T using three attributes. Let $M = \{p, q, r\}$. We define S by

$$S(x, p) = u, S(x, q) = v, S(x, r) = 0,$$

$$S(y, p) = S(y, q) = S(y, r) = 1, S(x, q) = v, S(x, r) = 0,$$

$$S(z, p) = 0, S(z, q) = u, S(z, r) = v.$$

In addition to the crisp binary concept $(\{y\}, \{K_1, K_2\})$ we get three fuzzy concepts (A_i, B_i), $i = 1, 2, 3$, such that

$$A_1 = \{x, y\}, B_1(p) = u, B_1(q) = v, B_1(r) = 0,$$

$$A_2 = \{y, z\}, B_2(p) = 0, B_2(q) = u, B_2(r) = v,$$

$$A_3(x) = u, A_3(y) = 1, A_3(z) = v, B_3(p) = u, B_3(q) = 0, B_3(r) = v.$$

So we can see that a new concept extent appears.

3 The Arrow and Fisher-Lynch-Paterson Impossibility Theorems

The impossibility theorems, including the Arrow and Fisher-Lynch-Paterson theorems, play an important methodological role. The lock these theorems put on significant and important constructions forces us to carefully analyze the conditions of these theorems and look for bypasses. This section compares two of the most well-known impossibility theorems. The comparison shows that the paradoxical conclusions of these theorems could disappear if we accept the hypothesis that group logic is not classical binary logic.

In his famous 1951 paper, Arrow [9] showed that the aggregation functions of individual preferences should be "dictatorial" (i.e., coincide with the preferences of one of the agents) if this function satisfies a particular set of "natural" requirements. Since then, a number of so-called impossibility theorems have been obtained [10]. The search for (non-dictatorial) methods of aggregation of preferences forces us to look for ways to leave aside the "natural" Arrow conditions. One of these paths leads to the use of non-classical logics [11]. It seems natural to assume that the logic of group decision-making may not be classical [12]. A similar situation has arisen in a seemingly distant field far from economics – the theory of distributed systems. The Fisher-Lynch-Paterson impossibility theorem (FLP-theorem) [13] was proved three and a half decades after the publication of Arrow's work. According to this theorem, there does not exist a deterministic algorithm for achieving consensus (satisfying "natural" conditions) in an asynchronous computing network if at least one of the network nodes may fail. This theorem has become widely known in connection with the emergence and development of blockchain technology. Consensus algorithms are key to blockchain technology, and developers of open blockchain platforms are forced to look for ways to circumvent the

FLP-theorem. The path proposed by Nakamoto [14] (the creator of Bitcoin) is associated with the rejection of determinism. Nakamoto's proposed method of achieving probabilistic consensus (proof of work, POW) is very costly with respect to computational resources. Algorithms using proof of stake (POS) should prevent excessive costs, see [15]. However, even there "impossibility" theorems appear [16].

Analyzing proofs of the Arrow and Fisher-Lynch-Paterson theorems, we can identify one common feature: the decisive step in the proof of both theorems is associated with a leap in the assessment of the truth of some statements.

Thus, one of the shortest proofs of Arrow's theorem is based on the following reasoning. For agent i, $i = 1, 2, ..., n$, let $r_i(x, y)$ be a logical assessment of the truth of the statement "x is preferable to y". We consider a sequence of profiles $r^{(0)}$, $r^{(1)}$, ..., $r^{(n)}$ such that the initial zeros in the estimate $r_i(x, y)$ are sequentially replaced by ones. So $r_i(x, y) = 0$ for all i in the profile $r^{(0)}$. In $r^{(1)}$, $r_1(x, y)$ is replaced by one, etc. Finally, $r_i(x, y) = 1$ for all i in $r^{(n)}$. The social preference should be zero for $r^{(0)}$ and one for $r^{(n)}$. There exists a profile where we have a jump from zero to one in the sequence of the aggregate values: $R^{(k-1)}(x, y) = 0$ for profile $r^{(k-1)}$ and $R^{(k)}(x, y) = 1$ for profile $r^{(k)}$. Then it is easy to show that agent k is a dictator.

Similar reasoning underlies the proof of the Fisher-Lynch-Paterson theorem. Let some Boolean variable v be given. The global state is called bivalent if the system can move from it, depending on the development of a sequence of events, to a global state in which the consistent value is $v = 0$, or to a global state in which the consistent value is $v = 1$. The global state is called univalent if only one value of the variable v is possible for any sequence of permissible events. Accordingly, univalent global states are called 0-valent or 1-valent.

Let us assume that consensus is achievable at any initial state of the system. If all nodes have a value of 0 in the initial state $S^{(0)}$, this state is 0-valent. If all nodes have a value of 1 in the initial state, this state is 1-valent. In the state $S^{(0)}$, we will sequentially, starting from the first node, replace zeros with ones. At some node i, the 0-valent state will be replaced by a 1-valent one. Let us denote by I_0 the initial state we had before this replacement, and by I_1 the one obtained after the replacement. Let us assume that node i failed before it could transmit its value. From the point of view of the other participants (nodes), the system states achievable from I_0 and achievable from I_1 do not differ. This means that this state is bivalent and consensus cannot be reached. According to this short reasoning, it can be seen that the failing node essentially performs the function of a dictator in the sense of Arrow.

Applying non-classical logics in the Arrow paradox is studied quite intensively and is primarily associated with the assessment of the intensity of preferences in various logical scales [17]. In particular, if the segment [0;1] with the t-norm

$$u * v = \max(u + v - 1, 0)$$

as a conjunction is used as a logical scale, a solution can be obtained by averaging profile estimates of agent preferences [18]. The reason for this is the existence of zero divisors in the logical scale. This result admits to a far-reaching generalization.

Suppose that the intensity of group preference is evaluated in a complete lattice L. A preference profile on the set of alternatives is given by an ordered set (r_i), where r_i is the characteristic function of the agent i preference relation valued in the binary scale $\{0, 1\}$. The aggregate preference is also given by the characteristic function, but this function takes values in the scale L. All individual preferences should be reflexive, complete, and transitive, i.e.

$$r_i(x, x) = 1; \text{ if } r_i(x, y) = 0 \text{ then } r_i(y, x) = 1;$$

$$\min(r_i(x, y), r_i(y, z)) \le r_i(x, z)$$

for any agent i and all alternatives x, y, z.

The aggregate preference should also be reflexive, complete and transitive. Taking into account the replacement of the logical scale, the transitivity condition looks as follows:

$$R(x, y) * R(y, z) \le R(x, z).$$

In addition, the aggregation rule must have the following properties:

(monotonicity) if an actor in a preference profile increases the position of x in their ranking then x cannot decrease in the ranking produced by the preference aggregation rule;

(independence) if in two profiles all agents rank alternatives x and y in the same way, then the group preferences corresponding to these profiles rank these alternatives equally;

(unanimity) if all agents prefer alternative x to y, the same is true for the corresponding group preference;

(neutrality) if a pair of profiles is given such that any agent in the first profile ranks alternatives x and y in the same way as they ranks alternatives z and w in the second profile, then the aggregate preference corresponding to the first profile ranks x and y in the same way as the aggregate preference corresponding to the second profile ranks w and z.

In order not to complicate the notation, we illustrate the proof with four agents. For each pair of alternatives x, y, the ranking profile r is given by a binary string. For example, $r(x, y) = (1, 1, 0, 0)$ this means that agents 1 and 2 prefer alternative x, and agents 3, 4 prefer alternative y.

Let x, y, z be three different alternatives. Consider a sequence of profiles such that

$$r^{(0)}(x, y) = (0, 0, 0, 0), r^{(1)}(x, y) = (1, 0, 0, 0), r^{(2)}(x, y) = (1, 1, 0, 0)$$

$$r^{(3)}(x, y) = (1, 1, 1, 0), r^{(4)}(x, y) = (1, 1, 1, 1).$$

According with unanimity, we have $R^{(0)}(x, y) = 0$ and $R^{(4)}(x, y) = 1$. There is a point in the profile sequence where the "zero" solution changes to a "non-zero" one. Assume for certainty that $R^{(1)}(x, y) = 0$, $R^{(2)}(x, y) = v$ and $v \ne 0$. It can be shown that agent 2 is a dictator unless there are zero divisors in L. In fact, consider a profile r such that

$$r(x, y) = (1, 0, 1, 1), r(x, z) = (1, 0, 0, 0), r(y, z) = (1, 1, 0, 0).$$

By the neutrality condition, we have

$$R(x, z) = R^{(1)}(x, y) = 0$$

since $r(x, z) = r^{(1)}(x, y)$. In a similar way $R(y, z) = v$.

Let $R(x, y) = u$. Then, by transitivity, $u * v \leq 0$. Thus, $u * v = 0$. If there is no zero divisors in L then $u = 0$. So

$$R(x, y) = 0 = r_2(x, y).$$

Then we can see that $R(y, x) = 1 = r_2(y, x)$. Therefore for profile r, the group decision coincides with the decision of agent 2. Further, using the properties of the aggregation function, it can be shown that agent 2 is a dictator.

Consider an example of a non-dictatorial aggregation rule when L is a nonlinear lattice with zero divisors. Put $a * b = a \wedge b$ by definition. Let u, v be non-zero elements of L such that $u * v = 0$. We define the aggregation rule as follows:

$$R(x, y) = 0 \text{ iff } r_1(x, y) = 0 \text{ and } r_2(x, y) = 0;$$

$$R(x, y) = u \text{ iff } r_1(x, y) = 1 \text{ and } r_2(x, y) = 0;$$

$$R(x, y) = v \text{ iff } r_1(x, y) = 0 \text{ and } r_2(x, y) = 1;$$

$$R(x, y) = 1 \text{ iff } r_1(x, y) = 1 \text{ and } r_2(x, y) = 1.$$

It can be easily seen that this aggregation rule is not dictatorial and satisfies all necessary conditions. We show, for example, that R is transitive, that is

$$R(x, y) \wedge R(y, z) \leq R(x, z)$$

for all x, y, z.

If $R(x, z) = u$ then $r_2(x, z) = 0$. Since r_2 is transitive we have $r_2(x, y) = 0$ or $r_2(y, z) = 0$. In the first case, $R(x, y) = u$ either $R(x, y) = 0$. In the second case $R(y, z) = u$ either $R(y, z) = 0$. In both cases

$$R(x, y) \wedge R(y, z) \leq R(x, z)$$

holds.

The case where $R(x, z) = v$ can be considered similarly.

Now suppose that $R(x, z) = 0$. Then

$$r_1(x, y) \wedge r_1(y, z) = 0 \text{ and } r_2(x, y) \wedge r_2(y, z) = 0.$$

If at the same time $R(x, y) \neq 0$ and $R(y, z) \neq 0$ then $R(x, y) = u$ and $R(y, z) = v$, either $R(x, y) = v$ and $R(y, z) = u$. In both cases we have $R(x, y) \wedge R(y, z) = 0$.

Note that in the nonlinear case, it is possible to build a non-dictatorial aggregation function without using averaging functions (it is the averaging functions that plays a key role in the case of a linear logical scale, see [18]).

As for blockchain, the use of intuitionistic logic, particularly, variations of Kripke models, looks adequate. For justification, we will give a brief formalization of the blockchain. The blockchain stores information about events of a distributed system in blocks. Miners (network nodes) are engaged in the formation of blocks. Each block b contains a reference to its predecessor $f(b)$, obtained using cryptographic hash functions, and a timestamp $t(b)$. Each block, taking into account its references to previous blocks (direct to the immediate predecessor and indirect to earlier ones), contains a description of a potentially possible history of events in the network. If we assume the latency of message delivery in the network, then candidate blocks form a tree with a common "trunk". The consensus of the nodes should be reached regarding the predicate of including the block in the chain of blocks $c(b,t)$, where t is the current moment in time, with the discarding of extra (orphan) blocks. The blocks on which consensus is reached are sinking deeper into the blockchain. With the depth of immersion, the probability increases that the block will not become an orphan. Logically, this process can be described within the framework of temporal logic [19]. However, unlike [19], states can form a tree that is not a chain, and the evaluation of the truth of $c(b,t)$ can be obtained by attributing (binary) truth values to the blocks-nodes of the corresponding tree. This brings the proposed logic scheme closer to the branching time logic. Thus, in the case of blockchain, the possibility of reaching consensus can be explained by the fact that the collective logic is non-classical. Note that even in this case, nonlinear logic scales come into play.

4   Efficient Market Hypothesis and Efficient Computability

In the introduction, we have already written that the use of non-classical logic can be considered as the movement of a light source, forcing the models to cast new shadows. An example is [1], where it is shown that under certain assumptions, the efficient market hypothesis (EMH) is equivalent to the hypothesis $P = NP$. Another move of the "projection center" makes it possible to establish a connection between the efficient market hypothesis and the Minsky's financial instability hypothesis (FIH). As a result, the latter becomes an unexpected argument in favor of the validity of $P \neq NP$.

Note that [1] uses a weak form of the efficient market hypothesis: future stock prices cannot be predicted based on past price data. The hypothesis $P = NP$ is also considered in a simplified form: if the solution of a problem can be effectively verified, then the problem can be effectively solved (efficiency in this case means the existence of an algorithm that works in polynomial time). Schematically, the justification for the equivalence of EMH and $P = NP$ looks as follows. The market's history is represented as a space of sets of ternary sequences (-1 – down, 1 – up, 0 – flat). The strategy attributes one of three values to sequences (buy, sell, neutral position). If some financial market player managed (perhaps by chance) to find a winning strategy, assuming $P = NP$, other market participants could find this strategy, and such a strategy could not be a winning one. Similar reasoning is used to prove the opposite. The ideas from [1] were further developed and generalized in [20], where the efficiency of markets was replaced by "almost efficiency," and the condition $P = NP$ was a condition for the existence of a specific quasi-polynomial algorithm.

Analyzing the proof, it is not difficult to notice that the equivalence of the two hypotheses can be established by including an economic agent in the model, whose behavior, on the one hand, is an exogenous factor; on the other hand, the behavior of economic agents is the source of uncertainty that causes complexity. In both models, we can simplify the representation of the agent, which in a certain sense corresponds to a reduction in dimension. This will lead to an efficient market model in an economy with rational (possibly limited rational) agents. In mathematics, we obtain a computational model in which an NP-class problem can be efficiently solved (in the latter case, efficiency, of course, does not mean the presence of a polynomial algorithm, but can be defined, for example, as the ability to find an approximate solution or a solution in subexponential time).

Let us now focus on the connection of Minsky's concepts with the efficient market hypothesis. Formulating his hypothesis of financial instability (FIH), Minsky looks at the EMH hypothesis, it would seem, from a completely different angle, see [21, 22]. Nevertheless, in the FIH concept, "additional dimension" is also determined by the peculiarities of the behavior of economic agents and the decisions they make. In this connection, we note that the assumption $P \neq NP$ does not contradict the fact that a particular solution can be found to an effectively unsolvable problem in general. Similarly, an investor, working in an efficient market can develop a strategy that will bring him success in some finite period of time. In both cases, the solution of the problem is determined not by algorithmic approaches, but by the ability to discover new facts and patterns characteristic of human thinking. In fact, it is also one of the most important foundations of FIH.

According to Minsky's theory, the financial structure of the capitalist economy becomes more and more fragile during the period of prosperity, evolving from a hedging regime to a speculative regime and then towards a Ponzi regime. During the growth companies in highly profitable sectors of the economy receive generous remuneration for taking on more and more debts. The success of these companies encourages others to act similarly. No one wants to be left behind because of insufficient investment. The increase in profits also fuels the trend towards higher debt, easing creditors' fears that new loans may remain unpaid.

Minsky described in detail the aspects of FIH that come to the fore during the expansion. One of them is the evolution of the economy (or sector of the economy) from a hedging regime to a speculative finance regime, and then towards a Ponzi regime. In hedging mode, borrowers can repay interest and principal when the loan matures. In speculative mode, they can only return interest, and, therefore, must prolong financing. In Ponzi mode, companies have to borrow even more to pay interest on their existing liabilities.

In the context of our analysis, a key aspect of FIH is the emphasis on lending as an innovative, profit-oriented business. Banks and other financial intermediaries seek innovation both in relation to the assets they acquire and in relation to the liabilities they sell. New financial instruments (such as securitization) allow for meeting the demand for money at the moment, postponing the fulfillment of obligations at a later date.

Problems arise when it becomes clear that it is necessary to sell assets in order to make their payments. Forced sale of assets may lead to their revaluation. While the accumulation of debt can last for years, revaluation can be fleeting. This can lead to a collapse, as a result of which the value of assets will fall sharply, and the volume of loans will dry up to such an extent that investment and output will fall, and unemployment will rise sharply.

Minsky's idea of the role of new financial instruments in the formation of excessive debt burden can be interpreted in the context of [1]. In fact, the price of a derivative instrument is defined as a function on the space of sequences describing the dynamics of the underlying instruments. Regardless of whether the execution of a contingent claim is connected with time or with the price level, the lengths of the corresponding ternary sequences can be arbitrarily long. Solving the arising optimization problem may take non-polynomial time. In that way the market turns to be inefficient.

Thus, innovations show market inefficiency, because according to EMH, even if individual decision makers incorrectly evaluate assets, the market as a whole evaluates them correctly, and financial instruments are driven by an "invisible hand" to a certain set of prices that reflect the underlying or fundamental value of assets. In models based on Minsky's ideas, cyclicity is inevitably generated by endogenous factors. According to Minsky, models of efficient markets arise due to simplification: in these models, money is considered as an exogenous factor. The inclusion of money in the model as an endogenous factor leads to an inevitable violation of efficiency.

Summing up, the hypothesis of financial instability of Minsky turns out to be a kind of additional confirmation of the hypothesis $P \neq NP$.

5 Conclusion

We have considered various models from different branches of mathematics, economics and finance theory. What they have in common is that the content of the underlying hypotheses is fully revealed with the complication of the basic logic.

The game-theoretic approach to substantiating probability theory and finance theory shed additional light on this problem (see [23]). In this book, the so-called Fundamental Interpretative Hypothesis introduced earlier is being developed and improved. This hypothesis from the metatheory connects the model with reality. Depending on its interpretation, one can come to the hypothesis of an efficient market or to the hypothesis of the impossibility of a betting system.

Note that the implementation of this approach gives rise to constructions where the logic of the decision-maker ceases to be classical. This leads to a more nuanced understanding of the probability measure, which splits into two (sometimes non-additive) measures: the measure of possibility and the measure of necessity. One way or another, there is an outgrowth of the classical binary logic.

The significance of the interpretative hypothesis is much broader than the above embodiments. It shows that, even developing an abstract mathematical theory, it is necessary to consider the observer's peculiarities. Furthermore, the vision of this observer will not necessarily be black and white.

The nonlinearity, the importance of which has become apparent for dynamic models, begins to play a role in static models, complicating their logic and thereby bringing them closer to the complexity of the real world.

References

1. Maymin, P.Z.: Markets are efficient if and only if $P=NP$. Algorithmic Finance **1**(1), 1–11 (2011)
2. Sergeyev, Y.D.: Numerical infinities and infinitesimals: methodology, applications, and repercussions on two Hilbert problems. EMS Surv. Math. Sci. **4**(2), 219–320 (2017)
3. Sergeyev, Y.D.: Blinking fractals and their quantitative analysis using infinite and infinitesimal numbers. Chaos, Solitons Fractals **33**(1), 50–75 (2007)
4. Tarasenko, V.V.: Fractal construction of sign reality and multiscale self-reference. Philosophical Sci. **6**, 41–49 (2007). (in Russian)
5. Morozov, M.: The concept of "fractality" as a logical category. Problems of ontological and epistemological substantiation of mathematics and science **11**, 65–74 (2020). (in Russian)
6. Poelmans, J., Ignatov, D.I., Kuznetsov, S.O., Dedene, G.: Fuzzy and rough formal concept analysis: a survey. Int. J. Gen Syst **43**(2), 105–134 (2014)
7. Volkova, E.S., Gisin, V.B.: Representation of Tolerance relations and granulation of information with respect to substructural logic. In: 2019 XXII International Conference on Soft Computing and Measurements (SCM), pp. 12–14. IEEE (2019)
8. Volkova, E.S., Gisin, V.B.: Fuzzy tolerance classes. In: 2019 XXII International Conference on Soft Computing and Measurements (SCM), pp. 15–16. IEEE (2019)
9. Arrow, K.: Social Choice and Individual Values. Wiley (1951)
10. Fleurbaey, M., Salles, M.: A brief history of social choice and welfare theory. In: Fleurbaey, M., Salles, M. (eds.) Conversations on Social Choice and Welfare Theory, vol. 1, pp. 1–16. Springer Nature, Switzerland AG (2021)
11. Balinski, M., Laraki, R.: Judge: Don't Vote! Oper. Res. **3**(62), 483–511 (2014)
12. Kliemt, H.: Public choice: A methodological perspective. In: Maki, U. (ed.) Philosophy of Economics, pp. 765–798. Elsevier, North-Holland (2012)
13. Fischer, M.J., Lynch, N.A., Paterson, M.S.: Impossibility of distributed consensus with one faulty process. J. ACM **32**(2), 374–382 (1985)
14. Nakamoto, S.: Bitcoin: A peer-to-peer electronic cash system. Decentralized Business Review, 21260 (2008)
15. Chang, Y.Z.: Blockchain Viewed from Mathematics. Notices AMS **68**(10), 1740–1751 (2021)
16. Brown-Cohen, J., Narayanan, A., Psomas, A., Weinberg, S.M.: Formal barriers to longest-chain proof-of-stake protocols. In: Proceedings of the 2019 ACM Conference on Economics and Computation, pp. 459–473. ACM, Phoenix (2019)
17. Subramanian, S.: Social Values and Social Indicators. Springer Nature, Singapore (2021)
18. Duddy, C., Perote-Peña, J., Piggins, A. Arrow's theorem and max-star transitivity. Soc. Choice Welfare **36**(1), 25–34 (2011).
19. Lamport, L.: The temporal logic of actions. ACM Trans. Program. Lang. Syst. **16**(3), 872–923 (1994)
20. da Costa, N.C.A., Doria, F.A.: On the O'Donnell algorithm for NP–complete problems. Rev. Behav. Econ. **3**(2), 221–242 (2016)
21. Ferri, P.: Minsky's Moment: An Insider's View on the Economics of Hyman Minsky. Edward Elgar Publishing (2019)
22. Neilson, D.: Minsky. Polity Press, Cambridge, Medford (2019)
23. Shafer, G., Vovk, V.: Game-Theoretic Foundations for Probability and Finance. John Wiley & Sons, Hoboken (2019)

Quantification of Textual Responses To Open-Ended Questions In Big Data

Gediminas Merkys[1] and Daiva Bubeliene[2(✉)]

[1] Vytautas Magnus University, LT-44248 Kaunas, Lithuania
[2] Kaunas University of Applied Sciences, Pramones pr. 20, 50468 Kaunas, Lithuania
`daivabubeliene@gmail.com`

Abstract. The article summarizes many years of methodological experience with large-scale quantitative surveys to measure satisfaction with public services. Methodological advantages of extremely short questionnaires based on open-ended questions over long inventory-type questionnaires are pointed out. At the same time, the irrationally high costs of coding text responses are emphasized. The corresponding function/operation cannot be completely delegated to the computer. The possibility of triangulating inductive and hypothetical deductive approaches in coding is shown. Based on the Laplace-Moivre and central limit theorems, normality of empirical distributions can be postulated for dichotomous/binary variables, with all the resulting favorable consequences for the statistical analysis process. Digital information generated from qualitative textual information through interpretation and coding requires specific statistical analysis approaches. There is a lack of discourse on this topic in the methodological literature.

Keywords: survey inventory · open-ended questions · coding · content analysis · maxqda · triangulation

1 Introduction to the Problem: "Open-Ended Questions" as a Big Challenge but also a Good Redoubt for Social Survey Research

The article reflects many years of methodological experience with quantitative mass social surveys. A decade-long research focus was the development of a standardized survey instrument to measure consumer satisfaction regarding public services [9, 10]. The experience and methodological reflection of the research, whose origins date back to 2000, led to an understanding of the outstanding epistemological and heuristic importance of the so-called open-ended questions. This is particularly important when aiming at really high-quality research that could perform a subtle social diagnosis that would really benefit the clients, in this case, important decision-makers in public administration.

The first reason for a new and respectful approach to survey design based on open-ended questions has to do with mental changes in the public sphere. The further it goes, the more difficult it becomes under the conditions of modernity to attract respondents for mass surveys. Individualism trends are increasing, people tend to save their time, and protect their privacy and peace. It is a trivial attempt to guard against the overwhelming stream of redundant information. The principle of voluntary participation in social surveys is not a secret to anyone (WAPOR; ESOMAR etc.). Mass refusal to participate occurs even in surveys directly related to the interests and well-being of the respondents. The guardians of their privacy are certainly also users of public services, so in principle, there should be a motivation to participate in the surveys.

The percentage of refusals in surveys, often over 50%, destroys the whole "high moral" of statistics and methodology textbooks, which always report about the enormous importance of random sampling [8]. A person who agrees to participate in a survey today and fills out a long quantitative questionnaire has a very specific psychosocial profile. Such a person is no longer a realistic average representation of the population. It is a person who is constantly interested in public affairs, characterized by increased social responsibility, etc. It is known from the practice of surveys that especially 35–55 years old women from the middle social class with university degrees participate very willingly and conditionally actively in public affairs surveys. "Status people" are very reluctant to participate in surveys, regardless of gender, e.g. public service and company managers. Less educated youth, especially young and uneducated men, are also very reluctant to participate in surveys. The essential postulate of sampling - "every individual in the population had an equal chance of being selected and surveyed" - simply no longer works because it goes beyond the actual truth.

It is pointless and damaging to deny the need for random sampling, but the real problem is how to fully meet this basic requirement from an organizational perspective? Honest researchers today avoid boasting about "true" random sampling. It is appropriate to speak only of the convergence of a single survey design to the ideal of a random sample. This is justified by the diversity of the subclusters in the sample, both geographically and in terms of how respondents are approached. An important tool for ensuring sample quality is the control within the sample of various sociodemographic parameters known from official statistics.

The proliferation of online surveys has brought researchers a number of organizational and resource-saving benefits but has only exacerbated the problem of refusing to participate in survey research. Under current conditions, any survey project based on a long questionnaire becomes a priori a risky project. The likelihood that such a project will fail in general or suffer significant losses in the quality of the research increases dramatically. However, a long questionnaire is not an empty ambition of the researchers. A rich variable structure is an aspiration of any correlational study, improving the diagnostic quality of the study as a whole [11]. Unfortunately, even conditionally motivated respondents often drop a long online questionnaire in the middle of completing it.... The researcher's decision to discard or include the questionnaires in the study is another undermining stone to the quality of the survey.

One way to solve the problem is to drastically shorten the length of quantitative questionnaires. As practice has shown and as this article will show, such an idea works. There are at least some starting points for researchers here. For example, in measuring satisfaction with public transportation, instead of 7 very specific Likert-type items, simply formulate an abstract question about satisfaction with service that offers a 10- or 100-point response format on the visual analog scale [13]. Below the question is a text table asking respondents to comment and add to their quantitative assessment. Of course, one should be aware that the rate for filling in such additional open-ended questions is on average only 10–30 percent.

Even more radical and effective is the switch to an extremely short questionnaire. Only a few open-ended questions can be formulated, providing for a completely free written response. Quantitative questions are completely abandoned, with the exception of a few socio-demographic ones. From an inventory-type questionnaire with 100–150 primary items, we move to an extremely short questionnaire based on generally formulated 3–5 questions. The practice has shown that such an approach has been successful in two respects: 1) the motivation and cooperation of the subjects has improved, and the reversibility of the answers has increased; 2) in a heuristic sense, the results thus obtained are usually very valuable.

Someone may wonder if there is no motivation to fill out a long quantitative questionnaire, in which the response is registered in a few seconds, why should the desire to fill out a short questionnaire, in which the respondent has to formulate the answers himself, suddenly wake up? However, it was shown that filling out extremely short questionnaires based on 3–4 open-ended questions is not so affected by the refusal of the survey. Why such a phenomenon is triggered, there are currently no closer answers. It would be useful to conduct a special study.

A second reason why researchers have turned to open-ended question design is related to the well-known limitations of quantitative surveys (and quantitative methods in general). One important issue is the openness versus closedness aspect of social research. Quantitative research is objectively closed. If researchers have not considered an indicator when designing a quantitative survey, there is no chance that the corresponding subtopic will appear in the same measurement and study. The great pity is that exactly what the researchers had no idea about, what science - the relevant research direction - had no idea about, is not included in the structure of the research variables. The conservatism of science, the tendency of researchers to rely on the work of previous studies, often results in such a closed structure of variables appearing to be "frozen" and constantly reproduced. The structure is systematically perpetuated into the future without any significant increase in knowledge or innovative component being gained. Herein lies a major methodological and heuristic limitation of quantitative surveys, despite the many analytical advantages of a standardized survey.

It is the methodology of open-ended questions that sets the stage for overcoming the aforementioned limitations of the closed nature of quantitative research. Of course, if the wording of the questions is correct. In open-ended questions, respondents generate topics and subtopics themselves and disclose all nuances. The phenomenon of imposing the researcher's subjective theory and vision of social problems on respondents disappears [1].

Some examples from the research practice. Since 2000, the inventory-type questionnaire "Residents' satisfaction with public services" has been developed. Around 2013–2015, the questionnaire received a complete, established structure. The latter included 190 primary items, which were divided into 8 thematic scales and 33 subscales [9, 10] using factorial validation. The inventory was adopted in many Lithuanian municipalities. In some municipalities, the surveys were repeated 3–6 times every two to three years.

After decades of hindsight, it is clear that the inventory served the common good. There would be communities whose managers trusted the survey data and consistently aligned their strategic planning and investments to meet residents' expectations. Many publicly accessible, free recreation and leisure infrastructure facilities have been created. It meant: bicycle and pedestrian paths, beaches, various sports fields, extreme sports fields for youth, parks, small boat docks, etc. Quantitative surveys have consistently shown that freely accessible, nearby, and free recreation facilities are among the most sought-after priorities.

Having recognized the high "utility factor" of quantitative stocktaking, the closed nature of the methodology must be mentioned. It was not from decades of repeated quantitative surveys, but from the switch to extremely short questionnaires based exclusively on open-ended questions that some completely new needs of the population were recognized. For example, it was recognized that seniors in the big city prefer to have their own public, free spaces in each neighborhood for communication, games, artistic activities, meetings with celebrities, etc. In addition, just from the open-ended questions, it was found that residents are very satisfied with the new traffic circles in the city, as traffic safety has improved and tensions due to congestion have decreased. The city government can now plan traffic circles knowing that residents/voters will not question the investment of public funds as a result.

The heuristic breakthrough, the innovation, the expansion of knowledge about the population's concrete needs for public services, did not come from the quantitative inventory of 190 indicators that had been cultivated over decades, but from some surveys based only on open-ended questions.

The use of open-ended questions in mass surveys is highly problematic and comes at a price. 1. The question arises of how to convert the qualitative information, what are the free-form texts written by the respondents, into digital information? No matter which of the known coding methods is used, everything depends on time and mental costs, which are always irrationally large. 2. What statistical strategies are applicable to quantified data of the relevant type?

2 Illustration of the Problem Solutions and New Methodological Issues

Mass surveys were conducted in two Lithuanian municipalities on the topic of residents' satisfaction with public services. These are the municipality of Siauliai, the fourth largest city in Lithuania, and the circular municipality of Kaunas, which surrounds the metropolis of Kaunas. Both municipalities have about 100,000 inhabitants each. The first is a typical urbanized area, while the second municipality is a mixed type, with both urbanized and non-urbanized areas. In Siauliai, 3,002 people were surveyed. In the Kaunas district, 1.8 thousand respondents[1] were interviewed. In both cases, a minimalist questionnaire (in terms of scope) was used, consisting of some rather abstractly worded open-ended questions with, of course, some standard questions on the socio-demographic status of the respondents.

---

[1] Such large samples are useful because diagnostic decisions are also made with respect to smaller administrative-territorial units of the community, which may number a dozen to two dozen.

Examples of open-ended questions:

1. What specific tasks and problems should the Siauliai City Government focus on during the remainder of its term of office? Please define at least 3–5 problems or challenges.
2. What is it about the activities of the Siauliai City Government that gives you dissatisfaction or doubts? Criticise, and make suggestions. Please define 3–5 aspects.
3. What would you like to praise the local government for? What works or activities do you enjoy? Please define 3–5 points.
4. What do you see as the untapped opportunities in Siauliai? Do you have specific insights and ideas on how to manage the city better? Suggest.

The questions are formulated in such a way that they survey the general semantic field of the problem under investigation, but in no way force the respondents to escalate in advance certain topics and contents. The concrete thematic content of the answers must be generated entirely by the respondents themselves.

The organization of large-scale survey research based exclusively on open-ended questions is still considered a rarity and innovation. Somewhat more frequently, such precedents occur when an additional and clarifying open-ended question is integrated into the quantitative questionnaire. The introduction of open-ended questions into such projects means that they move a bit closer to a multi-method and triangulated design. This undoubtedly increases the value of the study. In Germany, the ALLBUS[2] - General Population Survey of the Social Sciences - project usually uses large samples (N ≥ 3000), but open-ended questions are still used as a complement.

With large samples, open-ended questions are usually used to generate a large amount of textual information of a qualitative-interpretative nature, which then has to be converted into digital information, i.e., quantified. Here are some examples.

Answering 4 open questions, the surveyed residents generated 70,933 words in Kaunas County Municipality and 110,000 words in Siauliai Municipality, respectively. If we comment on the latter case, it results in over 600 printed sheets of A4 format.

Various popular computer programs, e.g. MAXQDA is simply good data management tool. Based on the interpretation of the answers, the quantification decision for a single sentence must be made by the researcher. This deeply creative function and operation cannot be completely delegated to a computer [5, 6].

In the case of the two studies mentioned above, a unique technique for encoding text responses was developed and tested. Initially, indivisible - "atomistic" - units of meaning were sought in authentic text utterances, as usual. Let us assume that the respondent answers: "… it is necessary to manage not only the city center, but also the outskirts; to install more traffic circles; to finish what has been started, to "eat" less among themselves in the Council, and to care more about the concerns of the city and its residents." In this fairly typical example of a response from a city resident, up to 4 different indivisible semantic units can be distinguished. These are statements: 1) about the even development of the city, non-discrimination of individual areas; 2) a desire to install even more traffic circles; 3) a call to finish the work and projects started; 4) fewer conflicts in the council and focus on joint work, representing the interests of residents and the city.

---

[2] German General Social Survey ALLBUS – Allgemeine Bevölkerungsumfrage.der Sozialwissenschaften.

The presence of an isolated semantic unit is coded as 1 - "the feature is present" and its absence is coded as 0 - "the feature is absent". This is a classic technique of quantitative content analysis. The research has a qualitative component only at the beginning but later transforms into a traditional quantitative study. The prerequisite is that the coding of the answers is carried out by at least two analysts, whose work results are statistically compared [12].

For the above surveys, coding was performed by two analysts (authors). Coding was done in two different ways using MAXQDA [4, 7]. The first method is purely induc-tive - from separateness to commonality, from bottom to top. When repeated semantic units are found, they are grouped into a summary subcategory. Later, when there is a reason, the subcategories are combined and expanded. Another way is to provide an analysis path from commonality to separateness, from top to bottom. It is appropriate to call this method of category formation hypothetic-deductive. A hypothetical estimate is made of which categories are likely to occur, and on this basis, a preliminary network of theoretically expected categories is created. For example, in coding the question "on which tasks should local government focus?", some of the categories can be formulated as successfully as possible before contact with the empirics. At least some of the cate-gories inevitably relate to individual sectors of public services such as education, social protection, primary health care, public transport, urban development, spatial planning, environmental protection, leisure, and recreation, etc. It is clear that in one case very concrete services and objects are desired, in another case the desires are formulated abstractly and only the general direction is mentioned. Moreover, such a network is con-stantly refined in the coding process, and harmonized in terms of data. The paradox is that in the later stages of coding, the networks of categories created by different analysts and with different methods are very similar to each other. Then, through group discus-sion among coders and expert consensus, a final list of categories with precise, purified labels is created.

Apparently, researchers can be blamed, so why not a quantitative statistical analysis of the correspondence of coding systems? Due to the phenomenon of synonymy, an identical object or phenomenon is very often named by different coders with different words whose roots hardly coincide. Without prior processing of the results of the two coding systems, it is simply not technically possible to proceed to correlation analysis. On the other hand, it has been found in practice that the phase of further processing and preparation for correlation analysis generates a mature system of categories whose logical/content validity is quite obvious. The formulations of category names obtained in different ways are definitively recorded. The limits of the logical/semantic scope of the categories are clarified. After that, it is possible to continue the quantitative research as a matrix of dichotomous (or binary) features is obtained - "the feature is present" (1) or "the feature is absent" (0).

In the methodological literature, the authors note, there is a lack of discourse on what statistical strategies might be applied to such data, which have evolved from free text to rigorously structured digital information? There are some risks and unanswered methodological questions. Some points are worth discussing here.

According to Moivre-Laplace and the Central Limit Theorem, the normality of their empirical distributions can be postulated for dichotomous/binary variables [2, 3]. This results in a number of normative advantages of statistical analysis. The distribution's mean indicates the corresponding category's empirical probability, expressed as relative frequencies or percentages. It is assumed that the scale in question meets the requirements for metric scales [13, 14]. It is possible to create ratings and apply inferential statistics to calculate a confidence interval. If the sample is large and the filling of most categories with empirical frequencies is not minimal, chi-square statistics, contingency analyses, factor analyses, and cluster analyses can be applied. The resulting category structure can be considered a closed system and diagnostic construct. It is possible to relate empirical frequencies of categories to sociodemographic variables. When it comes to surveys on satisfaction with public services, it is useful to identify specific categories "female" and "male," "seniors," "youth," and "families with children," or categories that are indifferent to sociodemographic status and relevant to all population groups.

Some problems are caused by extremely asymmetric distributions when the filling frequency of a category is only 1 percent or even part of it. Such distributions are not very attractive from a formal statistical point of view, but from a heuristic point of view, they can be diagnostically very meaningful and valuable. Typical of this is the aforementioned example of the desire of seniors in large cities to have free public facilities in each micro-neighbourhood. Even in a mixed natural sample of three thousand, of course, the relative frequency of such desires was extremely low. Most of the seniors interviewed were unfamiliar with the aforementioned idea and emphasized quite different things.

Another confusing, quite non-trivial question emerged: At what number of respondents should the category's percentage mention frequencies be calculated? If the respondent has answered at least one of several open questions in detail, there is nothing against including him/her in the survey database. In this case, we are talking about the N_{Total} indicator, which represents the total number of participants in the survey. Open-ended questions act as a stimulus to which respondents react with varying degrees of activity. In practice, we have yet to see a precedent where all open-ended questions would have the same percentage of responses. In this way, it is appropriate to distinguish such a quantity as $N_{question\text{-}response}$. The size represents the number of responses to a single question. Next, experience with statistical processing of open-ended questions on satisfaction with public services showed that it is necessary to distinguish between two relative quantities. These are 1) "empirical probability of issue escalation (%)" or simply escalation probability and 2) "percent mention of issue" or simply "percent mention." The first relative variable is calculated from N_{total} of all subjects, and the second mentioned variable is calculated from $N_{question}$ response of those who answered a particular question. When $N_{total} = N_{question\ response}$, both quantities - the probability of escalation ($P_{escalation}$) and the frequency of mentions - ($P_{frequency\ of\ mentions}$) coincide completely.

Percentages, especially when it comes to the frequency of agreement or disagreement in the classic 5-point Likert scale, are a fairly clear, trivial quantity. However, it would be a big mistake to equate Likert percentages and "topic escalation percentages" in a diagnostic sense. Escalation probability (%) has much more heuristic potential than common percentages calculated from a traditional quantitative questionnaire. In service satisfaction surveys based on open-ended questions that do not impose the content of the answers, a quantity such as escalation probability is extremely diagnostic. A high percentage means that the service in question, its availability, and quality is really becoming a very sensitive issue in the population being studied. If a topic receives a low percentage of escalation, it is relevant to a small population or highly relevant only to a small specific segment of users. If the topic in question does not generate an escalation percentage in the mass survey (size $P_{escalation} \approx 0$), then it is clear beyond doubt that the service in question is completely unproblematic because no one mentions it and it does not escalate. Like water and air, until these are not missing, no one will worry about it.

In the mentioned city of Siauliai at the population survey, an anomalous fact was discovered. In a sample of 3,002 inhabitants of a large city, there were practically no precedents when the inhabitants escalated the problems concerning the city's public transport. Only a few respondents expressed a desire to extend the route of one or another city bus by several neighborhoods. In Lithuania, the problem of public transport is highly disturbed[3] both in big cities and in non-urbanized areas. For various reasons[4], the city of Siauliai has managed to create a well-functioning mass transit system. This was shown by a mass survey based on open questions and especially by the fact that in a huge sample, almost nobody escalated the problem in question.

Another fact is striking. Around the same time, on the basis of the above-mentioned quantitative inventory, a service satisfaction survey was conducted among residents of the same city Siauliai. Seven Likert-scaled primary items, as already mentioned, were intended for the evaluation of public transport. A large number of indicators of the whole inventory allowed us to calculate the percentile rank of each service indicator. The percentile ranks for 7 service indicators ranged from 61st to 76th, with an average of 67th percentile. Such relative sizes indicate that the service is rated above average, but not very well. Service scores do not fall into the highest quartile of the rating (Q 4/4), which begins at the 75th percentile rank.

The question is, which of the results of nearly simultaneous surveys is more reliable, inventory surveys using hundreds of standardized indicators or surveys based on only a few open-ended questions? Why does this relative dissatisfaction with service still show up in a standardized survey with 560 respondents? Due to the influence of media and social stereotypes, public opinion is influenced, leading to the assumption that public transportation services in the country are neglected, which is partially true.

Hypothetically a standardized questionnaire is often quite routine, sometimes formal, without the deeper engagement of the respondent with his or her own assessment. One thing is clear, trust and reliability should be prioritized especially in open questions and not in standardized surveys. If 3 thousand of the respondents do not escalate the issue of local public transport, it does not mean otherwise that there are no serious problems with the service in question in the city at all.

The experience and methodological findings formulated on the basis of opinion surveys among users of public services can be transferred without hesitation to research in other directions and topics: market research, voter behavior research, etc.

---

[3] High-level decision-makers in Lithuania tend to treat mass transit as a commercial service and incorrectly ignore the social and environmental context of the service.

[4] Due to the total destruction in the First and Second World War, the city was redesigned. It is dominated by geometrically regular blocks and optimally wide streets. There are no natural obstacles to transportation in the city - rivers, mountains and so on. Besides the objective assumptions, the good management of transport services in the city also had a positive effect.

3 Conclusions

1. The use of open-ended questions in large samples of social surveys, if N≈3000, is associated with irrational organizational and mental costs. The interpretation and coding of free-text responses cannot be completely delegated to a computer.

2. The high costs are justified by several arguments. 1. The closed nature of quantitative surveys is overcome and mitigated. 2. High heuristic potential of the survey. 3. if extremely short questionnaires based on open questions are used, then the motivation and willingness to participate in the survey are also increased.

3. Using a triangulation of inductive and hypothetical-deductive approaches is worthwhile when coding the free-text responses.

4. Processing digital data generated by interpretation and coding from free text requires specific statistical approaches. There is a lack of discourse on this topic in the methodological literature.

References

1. Ferrario, B., Stantcheva, St.: Eliciting People's First-Order Concerns: Text Analysis of Open-Ended Survey Questions. AEA Papers and Proceedings, 112, pp. 163–69, (2022). https://doi.org/10.1257/pandp.20221071

2. Fischer, H.: A History of the Central Limit Theorem. From Classical to Modern Probability Theory, New York (2011)

3. Georgii, H.O.: Stochastik: Einführung in die Wahrscheinlichkeitstheorie und Statistik, 4. Auflage, de Gruyter (2009)

4. Gizzi, M.C., Rädiker, S.: The Practice of Qualitative Data Analysis. Research Examples Using MAXQDA. MAXQDA Press, Berlin, 1st edition. (2021) https://doi.org/10.36192/978-3-948768058

5. He, Zhoushanyue, Schonlau, M.: Coding Text Answers to Open-ended Questions: Human Coders and Statistical Learning Algorithms Make Similar Mistakes. methods, data, analyses, [S.l.], ISSN 2190–4936. 15(1), p. 17 (2021). Accessed: 29 Dec. 2022 https://mda.gesis.org/index.php/mda/article/view/2020.10/279. https://doi.org/10.12758/mda.2020.10

6. Zhoushanyue, H.: On the Automatic Coding of Text Answers to Open-ended Questions in Surveys. UWSpace, (2021). http://hdl.handle.net/10012/16643

7. Kuckartz, U., Rädiker, S.: Analyzing Qualitative Data with MAXQDA. Springer Nature Switzerland AG. (2019)

8. Lohr, Sh, L.: Sampling: design and analysis. Chapman and Hall/CRC, (2021)

9. Merkys, G., Brazienė, R.: Evaluation of public services provided by municipalities in Lithuania: an experience of applying a standardized survey inventory. Social Sciences, 4 (66), pp. 50–61. Kaunas, Technologija (2009)

10. Merkys, G., Brazienė, R.: New standardised survey inventory for evaluation of services provided by municipalities//Development of Services World: New Thinking, New Actions: proceedings of 4th international scientific seminar, Oct 16–17, 2009, Kaunas University of Technology. Kaunas: KTU EMTC, pp.1–14, (2009)

11. Merkys, G.: Design and composition of questionnaires: techniques for response behavior by extremely long instruments//Quality and Equity in Higher Education - International Experiences and Comparisons: International Workshop, Nov 2008 / Ed. T. Bargel, M. Schmidt, H. Bargel. Konstanz: Universität Konstanz. nr. 53, p. 112–116. (2009)

12. Mohler, P.Ph., Zuell, C.: Applied Text Theory: Quantitative Analysis of Answers to Open-Ended Question. In West, M. D. (ed).: Applications of Computer Content Analysis. Westport: Aplex Publishing, S. 1–16, (2001)
13. Reips, U.F., Funke, F.: Interval-level measurement with visual analogue scales in nternet-based research: VAS Generator. Behav. Res. Methods **40**(3), 699–704 (2008). https://doi.org/10.3758/BRM.40.3.699
14. Steyer, R., Eid, M.: Messen und Testen, 2nd edn. Springer, Berlin, Heidelberg, New York (2001)

Optimization of Works Management of the Investment Project

Alexandr Mishchenko[1], Oleg Kosorukov[2,3] , and Olga Sviridova[4,5(✉)]

[1] UNITECH LEONOV Moscow Region University of Technology, Gagarina St., 42, 141074 Korolev, Russia
[2] Lomonosov Moscow State University, GSP-1, Leninskie Gory, 119991 Moscow, Russia
[3] Institute of Control Sciences named after V.A. Trapeznikov Russian Academy of Sciences, Profsoyuznaya st., 65, 117997 Moscow, Russia
[4] Financial University under the Government of the Russian Federation, 49 Leningradsky Prospekt, 125167 Moscow, Russia
olshan@list.ru
[5] Plekhanov Russian University of Economics, Russia, Stremyanny Lane, 36, 117997 Moscow, Russia

Abstract. The article focuses on optimizing project management with varying durations of work. A deterministic model of scheduling theory is considered, which involves the use of non-storable resources, taking into account the matrix setting of the execution time of operations by performers. The branches and bounds method for obtaining the optimal solution is proposed. A two-criteria model for evaluating the effectiveness of the schedule for random durations of works is considered.

Keywords: theory of scheduling · calendar plan · non-stock resources · optimization · two-criteria model · random duration of work

1 Introduction

Many management problems are somehow related to the allocation of limited resources. Modeling of their optimal application is often reduced to solving problems of the theory of scheduling, network planning, the formation of production programs, planning the conveyor systems' processes, the transport routing. These issues are often used to evaluate the effectiveness of projects implemented in various spheres of the national economy such as industrial production, warehousing systems, transport, and information data centers. The general formulation of these issues is to organize the execution of certain actions in time if a number of conditions are met. Each action consists of elementary operations called jobs (applications or tasks), which can either be prepared in advance or arrive dynamically. The organization of work is carried out in such a way as to minimize one of the following indicators such as work execution time, the average

The research was partly supported by Russian Science Foundation (project No. 22-71-10131).

N. Agarwal et al. (Eds.): MSBC 2022, CCIS 1717, pp. 201–217, 2023.
https://doi.org/10.1007/978-3-031-33728-4_15

weighted time of work execution, the volume of incomplete processing of applications for a certain period, the loss of time waiting for processing applications. Modeling the distribution of limited resources is often reduced to solving linear and nonlinear discrete optimization problems, most of which are NP-hard. These problems are mostly characterized by an exponential increase in the volume of calculations with an increase in the dimension of the problem [1]. This circumstance, as well as the fact that it is often necessary to find the optimal solution in the conditions of inaccurate initial information, determines the relevance of developing effective methods for managing limited resources.

In this article, the main attention will be paid to optimizing project management with changing work durations. Despite the fact that numerous methods and models for optimizing project resource management have been created at the current time. Nevertheless, there is a certain shortage of appropriate quantitative tools when solving the problem of minimizing the investment phase of a project in conditions of uncertainty and risk. At the same time, it is the investment phase, as the most time-consuming and capital intensive, that plays a significant role in the success of the entire project. Planning errors during this period caused by an unaccounted risk, can lead to significant losses.

A deterministic model of the theory of scheduling is considered, which assumes the use of non-stackable resources, taking into account the matrix assignment of the execution time of operations by performers, and a method of branches and boundaries for obtaining an optimal solution is proposed.

The methods of assessing the stability of schedules when performing continuous project work with various methods of setting changes in their duration are obtained. In a situation where the duration of work is set as random variables, a two-criterion model for evaluating the effectiveness of the schedule is proposed.

Models of optimal management of limited resources have been considered in a number of publications by domestic and foreign authors. For example, optimization problems of evaluating the effectiveness of production programs under conditions of uncertainty are studied in these articles [2, 3].

Methods for assessing the stability of schedules when changing task parameters are analyzed in following articles [4, 5]. Dynamic and static models and methods for managing limited resources in transport issues are considered in articles [6–8]. The problem of optimal control of resources of reentrant type in the formulation of the optimal cotrol problem of speed is considered in [9]. Exact and approximate algorithms for constructing optimal schedules for planning the operation of multiprocessor equipment are presented in following articles [10–12]. Models and methods for managing limited resources, which are reduced to solving minimax problems, are given in [13–19].

2   Deterministic Problem Statement

Let's consider the problem of optimizing the investment phase of the project in the following formulation.

Let the technological sequence of performing the work of this phase be given by an oriented acyclic graph $G(m, n)$, where m is the number of arcs, n is the number of vertices. We will further assume that the arcs define the technological sequence of work, and the vertices correspond to the operations. To perform each type of operation i, the resources specified by the vector $a_i = (a_{i1}, ..., a_{im}, ..., a_{im+1}, ..., a_{im1})$ are required.

We will assume that the resources of the $1,2,...m$ type are non-stock resources, and the resources of the $m + 1,..., m1$ type are storeable resources. The work of type i ($i = 1,2,...,n$) can be performed in time t_i that is allocated resources in the amount a_i type. It is impossible to interrupt execution of the work. Under the conditions of technological constraints on the sequence of executed activities defined by the digraph G (m,n) and resource constraints defined by the vector $b = (b_1, ..., b_m, ..., b_{m+1}, ..., b_{im1})$, all activities of the investment phase of the project have to be executed. To solve this problem, the scheme of the branch and boundary method can be used, which consists in the following method.

Step 1. Calculating the lower bound of the duration of the schedule on the optimal solution. In a situation where each work is performed by one performer, and the total number of performers is given by M type (the stock resources for all types of work in the required volumes are allocated), the lower bound T_l is calculated by the following formula:

$$T_l = max\left\{ S_{cr}, \frac{1}{M} \sum_{i=1}^{n} t_i \right\} \tag{1}$$

where S_{cr} is the length of the critical path of the directed graph G (m, n)

Step 2: Calculating the upper bound of the duration of the calendar plan on the optimal solution.

The upper bound T_u can be obtained by forming an admissible calendar plan and calculating its duration, which will be taken as T_u.

Step 3. If $T_u = T_l$, then the solution of the problem is obtained and it will be a schedule whose length is equal to T_l.

Step 4. If $T_u > T_l$, then continue the analysis of admissible schedules, calculating each time the current bottom estimate $T_l^{cur}(\tau)$ at the time of completion of the next job by the formula:

$$T_l^{cur}(\tau) = \tau + \max_{i=1,k}\left\{ S_i, \frac{1}{M} \sum_{i=1}^{n} t_i \right\}, \tag{2}$$

where

τ - the time of completion of one of the works in the formation of the current allowable schedule;

k - the number of paths in the graph G (n, m);

S_i - the path length of the oriented graph S_i, taking into account the complete or partial fulfillment of the work included in the path with the number i;

t_i - the length of the work with the number i taking into account its full or partial completion by the time τ;

M - number of the work performers.

If $T_l^{cur}(\tau) \geq T_u$, then the formation of the current schedule stops, because its duration will not be less than T_u and, therefore, it will not be optimal.

If $T_l^{cur}(\tau) < T_u$ then continue to form this calendar plan.

Thus calculating $T_l^{cur}(\tau)$ each time after the end of the next work the formed plan will either be discarded, or will be fully formed.

Denote the duration of the resulting new schedule by T^*. If $T^* < T_u$, then in the future we assume that the value of T_u is equal to T^*.

If the new value is presented by the following equation: $T_l = T_u$, then the optimal schedule is formed. If $T_u > T_l$, then proceed to the analysis of the next allowable schedule.

Continuing the described procedure of analyzing all the admissible schedules, we finally obtain one of two situations:

1. At the next adjustment value of T_u we get the following equation: $T_l = T_u$, and in this case the duration plan of T_l will be optimal.
2. After analyzing all admissible plans we obtain that $T_u > T_l$. In this case, the optimal plan is the one that corresponds to the last (minimum) value of T_u.

In the situation of high-dimensional problem when the number of works from several hundred to several thousands, we can use the scheme of truncated branch and boundary method, the essence of which is that we should not achieve the following equality: $T_u = T_l$, and it's necessary to stop after reaching the ratio $(T_u - T_l) \leq \Delta$, where Δ is the given accuracy of solving the problem.

Considering the previous problem, we did not take into account the influence of the intensity of supply of stored resources on the duration of work.

We will further assume that the intensity of the supply of the stored resource for the performance of work i over time t should be no less than $q_i(t)$ on the time interval for the performance of the work i $(\tau_i, \tau_i + t_i)$.

If there is a segment $(\Delta_i^1, \Delta_i^2) \subseteq (\tau_i, \tau_i + t_i)$ on which the real intensity of supplies $M_i(t) < q_i(t)$ $\forall t \in (\Delta_i^1, \Delta_i^2)$, then the duration of work t_i will obviously increase by the value Δ_i where

$$\Delta_i = t_i * \left(1 - \frac{\int_{\tau_i}^{\tau_i+t_i} u_i(t)dt}{\int_{\tau_i}^{\tau_i+t_i} q_i(t)dt} \right) \tag{3}$$

Here $u_i(t)$ - the real intensity of the supply of the stored resource;

$q_i(t)$ - the intensity of the supply of the stored resource, which ensures the completion of work i in the minimum time t_i.

After adjusting all work durations taking into account this formula, the branch and bound method described above can be used to optimize the schedule.

3   Two-Criteria Models for Assessing the Effectiveness of Schedules

If there is accumulated statistic of project works, the duration of each work can be specified as a random variable with a specified distribution law, i.e.

$$t_i = \begin{bmatrix} t_i^1 & p_1 \\ \dots\dots\dots \\ t_i^m & p_m \end{bmatrix}; \qquad p_j \geq 0; \quad \sum_{j=1}^{m} p_j = 1. \tag{4}$$

In this situation, the effectiveness of the calendar plan can be evaluated by two indicators:

1. The mathematical expectation of the duration of the calendar plan, calculated on the basis that each work is chosen as its mathematical expectation:

$$\overline{t_i} = \sum_{j=1}^{m} t_i^j P_j \tag{5}$$

2. The risk of the calendar plan. As a quantitative assessment of the calendar plan risk can be chosen either the variance of its duration, or the probability that the duration of the calendar plan is greater than some threshold value of Δ_{bord}.

Consider an example of evaluating the effectiveness of the schedule according to these criteria.

Let there be five works of the project $G(m, n) \equiv G(0, n)$ and its durations are given by the following table data:

Table 1. Distribution of duration of project activities

Probabilities	Works				
	1	2	3	4	5
0,2	1,1	2,1	3,1	4,1	5,1
0,3	0,9	1,9	2,9	3,9	4,9
0,5	1	2	3	4	5

Let's calculate the mathematical expectation of the duration of the work performed by the formula:

$$\overline{t_i} = \sum_{j=1}^{3} t_i^j P_j \tag{6}$$

We'll get: $\overline{t_1} = 0,95$; $\overline{t_2} = 1,93$; $\overline{t_3} = 2,97$; $\overline{t_4} = 3,98$; $\overline{t_5} = 4,98$.

Obviously, the optimal schedule for 2 performers can be represented by the following Gantt chart (See Fig. 1):

The duration of the schedule, assuming that the duration of the activities is taken as their mathematical expectation

$$T_{opt} = \overline{t_1} + \overline{t_2} + \overline{t_5} = 7,9$$

Next, we determine the risk of this schedule based on the variance of its duration using the formula (7):

$$R_1 = \sum_{i \in D_b} d_i^2 \tau_i^2 + 2 \sum_{i \in D_b} \sum_{j \in D_b} d_i d_j \cdot cov_{ij} \tag{7}$$

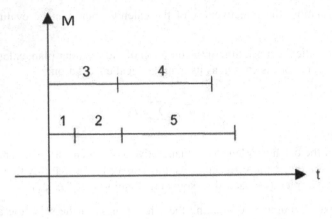

Fig. 1. Optimal schedule according to the criterion of minimizing the mathematical expectation of its duration.

Given that D_b includes activities 1,2,5 and calculating d_i by formula (8)

$$d_i = \frac{\bar{t}_i}{\sum_{j \in D_b} \bar{t}_j},$$
(8)

thus obtaining that d_i is the share of the mathematical expectation of the duration of the activity i-type in the mathematical expectation of the duration of the schedule, let us calculate R_1 with the formulas (9), (10):

$$\tau_i^2 = \sum_{e=1}^{m} \left(\bar{t}_i - t_i^e\right)^2 \cdot P_e;$$
(9)

$$cov_{ij} = \sum_{e=1}^{m} \left(\bar{t}_j - t_j^e\right)\left(\bar{t}_i - t_i^e\right) \cdot P_e$$
(10)

The second approach to quantifying schedule risk is based on determining the probability that $T_{opt} \geq \Delta_{bord}$.

If this threshold is taken to be $\Delta_{bord} = 8,05$, then, taking into account Table 1, risk estimate for this criterion is $R_2 = P\{T_{opt} \geq 8,05\} = 0,2$.

4   Sustainability Analysis of Timetables

When developing a project schedule, due to a high degree of uncertainty and risk, there is a need to analyze the stability of the plan under variation of some indicators.

Once again, let us consider the situation when the technological sequence of project activities is defined by an oriented acyclic graph $G(m, n)$, where m is a number of arcs and n is a number of vertices. Let us further assume that arcs define technological sequence of works, and vertices correspond to activities. Work i – type ($i = 1,2,..., n$) can be done in time t_i. Work cannot be interrupted. Each work is performed by a single performer.

When estimating the duration of the activities on the schedule, the decision maker (DM) can determine their durations either on the basis of accumulated statistics or on the basis of an expert's opinion. Therefore, deterministic estimation of the duration of each activity is often not possible in real conditions.

Thus, the duration of work in most cases can be estimated either as an interval $t_i \in [t_i^1, t_i^2]$, or by taking into account some possible perturbation. In the first case, it is assumed that the duration of work i can be any number from the interval $[t_i^1, t_i^2]$. In the second case, it is assumed that the most probable duration of work is t_i, but deviations from this duration are possible by an amount no more than $\varepsilon(\varepsilon > 0)$.

Thus, the length of the work i is the range $(t_i - \varepsilon, t_i + \varepsilon), (i = 1, 2, \ldots, n)$.

Let's look at an example to illustrate the difference between the two approaches.

In the first case, the work durations take different values on the multidimensional parallelepiped:

$$P = \prod_{i=1}^{n} \left[t_i^1, t_i^2 \right] \tag{11}$$

The range of acceptable values for interval times is shown in Fig. 2.

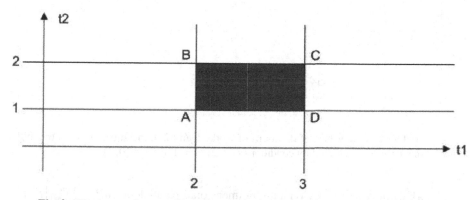

Fig. 2. The range of acceptable values in the interval assignment of work durations

In the two-dimensional case, the work durations are all points of the rectangle ABCD provided that $t_1 \in [2, 3]$; $t_2 \in [1, 2]$.

In the second case, if the following equation is met: $t_1 = 2$; $t_2 = 1$ and the duration of work can increase at the interval $\forall \varepsilon > 0$, then the set of work durations t_1, t_2 can be graphically represented as follows (Fig. 3):

Therefore, the possible durations of works 1 and 2 is a half line whose origin is a condition $t_1 = 2$; $t_2 = 1$, and whose inclination angle to the axis t_1 is equal to $45°$.

Obviously, if the magnitude of perturbation ε is bounded, for instance, by a condition $\varepsilon \in [0, 2]$, then the set of admissible values of durations of works 1 and 2 in the situation $t_1 = 2$; $t_2 = 1$ will be a line segment with coordinates $t_1^1 = 2, t_2^1 = 1$ and $t_1^2 = 4, t_2^2 = 3$. This situation is illustrated in Fig. 4.

In the conditions of imprecise assignment of work durations, it is necessary to find out how the optimal schedule will change when these durations are varied.

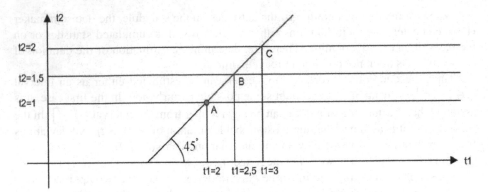

Fig. 3. Set of durations of two works at perturbation $\varepsilon \in (0, \infty)$.

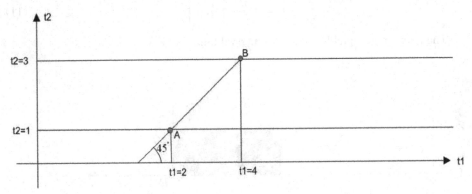

Fig. 4. Set of acceptable values of durations of works 1 and 2 in the situation when the initial values of durations are presented by conditions $t_1 = 2; t_2 = 1$ and $\varepsilon \in [0, 2]$.

If work durations can vary on a multidimensional parallelepiped $P = \prod_{i=1}^{n} [t_i^1, t_i^2]$, then P can be broken down into a finite number of polyhedrons M_j $(j = 1, 2, ..., N)$, having the following properties: $\bigcup_{j=1}^{N} M_j = P$.

For any polyhedron M_j $(j = 1, 2, ..., N)$ there exists a schedule K_j, which remains optimal for any parameters $t \in M_j$, $(j = 1, 2, ..., N)$. Here is a vector $t = (t_1, ..., t_n)$ whose coordinates specify durations of works i $(i = 1, 2, ..., n)$.

If the works are not intermittent, the duration of the optimal plan can be represented as follows:

$$T_{opt} = \sum_{i \in D_d} t_i \qquad (12)$$

where D_d is some subset of the activities of the original set of works Q-type, i.e. $D_d \subseteq Q$.

Let us illustrate this statement with the following example. Let there be three works $G(m, n) = G(0, n)$. The durations of activities are defined by interval $2 \leq t_i \leq 5, i = 1, 2, 3$.

Consider the following schedule when the works are performed by two performers (Fig. 5).

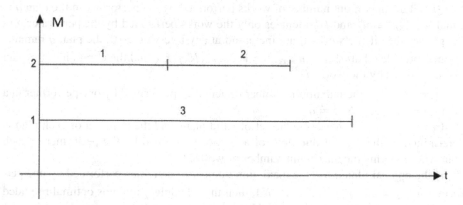

Fig. 5. Gantt Chart of the Time Schedule

Here works 1 and 2 are performed by performer 2, and work 3 is performed by performer 1. Obviously, this plan is optimal on the following set of points giving the duration of the works:

$$\begin{cases} 2 \leq t_1 \leq 5 \\ 2 \leq t_2 \leq 5 \\ 2 \leq t_3 \leq 5 \\ t_1 < t_3 \\ t_2 < t_3 \\ t_1 + t_2 < t_3 \end{cases}$$

The length of the optimal plan is t_3. Consequently, only work 3 is included in parameter D_d.

Consider a situation where the durations of all works can be increased by value $\varepsilon > 0$.

If uninterrupted works are performed by performers K, there are allowable schedules N, then the duration of the optimum plan is determined by the formula:

$$T_{opt} = \min_{e=\overline{1,N}} \max_{j=\overline{1,K}} \left\{ \tau_j^e \right\} \qquad (13)$$

where T_{opt}– the duration of the optimum plan;

K - the number of employees in the timetable;

τ_j^e – the moment when a performer j completes the work in the schedule e.

If the duration of all activities is increased in interval $\varepsilon > 0$, then formula (13) will take the following form:

$$T_{opt}(\varepsilon) = \min_{e=\overline{1,N}} \max_{j=\overline{1,K}} \left\{ \tau_j^e + m_j^e \varepsilon \right\} \qquad (14)$$

where m_j^e – the number of works performed by the performer j in the schedule e;

   ε – the incremental duration of each work.

From formula (14), in particular, it follows that if the plan q was optimal in condition $\varepsilon = 0$ and the maximum number of works performed by the performer in the plan q is equal to $m_{max}^q \equiv m_b^q$ and D_d^q includes only the works performed by the performer b in the plan q, then if the works t_i are increased at any interval$\varepsilon > 0$, the plan q remains optimal provided that$m_{max}^q \leq m_{max}^j, j = 1, 2, \ldots, N, j \neq q$ and the duration of the plan j is determined by the works D_d^q.

Here m_{max}^j – is the maximum number of activities performed by one performer in a plan $j, j = 1, 2, \ldots, N, j \neq q$.

In other words, if there is some set of valid plans and the duration of each plan is determined by the sum of durations of activities performed by the performer in each plan who performs the maximum number of works.

If the optimal plan q has the maximum number of activities performed by one performer $m_{max}^q = m_{max}^j (j = 1, 2, \ldots, N)$, then the schedule q remains optimal provided that all activity durations are increased by any interval $\varepsilon > 0$.

The confirmation of this fact follows from the fact that, the length of the optimal plan is defined by the set of works D_d^q, the number of which is equal to m_{max}^q, i.e.

$$T_{opt} = \sum_{i \in D_d^q} t_i. \tag{15}$$

For the remaining schedules, their duration is presented by formula 16:

$$T_j = \sum_{i \in D_d^j} t_i > T_{opt}, \quad j = 1, 2, \ldots, N \tag{16}$$

If the duration of work is increased by any interval $\varepsilon > 0$, the durations of all plans will be equal accordingly:

$$T_{opt}(\varepsilon) = \sum_{i \in D_d^q} t_i + m_{max}^q \cdot \varepsilon, \tag{17}$$

$$T^j(\varepsilon) = \sum_{i \subset D_d^j} t_i + m_{max}^j \cdot \varepsilon. \tag{18}$$

By virtue of relation (16) and the fact that $m_{max}^q \leq m_{max}^j, j = 1, 2, \ldots, N$, we obtain following inequality $T^j(\varepsilon) > T_{opt}(\varepsilon)$ for any $\varepsilon > 0$.

In general, the length of any allowable timetable can be determined by formula 19:

$$T^e = \max_{j=\overline{1,m}} \left\{ \sum_{i \in I_e^j} t_i \right\}, e = 1, 2, \ldots, N. \tag{19}$$

where:

   m is the number of performers;

   I_e^j is the set of activities performed by the performer j in the plan e.

Obviously, if the duration of all activities is increased by the interval $\varepsilon > 0$, then the duration of the plan e will be calculated as formula 20:

$$T^e(\varepsilon) = \max_{j=\overline{1,m}} \left\{ \sum_{i \in I_e^j} t_i + n_e^j \cdot \varepsilon \right\} \tag{20}$$

Here is n_e^j is the number of works performed by the performer j in the plan e.

From formula (20) in particular, it follows that there exists $\varepsilon*$, starting from which ($\varepsilon* < \varepsilon < \infty$) the length of the plan e will be determined by the total duration of the works of the performer who performs the maximum number of activities in the given schedule.

Denote r_e^j as the time of completion of the works carried out by an performer j in the schedule e.

Let's renumber the performers in ascending order of number of works performed by each performer, i.e. p > q provided that $n_e^p > n_e^q$.

Let the performer with the number finish the work last, i.e.

$$T^e = max\left\{\sum_{i \in I_e^j} t_i\right\} = \sum_{i \in I_e^\lambda} t_i \quad 1 \leq \lambda \leq m. \qquad (21)$$

If $\lambda < m$, then graphically the change in plan duration $T^e(\varepsilon)$ with growth ε can be represented as follows (Fig. 6):

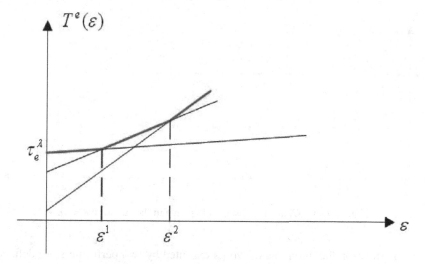

Fig. 6. Plan e length change graph with increasing value ε

At points ε_1 and ε_2 the growth trajectory $T^e(\varepsilon)$ changes due to the fact that the completion time of activities performed by other performers grows faster with growth of e value, than the completion time of the performer λ.

Therefore, the dynamics of plan e duration change with growth ε is a piecewise linear increasing function $T^e(\varepsilon)$.

Let us give an example to illustrate the formulated statement.

Denote $T_j^e(\varepsilon)$ as the moment of completion of the work by a performer j in the schedule e in perturbation ε. As follows from (20):

$$T_j^e(\varepsilon) = \sum_{i \in I_e^j} t_i + n_e^j \cdot \varepsilon \qquad (22)$$

It is obvious that $\frac{dT_j^e(\varepsilon)}{d\varepsilon} = n_e^j$.

Consequently, if there is a condition $\varepsilon = 0$ the duration of the plan e is defined as formula 23:

$$T_e(0) = \sum_{i \in I_e^k} t_i, \quad 1 \le k \le m \tag{23}$$

and there is a performer p for which there is also several conditions 24:

$$\frac{dT_p^e(\varepsilon)}{d\varepsilon} > \frac{dT_k^\varepsilon(\varepsilon)}{d\varepsilon} \text{ and } \frac{dT_p^e(\varepsilon)}{d\varepsilon} > \frac{dT^j(\varepsilon)}{d\varepsilon} \quad \forall j = 1, 2, .., m, \tag{24}$$

then there is $\varepsilon*$ starting from which

$$T^e(\varepsilon) = \sum_{i \in I_e^p} t_i + n_e^p \cdot \varepsilon \tag{25}$$

for all $\varepsilon \in (\varepsilon*, \infty)$.

As an example, consider the following Gantt diagram (Fig. 7).

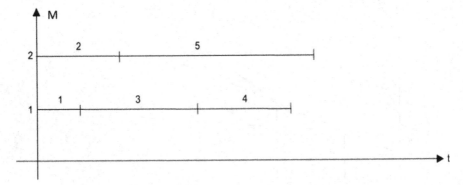

Fig. 7. Gantt Chart of the schedule plan e in the situation $\varepsilon = 0$.

In this situation the durations of works executed by two performers are defined as follows $t_1 = 1$; $t_2 = 2$; $t_3 = 3$; $t_4 = 2,5$; $t_5 = 5$.

In the case when $\varepsilon = 0$, the duration of calendar plan is determined by the sum of durations of works executed by the second performer $T(0) = 5 + 2 = 7 = T_2(0)$, i.e. the duration of the plan is determined by the time of completion of the activities performed by the second performer.

Let $T_1(\varepsilon)$ and $T_2(\varepsilon)$ be the moment when the first performer and the second performer finish the work.

Accordingly, we obtained these equations:

$$\frac{dT_1(\varepsilon)}{d\varepsilon} = (1 + 3 + 2, 5 + 3\varepsilon)' = 3; \tag{26}$$

$$\frac{dT_2(\varepsilon)}{d\varepsilon} = (2 + 5 + 2\varepsilon)' = 2. \tag{27}$$

Define the value of $\varepsilon*$, from which the duration of the schedule is given by the time of completion of the work performed by the first performer.

To do this, we solve the equation:

$$T_1(\varepsilon*) = T_2(\varepsilon*); \tag{28}$$

$2 + 5 + 2\varepsilon = 1 + 3 + 2, 5 + 3\varepsilon$, where we get that $\varepsilon* = 0, 5$.

Therefore with $\varepsilon \geq 0, 5$ the duration of the schedule is determined by the time the first performer completes the work.

Consequently, $T_e(\varepsilon)$ is defined as follows:

$$T_e(\varepsilon) = \begin{cases} 7 + 2\varepsilon & 0 \leq \varepsilon \leq 0, 5; \\ 6, 5 + 3\varepsilon & 0, 5 \leq \varepsilon \leq \infty. \end{cases} \tag{29}$$

By looking at the changing dynamics of the durations of all permissible schedules, it is possible to determine the zone of change $\varepsilon \in (\varepsilon', \varepsilon'')$ for each plan in which it will be optimal. The procedure for determining this zone is as follows.

Suppose there are N-calendar plans and among them there is an optimal plan e for the situation when there is a perturbation $\varepsilon = 0$.

For this plan, we form a function $T^e(\varepsilon)$ that defines the length of the plan depending on the size of the disturbance ε, using formula (20). Similarly, we define a function $T^j(\varepsilon)$ for any other plan. Then we define $\frac{dT^j(\varepsilon)}{d\varepsilon}$ at a point $\varepsilon = 0$ for all values $j = 1, 2, \ldots, N$ and therefore we form a subset of schedules D_1 for which the relation (31) is fulfilled:

$$\left. \frac{dT^i(\varepsilon)}{d\varepsilon} \right|_{\varepsilon=0} < \left. \frac{dT^e(\varepsilon)}{d\varepsilon} \right|_{\varepsilon=0}, \quad i \in D_1. \tag{30}$$

Next, we solve an equation of the form

$$T^i(\varepsilon) = T^e(\varepsilon), i \in D_1 \tag{31}$$

and obtain a solution of the form $\varepsilon_1^1, \ldots, \varepsilon_{M_1}^1$, where M_1 is number of elements in the set D_1.

We need to choose an option

$$\min_{j \in D_1} \varepsilon_j^1 = \varepsilon_{min}^1 = \varepsilon_k^1. \tag{32}$$

Consequently, with a perturbation $0 \leq \varepsilon \leq \varepsilon_k^1$, the optimal plan will remain the schedule e. Starting from the value of perturbation ε_k^1 and more, the plan k becomes optimal. To determine the right perturbation boundary of the change interval ε at which the optimal plan will be k, it is necessary to follow this procedure.

Form the set of calendar plans D_2 as follows.

Include into the set D_2 all schedules are satisfying the following condition (33):

$$\left. \frac{dT^i(\varepsilon)}{d\varepsilon} \right|_{\varepsilon=\varepsilon_k^1} < \left. \frac{dT^k(\varepsilon)}{d\varepsilon} \right|_{\varepsilon=\varepsilon_k^1}. \tag{33}$$

Then we solve the equations of the form

$$T^i(\varepsilon) = T^k(\varepsilon), i \in D_2 \qquad (34)$$

on the interval of change $\varepsilon \in [\varepsilon_k^1, \infty)$.

Thus, we obtained solutions of form $\varepsilon_1^2, \ldots, \varepsilon_{M_2}^2$.

Next step is based on choosing of the minimum of these solutions

$$\min_{j \in D_2} \varepsilon_j^2 = \varepsilon_{min}^2 = \varepsilon_m^2. \qquad (35)$$

Therefore, the solution k will be optimal when the perturbation changes on the interval $[\varepsilon_k^1, \varepsilon_m^2]$. Given the finiteness of the number of solutions for each equation of the form:

$$T_i(\varepsilon) = T_j(\varepsilon); i = 1, 2, \ldots, N, \quad j = 1, 2, \ldots, N; i \neq j, \ \varepsilon \in (0, \infty); \qquad (36)$$

we obtain that the interval of variation of its values $\varepsilon \in (0, \infty)$ can be divided into a finite number of intervals such that one and the same schedule remains optimal if the perturbation changes within the boundaries of one interval.

Consider an example interpreting this statement. Let there be 6 works performed by two performers $M = 2$; $G(m, n) \equiv G(0, n)$. The durations of the activities are equal to $t_i = 1, i = 1,2,3,4$; $t_5 = 1,9$; $t_6 = 2,1$. Consider two schedules (Fig. 8 and 9).

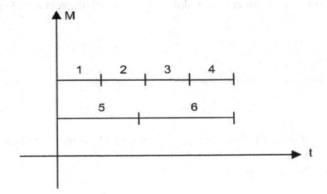

Fig. 8. Gantt Chart of the first timetable

It is easy to see that the first timetable would be optimal with $\varepsilon = 0$

$$T^1 = max\{1 + 1 + 1 + 1; 2, 1 + 1, 9\} = 4$$

$$T^2 = max\{1 + 1 + 1, 9; 1 + 1 + 2, 1\} = 4, 1.$$

If the durations of all activities are increased by an interval $\varepsilon > 0$, then the durations of the plans will respectively be equal:

$$T^1(\varepsilon) = max\{4 + 4\varepsilon; 4 + 2\varepsilon\}$$

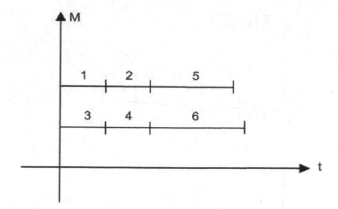

Fig. 9. Gantt Chart of the second timetable

$$T^2(\varepsilon) = max\{3, 9 + 3\varepsilon; 4, 1 + 3\varepsilon\}$$

Obviously, the length of the first plan at perturbation ε will be equal to $T_1(\varepsilon) = 4 + 4\varepsilon$ while the length of the second plan will be presented by a following formula $T_2(\varepsilon) = 4, 1 + 3\varepsilon$.

Taking into account that $\frac{dT_1(\varepsilon)}{d\varepsilon} > \frac{dT_2(\varepsilon)}{d\varepsilon}$ for some value $\varepsilon* > 0$ there will be a transition to another optimal plan.

In order to determine this boundary value $\varepsilon* > 0$, it is necessary to solve the following equation:

$$4 + 4\varepsilon = 4, 1 + 3\varepsilon$$

We get from here that $\varepsilon = 0, 1$.

Consequently, the perturbation from which the second schedule would be optimal could be illustrated by an equation $\varepsilon* = 0, 1$.

Graphically, this situation can be shown as follows (Fig. 10):

In this manner this paper presents an example of how to evaluate the stability interval of a schedule.

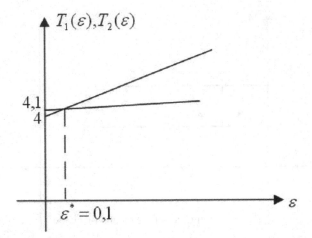

Fig. 10. Transition point to the new optimal schedule.

References

1. Garey, M.R., Johnson, D.S.: Computers and Intractability: A Guide to the Theory of NP-Completeness. W. H. Freeman, New York (1979)
2. Mishchenko, A.V., Khalikov, M.A.: Distribution of limited resources in the problem of optimizing the production activities of an enterprise. Izv. Akad. Nauk SSSR, Tekh. Kibern. **6** (1991)
3. Mishchenko, A.V., Pilyugina, A.V.: Dynamic models of research and manufacturing system management. Vestn. MGTU im. Baumana, Ser. Priborostr. **2** (2019)
4. Mishchenko, A.V., Sushkov, B.G.: The problem of optimal resource allocation on a network model with linear constraints on the time of work execution. Zh. Vychisl. Mat. Mat. Fiz. **10**(5) (1980)
5. Mishchenko, A.V., Kogalovskii, V.M.: Problems of stability of production planning tasks in mechanical engineering. Ekon. Mat. Metody. **3** (1992)
6. Mishchenko, A.V., Stability of solutions in the problem of redistribution of vehicles in the event of an emergency closure of traffic on a metro section. Izv. Akad. Nauk SSSR, Tekh. Kibern. **3** (1990)
7. Mishchenko, A.V.: The problem of distributing vehicles along bus routes with an inaccurately specified matrix of passenger traffic correspondences. Izv. Akad. Nauk SSSR, Tekh. Kibern. **2** (1992)
8. Katyukhina, O.A., Mishchenko, A.V.: Dynamic models of transport resources management by the example of bus fleet work organization. Audit Fin. Anal. **2**, 156–167 (2016)
9. Kosorukov, O.A., Belov, A.G.: Resource management problem on network diagrams as an optimal control problem. - Vestn. Moscow university Ser. 15, Comput. mathematics and cybernetics, vol. 2, pp. 29–33 (2014)
10. Kosorukov, O.A., Furugyan, M.G.: Some algorithms for resource allocation in multiprocessor systems. Moscow Univ. Comput. Math. Cybernet. **33**, 202 (2009)
11. Furugyan, M.G.: Computation planning in multiprocessor real time automated control systems with an additional resource. Autom. Remote. Control. **76**(3), 487–492 (2015). https://doi.org/10.1134/S0005117915030121

12. Kosorukov, O.A., Furugyan, M.G.: Algorithms for resource allocation in multiprocessor systems with nonfixed parameters. In: Some Algorithms for Scheduling Calculations and Organizing Control in Real-Time Systems (VTs RAN, Moscow, 2011), pp. 40–51 (2011). (in Russian)
13. Mironov, A.A., Tsurkov, V.I.: Transport-type problems with a criterion. Avtom. Telemekh. **12**, 109–118 (1995)
14. Mironov, A.A., Tsurkov, V.I.: Hereditarily minimax matrices in models of transportation type. J. Comput. Syst. Sci. Int. **37**, 927 (1998)
15. Mironov, A.A., Levkina, T.A., Tsurkov, V.I.: Minimax estimations of expectates of arc weights in integer networks with fixed node degrees. Appl. Comput. Math. **8**, 216–226 (2009)
16. Mironov, A.A., Tsurkov, V.I.: Class of distribution problems with minimax criterion. Dokl. Akad. Nauk **336**, 35–38 (1994)
17. Tizik, A.P., Tsurkov, V.I.: Iterative functional modification method for solving a transportation problem. Autom. Remote Control. **73**, 134–143 (2012)
18. Mironov, A.A., Tsurkov, V.I.: Hereditarily minimax matrices in models of transportation type. J. Comput. Syst. Sci. Int. **37**(6), 927–944 (1998)
19. Mironov, A.A., Tsurkov, V.I.: Minimax in transportation models with integral constraints. 1. J. Comput. Syst. Sci. Int. **42**, 562–574 (2003)

Author Index

A
Agarwal, Nitin 3
Al-khateeb, Samer 3

B
Baboshin, Evgeniy 148
Bochkarev, Vladimir 126
Borisova, Ludmila 14
Bubeliene, Daiva 191
Byvshev, Viktor 97

D
Denisov, Artem 115
Duan, Changxu 161

E
Efimova, Olga 148

F
Fridman, Mira 14

G
Gorbaneva, Olga 27

K
Kleiner, George 48
Kosorukov, Oleg 201
Kumacheva, Suriya 63

L
Levina, Vera 126

M
Malysheva, Olga 148
Matveeva, Irina 148
Merkys, Gediminas 191
Mikhalkovich, Stanislav 27
Mishchenko, Alexandr 201
Murzin, Anton 27

N
Nestik, Timofei 126

O
Ougolnitsky, Guennady 27

P
Pyrkina, Olga 78

Q
Qian, Wang 115

R
Rybachuk, Maxim 48

S
Steblianskaia, Elizaveta 115
Steblyanskaya, Alina 137
Sviridova, Olga 201

T
Tomilina, Galina 63

U
Ushakov, Dmitry 48

V
Vasiev, Maksim 148
Vladimir, Gisin 179

W
Wang, Zhinan 137

Y
Yu, Tian 161
Yudanov, Andrey 78

Z
Zhitkova, Ekaterina 63

Printed in the United States
by Baker & Taylor Publisher Services